Ethics of the Body

Basic Bioethics
Glenn McGee and Arthur Caplan, editors

Pricing Life: Why It's Time for Health Care Rationing,
Peter A. Ubel

Bioethics: Ancient Themes in Contemporary Issues,
edited by Mark G. Kuczewski and Ronald Polansky

The Human Embryonic Stem Cell Debate: Science, Ethics, and Public Policy,
edited by Suzanne Holland, Karen Lebacqz, and Laurie Zoloth

Engendering International Health: The Challenge of Equity,
edited by Gita Sen, Asha George, and Piroska Östlin

Self-Trust and Reproductive Autonomy,
Carolyn McLeod

What Genes Can't Do,
Lenny Moss

In the Wake of Terror: Medicine and Morality in a Time of Crisis,
edited by Jonathan D. Moreno

Pragmatic Bioethics, 2d edition,
edited by Glenn McGee

Case Studies in Biomedical Research Ethics,
Timothy F. Murphy

Genetics and Life Insurance: Medical Underwriting and Social Policy,
edited by Mark A. Rothstein

Ethics and the Metaphysics of Medicine: Reflections on Health and Beneficence,
Kenneth A. Richman

DNA and the Criminal Justice System: The Technology of Justice,
edited by David Lazer

Is Human Nature Obsolete? Genetics, Bioengineering, and the Future of the Human Condition,
edited by Harold W. Baillie and Timothy K. Casey

End of Life Decision-Making: A Cross-National Study,
edited by Robert H. Blank and Janna C. Merrick

Deciding for the Profoundly Mentally Disabled,
by Norman L. Cantor

Ethics of the Body: Postconventional Challenges,
edited by Margrit Shildrick and Roxanne Mykitiuk

Ethics of the Body

Postconventional Challenges

edited by Margrit Shildrick and Roxanne Mykitiuk

The MIT Press
Cambridge, Massachusetts
London, England

MIT Press books may be purchased at special quantity discounts for business or sales promotional use. For information, please email special_sales@mitpress.mit.edu or write to Special Sales Department, The MIT Press, 5 Cambridge Center, Cambridge, MA 02142.

This book was set in Sabon by Achorn Graphic Services, Inc.
Printed on recycled paper and bound in the United States of America.

Library of Congress Cataloging-in-Publication Data

Ethics of the body: postconventional challenges / edited by Margrit Shildrick and Roxanne Mykitiuk.
p. cm.—(Basic bioethics)
Includes bibliographical references and index.
ISBN 0-262-19523-2 (alk. paper)—ISBN 0-262-69320-8 (pbk. : alk. paper)
1. Bioethics. I. Shildrick, Margrit. II. Mykitiuk, Roxanne, 1962– III. Series.

QH332.E736 2005
174′.957—dc22

2004061361

10 9 8 7 6 5 4 3 2 1

Contents

Series Foreword

We are pleased to present the sixteenth book in the series Basic Bioethics. The series presents innovative works in bioethics to a broad audience and introduces seminal scholarly manuscripts, state-of-the-art reference works, and textbooks. Such broad areas as the philosophy of medicine, advancing genetics and biotechnology, end-of-life care, health and social policy, and the empirical study of biomedical life are examined.

Glenn McGee
Arthur Caplan

Acknowledgments

As with any intellectual enterprise, many friends and colleagues have contributed both knowingly and unknowingly to the generation and completion of this collection. Some have been encouraging, others skeptical, but all have had an influence. The initial idea came about as the result of a kind invitation from Anne Donchin independently to both editors to take part in a panel for the third International Conference of Feminist Approaches to Bioethics (FAB) held in London in 2000. Although Anne and other members of the executive committee of FAB had hoped we would edit a collection of papers drawn from that conference, we decided instead on a different approach that more clearly reflected our own postmodernist interests. Nonetheless, we sincerely hope that they will find this book both surprising and stimulating. Our main thanks, then, to the present contributors—of whom just two presented papers in London—for their enthusiasm, support, and patience throughout a somewhat lengthy process.

Margrit: my personal thanks to Roxanne for making this long-distance collaboration such a pleasurable and care-free experience and to my long-term collaborator Janet Price, whose sharing and discussion of ideas over many years remains invaluable.

Roxanne: Misha Mykitiuk has been a patient and understanding child during the completion of this project. I am also grateful to Margrit for her good-humored patience and perseverance.

I

Introduction

1

Beyond the Body of Bioethics: Challenging the Conventions

Margrit Shildrick

As a recognizable and credible discipline entitled to comment, guide, and pass judgment on the broad operation of biomedicine, bioethics has become fully established only during the past few decades. Taking in aspects both of ethics in general—with a particular focus on the practicalities of applied morality—and of relevant legal tenets, the discipline has recently emerged as the source of authoritative evaluation for a range of biomedical issues covering not only the behavior and practice of professional providers and users of health care systems but also bioscientific research and development. At the same time, contemporary bioethicists are increasingly expected to participate in the public debate about what are broadly seen as biomedical dilemmas, particularly those arising from the new technologies. They are called on to resolve problems, to adjudicate between rival opinions or suggested courses of action, and above all, to lend the imprimatur of the moral good to this or that decision, usually without recourse to too much high theory.

The primary issues of concern to bioethicists are taken to be the pragmatic ones that in one way or another make a direct difference in how biomedicine conducts itself. Although there is always a place for exploration of the theoretical frameworks—the metaethics—that support or preclude the relevance of any one model of behavior, the real test of bioethics is whether it is able to operate adequately in practice. In other words, the question is one of the extent to which it answers the different needs and desires of individual agents faced with a complexity of possible courses of action, and uncertain as how to proceed for the best result. Nonetheless, it is our contention in this book that despite such worthy aims, and for all its high profile, bioethics is out of touch. It is out of touch with bodies themselves, in the phenomenological sense in which the being, or rather the becoming, of the self is always intricately interwoven with the fabric of the body; it is out of touch with the developments in and impact of postmodernist theory as it problematizes the hitherto unchallenged certainties of binary thinking; and it is out of touch with a postmodern culture in which bioscience itself forces us to question what is meant by the notion of the human self.

The publicly acknowledged and newly persuasive status of bioethics in the twenty-first century—in the West at least—can be no surprise to those aware of the transformatory changes in biomedical practice that have taken place during the past few decades. In the areas both of lay opinion, in which the media play no small part, and of specialist concerns, there is a growing awareness that decisions made in the field of bioscience have far-reaching effects. They not only relate to traditional concerns with the direct operative possibilities of any health care delivery, but more fundamentally they question some of the taken-for-granted parameters of what it means to be a human being. Issues of where the limits of reproduction lie, what constitutes a "normal" body, whether species distinction should be rigidly maintained, how to determine the boundaries of life and death, the value of individuality, and many other equally urgent and troubling concerns, have entered public discussion. Although the power of biomedical discourse to shape as well as to respond to social norms, needs, and desires has long been recognized, there has been relatively little long-term dissent from the view that an expanded understanding of the human body equates unproblematically with progress. Religious teaching and popular prejudice alike have periodically railed against certain developments such as postmortem examination, the use of blood transfusions, or more recently the introduction of effective contraception for women, but for the majority, the successful application of such techniques has rapidly led to their acceptance. They are plainly seen to do good, to advance, in other words, what we understand to be the paradigm of health. It is too soon to know whether current innovations in the knowledge base of bioscience will in turn come to be seen as a self-evident good, but what is perhaps different in the process is the expectation that particular "experts" in moral reasoning—bioethicists—will be able to guide evaluation in the direction of clear and distinct answers.

The difficulty as I see it—and it is one that bioethicists themselves have largely failed to address—is that the desire to distinguish between right and wrong, between good and bad actions, or to have a determinate assessment of consequences remains undiminished in the face of a set of developments that are marked by their problematization of normative, oppositional, binaries. In other words, in the period we might term the era of postmodernity, precisely our own time, the problems created by a bioscience that has become highly technological, with its ever-accelerating, expanding, and unpredictable datasets, are intrinsically unfamiliar. Yet there is a strong tendency to continue to rely on models of moral evaluation that derive from a belief in fixed and normative templates as adequate for all new knowledge. The argument is that although understanding of the body might vary, the ontology of being human, of having potentially fixed standards of judgment, and thus of proper or improper moral agency, does not. This conventional morality relies predominantly on such qualities of mind as rationality, self-sovereignty, and impartiality, and although bioethics—with its putative focus on the practices of the body—might be expected to break with such abstraction and offer a more dynamic model, there is little sign of such a change. Instead, the discipline has effectively duplicated the master discourse and maintained the split between a secure sense of the transcendent self as moral agent, and a more or less unruly body that must be subjected to its dictates. Even in the era of postmodernity where no such certainties about the nature of the human self can endure, bioethics clings to the familiar philosophical models of consequentialism, with its confidence in a determinable calculus of harms and benefits, to deontology with its fixed principles of right and wrong action, or to the notion of virtue where what counts is precisely *human* flourishing.

While it is not my argument that there is no place at all for certain conventional moral and legal judgments—for they continue to act as practical safeguards against the abuse of biomedical power—I prefer to see them as second-order considerations. Rather than simply outlining a set of moral precepts geared to the delivery of a working relationship between the needs and desires of those involved in biomedicine and some concept of the good, the contributors to this book believe it is the task of bioethicists to step back and ask whether the ethical frameworks inherited from modernist discourse are adequate for the developments of a postmodern age, in both its theoretical and practical contexts. The latter is perhaps easier to appreciate in that it is a common observation that the pace of actual and potential innovation in the biosciences has accelerated far beyond anything that the ethical imagination has anticipated. That in itself has created an impossible pressure on the efficacy and adequacy of modernist conventions that are ill-adapted to take account of the new contingencies. Even philosophers well versed in the use of arcane thought experiments must struggle to apply the familiar paradigms of western ethics to scenarios that fundamentally contest normative conceptions of biology and of human life. I am thinking here of issues such as persistent vegetative state, prenatal gene manipulation, cloning, and even the growing use of high-tech prosthetics. The concern, then, is not so much to debate what changes and reforms could be made to existing moral precepts, but to ask what difference it would make to accept that the issues raised by the potential to vary the conditions of reproduction, of life or death, of embodiment, and indeed of human being itself, are ones that demand a radical reconfiguration of bioethical thought. The suggestion, developed throughout this volume, is that the issues would be better addressed by a postconventional or postmodernist approach that specifically seeks to break down such binary categories as those of the normal and the abnormal, of health and illness, of self and other, which are the bases of normative bioethics.

What then are the key features of the approach we favor? Postmodernism is itself a notoriously slippery term, and it should be clear from the start that my purpose is not to attempt to pin it down to a few definitive points, but to make use of some of its facets that lend themselves to rethinking an ethics of the body. Moreover, it is debatable whether all postconventional theory could be seen as postmodern. Feminism, for example, clearly rejects many of the conventions of modernism without necessarily engaging in a radical critique of the fundamental structure of western thought. For the purposes of this volume, however, it is just such a radical move, which goes far beyond the possibility of simply reforming existing systems, that concerns us, and to that end the contributors employ critiques that could be termed phenomenological, poststructuralist, deconstructionist, or postmodernist. What all these approaches have in common is that they contest the grounding certainties of the modernist project, particularly as it is manifest in the form of liberal humanism.

That system, which has been dominant in the West since the seventeenth-century Enlightenment, is characterized by a moral and social order in which autonomous individuals—supposedly neutral with respect to gender and race, for example—have sovereignty over their own lives, and enter into contractual relations with other similarly sovereign individuals, on the basis of free will and rationality. They are immediately recognizable as the normative agents—the actors—of conventional moral and bioethical theory. The specifically liberal humanist qualities of liberty, equality, rights, duties, and impartiality are then at the heart of the convention. Moreover, in that same intellectual tradition, all categories of thought, knowledge itself, are organized according to a thoroughgoing system of binary opposites that set in place unequivocal distinctions between self and other, mind and body, subject and object, right and wrong, truth and falsity, human and animal, health and disease, natural and artificial, and so on. In such a brief account some oversimplification is inevitable, but the point is that in its ideal form, it is a system that allows little in the way of uncertainty, mutability, or provisionality. In terms of an ethical application, it lends itself—indeed demands—clarity and resolution.

In contrast, the perspectives that fall under the umbrella term of "postmodernism" challenge and disrupt the foundations of mainstream western thought in a variety of ways. Their claim is that the rationalist and scientific project that characterized the European Enlightenment, with its appeal to the notion of progress and an ever-growing body of certain knowledge, is at an end. In place of a fixed and coherent notion of "truth," there are only multiple and provisional "truths," a series of dispersed and possibly conflicting discourses, none of which can claim ultimate authority. In consequence, because the notion of a unified rationality is fragmented, the so-called "grand narratives" of western thought—liberal humanism, including the discourses of bioscience and the law, and even conventional morality itself—have no enduring power. At the same time, the boundaries between the supposedly discrete categories by which thought is organized—natural and artificial would be a pertinent example—are shown to be blurred and leaky. Instead of the certainty of the separation and distinction of binary pairs that allowed a hierarchical ordering of value, and in which one term was consistently dominant, simple difference is replaced not just by multiple differences, but what Derrida (1973) calls *différance,* in which no term has independent meaning or value. Rather, there is an overflowing and intermingling of categories, a mutual dependence that belies the traditional insistence on clear and distinct divisions. Moreover, nothing is fixed in essence or given in advance of its representation; on the contrary, insofar as it is constructed through a tissue of mobile differences, meaning is fully discursive. This radical problematization of the known—what is often referred to as deconstruction—is as much a matter of the ontology of the subject as it is of epistemic categories. It is not simply that the binary of self and other is disrupted, but that the self, as a unified and identifiable entity, does not precede its own discursive construction. In other words, there is no sovereign subject, no central arbiter of truth or authority, no preexisting agent of moral action.

When it comes to the materiality of the body, postconventional and deconstructionist approaches are no less radical. In place of the implicit Cartesian split between mind and body, which is just one of the central binaries that is shown to be untenable, the notion of embodiment is employed to express an intertwining of the two elements. Rather than a traditional model in which the transcendent mind is unconstrained by the immanent flesh, at least insofar as the subject is white and masculine, the subject's very being—or more accurately, becoming—is dependent on the body. It is not simply a matter of having or owning a body, or of using it as an instrument, where the subject might yet be seen as a controlling overseer, but one in which embodiment is the condition of being a self at all. Just as that self is never separable from its own materiality, it is also not fully separable from other embodied selves. In postmodernist thought, the categorical distinctions among bodies are not natural givens, as bioscience has traditionally insisted, but normativities imposed and maintained by a combination of disciplinary and regulatory controls, not least of which is the practice of biomedicine itself. The extent of the control required to prop up such normative categories is readily apparent in at least two issues addressed in subsequent chapters: the treatment of intersexuality and the potential genetic limitation of disability. Against the inherent failure of the modernist model in which each form is bounded and self-complete, the postmodernist claim is that all corporeality is inherently leaky, uncontained, and uncontainable (Shildrick 1997). In other words, morphology is not something given once and for all, but is a process without an end.

The implications for a conventional understanding of the body, and by extension any material interaction with it, are far-reaching. The ideal configurations around which western thought is organized are exposed as precisely that—simply flawless templates that the bodies of everyday life more or less approximate, and are more or less valued as a consequence. All evidence of the actual instabilities, imperfections, breakdowns, and sheer messiness of corporeality—the very things that might be the subject of bioethics—is seen as a failure of form, a lack of wholeness and integrity, that is pushed to the margins as different or is even disavowed. In the cultural imaginary, the manifestation of lack as a material condition of bodies causes great anxiety and must be kept out of touch lest it undermine the security of the supposedly normatively embodied subject (Shildrick 2002). Yet although our overriding concern is to buttress our sense of unity and autonomy—the cherished attributes of the modernist subject—by centering on what Julia Kristeva has called "the self's clean and proper body" (1982: 71), that other body always returns. In disability and disease, in dreams, in reproduction and pregnancy, in growing old, in sexual practice, in cybernetics and genetic manipulation, the body transgresses its normative boundaries and draws attention to its own constructionist dynamic. Indeed, it is just such a scenario that Karen O'Connell (chapter 11) describes in her reflections on the limits of the body in law. Underlying our individual and cultural investments in order and distinction, then, underlying the normative exclusions and denial that so often are apparent in a reluctance to touch, another less comforting and far less determinate picture emerges.

What this means in terms of ethical transactions is that the encounter between one and another might be modelled on something other than autonomous abstract entities negotiating the safe space of separation and distinction. Instead, the interval is dissolved, and as embodied selves, who are not just interdependent but whose morphology is without divisive boundaries, the self and other are opened up to one another in a relationship in which the metaphorics of touch can play a primary part. One clear way in which this has been taken up in ethics is through the phenomenology of Merleau-Ponty (1962, 1968), who insists that the self and every other materiality is constituted in mutual relation. For Merleau-Ponty, there is no autonomous subjectivity, only the highly mediated experience of becoming-in-the-world-with-others. As he says of the tactile body: "its own movements incorporate themselves into the universe they interrogate. . . . the world of each opens upon that of the other" (1968: 133, 141).

The focus on the phenomenology of embodiment—which is especially evident in the work of Rothfield and Diprose in this collection—lends itself to an ethical development that finds particular expression in the work of Luce Irigaray, whose project is both to in-corporate ethics and to give voice to the hitherto unexpressed feminine. She is particularly concerned to rewrite the notion of sexual difference, not as a binary opposite that reduces the feminine to the other of the same, but as a radical difference, a difference otherwise, in which both terms are valued (Irigaray 1993). Following—albeit with some clear criticisms—the lead of Merleau-Ponty, however, she sees the ethical relation, not in terms of separation, but as a mode that occurs between subjects. The clarity of self and other is blurred in the acknowledgment of a mutual fluidity. It speaks to a circuit of embodied exchanges. Irigaray, like Merleau-Ponty, stresses the significance of a reversible and ambiguous touch—without reducing the difference(s) of the other to the standards of the selfsame.[1] For Irigaray, the threshold of ethics lies in the materiality and tangibility of the self–other relation: "Nearness so pronounced that it makes all discrimination of identity, and thus all forms of property, impossible. . . . This puts into question all prevailing economies" (1985: 31). Put like this, it is easier to see why the materiality of even everyday conditions like pregnancy might lend itself to ethical reflection.

Clearly all this has enormous implications for mainstream bioethics which, in both its theoretical bases and practical applications, is posited on precisely the certainties and distinctions that postmodernist analysis contests. The mutually exclusive categories of right and wrong, or human and animal, for example; the status of the subject, the meaning of autonomy, even the givenness of the body, are all called into question. What does not happen, contrary to fears that postmodernism will be unable to respond to an everyday materiality, or to a substantive conflict here and now, is that the more familiar models of modernist thought are made entirely redundant. Critique is not destructive per se. Its purpose is to expose the shortcomings, the unreflective assumptions, the hidden contradictions and elisions of hitherto unchallenged structures; to bring them into question but not to make them unusable. Insofar as bioethics continues to occupy a problem-solving role, there remain contexts in which an appeal to those categories that promise resolution is both inevitable and necessary. What does change, however, is the certainty with which such resolutions are invested. The point is that things could always be otherwise, and that the answers we give ourselves—often the basis for far-reaching actions—must never be allowed to settle, to take on the timeless mantle of absolute truth or moral right or universality.

Postmodernism entails an acceptance of provisionality, instability, and multiplicity, and an awareness that the task of ethics is never finally done, that the critique must be interminable. In advocating the adoption of such an alternative strategy, then, I am not proposing the kind of anything-goes approach of which postmodernism is so often, and wrongly, accused, but a more fluid and open model that is responsive to the rapid transformations that are occurring in both the theoretical and practical arenas. Although there is a tradition in which epistemology and ethics are seen to constitute quite separate and independent fields of enquiry, bioethics—in the form of an applied morality—has never fully endorsed such a distinction, and has at the very least considered an understanding of substantive issues as relevant to its operation. The point now is that the changes of postmodernity themselves contest traditional knowledge to the extent that new epistemic models are called for, which in turn go hand in hand with a very different type of ethics.

The problem with—and, I would argue, the relative limitations of—mainstream bioethics is that its concentration on issues such as choice and consent, property interests, rational decision making, and equality of access still relies on the traditional ethical model in which the ultimate determinants of moral agency are individuality and rationality (Shildrick

1997). It is not that these things are unimportant, but that they are rooted in a world that is being radically transformed by the capacities of bioscience to vary and extend the hitherto limited things of which bodies seem capable. Where once the material body could be taken as relatively stable and predictable (although postmodernists would argue that has always been an illusion), the technological possibilities of a postmodern age—and this is especially clear in the area of reproduction and genetics—continually disrupt humanist certainties.[2] Yet it is important to note that the relevance of a postconventional approach is not limited simply to those questions where the material circumstances themselves are characteristic of postmodernity—as, for example, in the areas of genetic engineering or xenotransplantation. On the contrary, we want to push for a reconsideration of *all* bioethical concerns in the light of postmodernist insights. The simplest technologies and practices of the body are as much subject to ethical and critical reflection as the most high-tech procedure. In other words, it is as fruitful to rethink the experience of cancer or the transcultural biomedical encounter as it is to reflect on the implications of sequencing the human genome.

Alongside the realization that there is no guarantee of an unchanging biology as the material base for the sovereign self, we need to look afresh, not just at how all interventions work for better or worse in terms of their own ostensible remit of enhancing human well-being, but also at the ethical implications of reconfiguring identity itself. Although it may be more or less evident that the conditions of, and responses to, madness or even addiction concern identity, is the same not true of cancer or HIV/AIDS? Similarly I would argue that a sense of self is disrupted differently, but just as significantly, in, for example, having a broken leg put in plaster, or having a robotic limb attached. Both affect the phenomenology of one's felt experience and interface with the world of others. The focus of enquiry, then, cannot be a matter of abstraction as though the materiality of the body had nothing to do with the makeup of the ethical, ontological self, but rather should be a matter of how any self is always irreducibly embodied. In other words, the concern is as much a matter of ontology as of ethics, where those two terms are intertwined and materially embedded. What is at stake throughout is a reconceived understanding of what it means to be an embodied human subject acting in a moral and legal landscape, and one, moreover, that takes none of the terms of selfhood for granted.

Once it is accepted that it is not the aim of the postmodernism advocated in this volume to simply invalidate existing forms of thought and action, it becomes easier to think through the significance of what is being offered. Most of the examples in the preceding two paragraphs refer to issues that are subjected to what may be unfamiliar postconventional modes of analyses in the chapters that follow. In light of the real confusions, complexities, and misunderstandings that characterize everyday experiences and decision making, subjecting the normative structures of modernity to a critique that exposes rather than covers over their shortcomings and inevitable aporias—in other words, places of paradox and impasse—seems well-conceived. But in postmodernist thinking, it is not only the evidently disordered contexts that clearly stretch our ability to impose predetermined rules, but the normative structure as a whole that is questioned. If nothing can be taken as given, then there is always an intrinsic undecidability at work.

In his turn to ethics, the poststructuralist philosopher Jacques Derrida uses the term "undecidable" to denote the inherent impossibility of ever arriving at a definitive resolution. How, we might reasonably ask, can there be ethical responsibility where decision itself is apparently stalled? To those familiar only with the clear-cut accountability of liberal humanist morality, the answer is perhaps surprising, but it is one that points the way to a new and arguably more encompassing way of understanding ethics. Far from abandoning the search for the ethical, Derrida takes up the notion of the undecidable as precisely the mark of a highly responsive and responsible ethics. His argument is that in the face of complex and incommensurable demands that suggest at best a multiplicity of competing ways forward, the imposition of one set of moral principles rather than another simply sidesteps the need for ethical decision. Rather than an effort to engage with the undecidable, the resort to preexisting rules or laws represents a retreat to the security of the known, not a real encounter with the ethical issues in hand. As he puts it:

> I will even venture to say that ethics, politics and responsibility, *if there are any*, will only ever have begun with the experience and experiment of the aporia. When the path is clear and given, when a certain knowledge opens up

the way in advance, the decision is already made, it might as well be said that there is none to make. . . . one simply applies or implements a program. (Derrida 1992: 41)

Undecidability figures, then, not a moment of indecision, but one of high personal responsibility. In Derrida's view, the nexus of principles, laws, and calculus that are usually taken to determine the direction of the good is empty of ethical content, and its operation is no more than an exercise in management. The ethical task is very different from that of "proper" moral procedure. It involves the risks of thinking beyond the boundaries of the familiar; thinking, in other words, for oneself.

For Derrida, the repositioning of ethics as distinct from morality is paralleled by a similar move in which justice is not unproblematically coincident with the established legal principles and procedures that constitute the law. This is to some extent a truism, but what Derrida intends is that the laws of any socius are not—cannot be—sufficient to deliver an ethical justice. This is so not simply in cases where normative expectations are already breached, but in every instance. Given the close association between bioethics and the law, this is especially apposite, for it reminds us that any attempt to systematize the issues must do injury to their full complexity, whether they arise from the intervention of high technologies or from everyday bodily concerns. To give one well-established example, the fundamental legal principle of bodily autonomy—broadly interpreted in lay discourse as property rights in one's own body—is contested both by the commercial exploitation of genetic information and material obtained from human bodies (as chapter 10 discusses) and by the status of the maternal–fetal relation. The application of law to such cases relies all too clearly on a system in which the constitution of the embodied self is thought to be unproblematic and given, rather than always and everywhere mediated.

What is at stake in normative morality and normative laws alike is a retreat to the supposed stability and certainty of conceptual definition in the face of an unknowable otherness that cannot be grasped without a certain reductive violence. In contrast, the ethics that Derrida offers—and it is a highly demanding one—aims to hold open the possibility of thinking the impossible. There is no attempt to ground an alternative program, for that would be to fall back into the limits of a systematized approach, the very predetermination and closure that he seeks to avoid. Above all, a Derridean ethics is not intended to provide prescriptive pathways, but rather to mobilize a critical reconfiguration of existing paradigms, not as a once-and-for-all corrective, but as an open-ended exercise. In recent years, Derrida has been perhaps the most ethically committed of those criticizing modernism, and for all his intellectual complexity, it is notable that he addresses some of the substantive issues of day-to-day life such as the topics of asylum (2001) or nationalism (1992). While his bioethical concerns are as yet peripheral, there is no reason to suppose that his approach, taken up by Nancy Potter in chapter 6, would not fruitfully lend itself to an ethics of the body.

It is not that mainstream bioethicists are necessarily uncritical of the dominant discourse, or unaware of the radicality of the changes in hand, but that in focusing on a practical and normative ethics, on asking primarily what is to be done, too little attention is directed to the task of thinking differently. At its most challenging, a move toward the risk of uncertainty and exposure of the limitations of the principles and rules that are supposed to order moral judgment, must entail an acknowledgment of one's own lack of secure grounding. It surely admits a personal vulnerability that reveals the self-reflective ethicist as no mere commentator or interpreter, but one whose own being is implicated in the ethical deliberation. Just as the perspective of phenomenology makes it clear that health care professionals and the users of their services are mutually constructed in their transactions, so too bioethicists cannot stand aside from the situations they presume to adjudicate. A postmodernist approach is not simply a matter of taking on epistemic uncertainty, but of opening one's self to other possibilities. Whether an issue involves something as everyday as a minor disability—a limp perhaps—or as futuristic as human cloning, it resonates with what we understand proper human form to be, our own included. The advent of advanced technologies has undoubtedly pushed such questions to the fore, but of course they have been there all along. What a postmodernist bioethics demands is an openness to the risk of the unknown, a commitment to self-reflection, and a willingness to be unsettled. Far from being playful in any derogatory sense, it is rather an enterprise of high responsibility. At the same time, it moves out from the questioning self to engage with the needs and desires of others.

The claim, then, is that it is only through a radical and potentially risky rethinking of the underlying ontological, epistemological, and ethical assumptions dominating existing bioethical analyses that new practical responses can be initiated that will widen the bases of adequacy.

Feminist Openings

With this in mind, the purpose of the essays gathered here is not to pursue a single theoretical perspective throughout, but to be open to the operation of thinking differently. There is no one word to encompass what is being attempted, for while some contributions are clearly poststructuralist in inspiration and intent, others are indebted to somewhat earlier traditions of phenomenology, or deal in a culturally marked postmodernism. Moreover, our commitment to theory and practice entails the embrace of an interdisciplinarity that poses the crucial ethical questions, not only in the traditional domain of philosophy, but also within a context of mutually informed fields, including legal studies, bioscientific research, psychiatry, cultural studies, and feminist theory. What holds the contributions to this volume together is that all are firmly postconventional in their determination to go beyond the familiar body of bioethics in both its theoretical and material manifestations. For the editors, the initial impetus to work on such a collection arose from a mutual dissatisfaction with the overly safe and constrained parameters of conventional inquiry that looks on postmodernist approaches—to use the term broadly here—with an ill-disguised skepticism, even contempt. Any analysis that refuses to take for granted the stability and continuity of the unified sovereign self—the archetypal moral agent—runs the risk of being seen as unable to address, still less influence, the ethical dimensions of the impact of the biosciences on all our lives. Rather than mount a detailed rebuttal of such a view, we offer here a series of essays, more or less committed to the guiding paradigms of postmodernism, that belie the central charge. The issue is not to "prove" the superiority of one system over another, and indeed the contributors have no unified approach, but to take the risk of thinking otherwise. In place of certainty, determinacy, and resolution, there is a reflective awareness that outcomes are intrinsically uncertain. Real lives are not conducted singly on any neat, logical plane of abstraction, but as messy and complex constructs that are interwoven with one another in unpredictable and highly changeable ways. In the face of such a dynamic, the task cannot be to impose the order of answers that will prevail unchallenged over time, but to let go of the solid ground where certain analytical categories and concepts are fixed in advance, and to continually reopen the questions themselves. Each contributor in her own way has done this.

Given the widely accepted perception that the recent emergence of bioethics as a powerful voice in its own right owes much to its having been taken up by theoretical and activist feminism, all the essays collected here respond in part to that history. That is not to say that the mutually motivating links are celebrated without critique. Since the beginning of its rejuvenation in the second half of the twentieth century, feminist theory has been marked by the recognition that many of the most fundamental tenets of modernist discourse have supported schemata in which not only women, but other others, have been systematically devalued. In response, feminism has set up alternative models of ontology, epistemology, and not least ethics, which challenge both the discursive primacy of the universal, white, able-bodied, masculinist subject and the normative codes by which that subject is supposed to live. At the same time, however, the desire to mount an effective challenge that would be taken seriously outside feminism has served to justify a certain conservatism at work that limits the extent to which the existing paradigms are taken apart and examined. Nonetheless, in the general field of ethics, feminism has mounted a sustained critique of the supposed neutrality of universalism and a concomitant attention to gender, race, and class in their specifics, and a wariness with regard to favoring abstraction at the expense of the particularities of embodiment, emotion, and affect. The ethics of care, introduced originally by Carol Gilligan's work (1982), has proved especially influential in providing a seemingly solid foundation on which to build a feminist ethics that not only looks very different from its masculinist counterparts, but has empirically descriptive as well as normative components. Its appeal as an important component in the context of bioethics is hardly surprising. Aside from the developments pursued by avowed postmodernists, however, that first confident challenge to the script of modernism hasn't greatly disrupted the enduring notion that ethics is fundamentally concerned with standards of good and evil, right and wrong (Shildrick 2001).

As far as feminist *bioethics* is concerned, there has been a similar disinclination—as is the case within bioethics more generally—to rigorously critique some of the most fundamental theoretical underpinnings of conventional paradigms. It is a task that both explicitly and implicitly propels this collection. At the same time, we want to acknowledge that some enduring changes in the shape of the discipline have already been effected. What has been achieved is considerable: a more interdisciplinary approach (characteristic of feminist scholarship in general); a highly effective critique of the masculinist, ableist, racial, and sexual biases of the mainstream; an attention to context and specificity; and not least, a powerful challenge to what counts as the legitimate ground for bioethical enquiry. As well as insisting on the ethical relevancy of the doctor–patient encounter itself, feminist bioethicists have drawn attention to larger systemic issues. Where at this level the convention is concerned primarily with the allocation of resources, feminist approaches have seen in issues such as the social determinants of health, the hierarchies of research funding, and the global politics of health care, further cause for bioethical reflection. Many influential writers in the field are highly persuasive in laying out the inadequacies of orthodox bioethics, and their contributions have been received positively both within and beyond feminism. Nonetheless, as the essays here indicate, there are reservations. The pervasiveness of the ethics of care throughout the area of bioethics, for example, indicates perhaps the most far-reaching of feminist interventions, but it has come to overshadow other developments. Although scholars like Susan Sherwin (1992) and Rosemarie Tong (1997) are by no means uncritical of such feminist-inspired models, there has been a certain caution, even suspicion, about exploring the avenues opened up by postmodernist perspectives. In short, what has been evident over the past couple of decades is more a matter of radical reform than one of taking the risk of a thoroughgoing deconstruction.

The point is that even where in limited cases feminist ethics in its wider application is slowly coming to terms with, or even enthusiastically engaging with, the implications of recent continental theory, bioethics has remained relatively resistant. Given its marked absence from most feminist texts, one might conclude that postmodernism has little to offer bioethics.[3] What has long been evident for feminists of all persuasions—and is a major reason for our involvement in the field—is that biomedical discourse is an incredibly powerful force in the construction of social identities and normative categories. Far from being a putatively neutral intervention dealing only with natural givens that may be modified for the better, bioscience itself is always ethically loaded from the start. The view that the primary purpose of biomedicine is to cure, or to care for, is contested by the realization that health care is as much about control, containment, and normalization as it is about treatment. As such it is a major site of power/knowledge in the Foucauldian sense (Foucault 1980; Singer 1993; Jones and Porter 1994; Shildrick 1997). Moreover, in inscribing itself on the body, biomedicine reveals itself as a textual practice that produces particular modes of identity and politics. These are all intrinsically ethical considerations, not in the familiar mode of conventional morality with its concentration on the parameters of right and wrong behavior, but as a matter of the dynamic becoming of the embodied self. The focus of concern then, cannot be limited to the practical mechanics of bioscience as it affects preexisting subjects and pregiven bodies, but must include a fully developed notion of embodiment as a process without end. Viewed in such a light, it becomes less contentious to claim that many of the major features of postmodernist perspectives have direct bearing, not only on contemporary bioscientific developments, but also on any attempt to reconsider bioethics per se, which is above all an ethics of the embodied self.

Alongside its attention to the nature of power—which in postmodernism does not disappear as a category so much as reappear as fully discursive—feminist theory has been particularly committed to exposing the ways in which sameness and difference operate, not simply as opposites, but in a hierarchical relation of privilege. Starting from the initially self-evident binary concept of sexual difference, progressive feminism has moved on to concede that differences are always multiple, indeterminate, and mobile. The categories of gender, race, and class—to name the usual suspects—make little sense as isolated components of any form of embodied identity, but are mutually constructed, albeit in an unfixed relation to one another. For postmodernists the deconstruction of difference goes further yet toward the Derridean concept of *différance* in which the distinctions between categories are exposed as intrinsically unstable. None of this is to say, however, that postconventional thought is unable to acknowledge the actual here and now operation of normative difference, particularly as it is manifest in various strategies of power. It is of no small significance that the essays in this volume, while encompassing a range of personal, cultural, and political differences, and despite their internationalism, are nevertheless alike in emerging from a broadly generic western European and North American perspective. This is not, we would stress, because postmodernism surreptitiously imports a new form of indifferent universalism under the guise of deprivileging binary difference, but is rather a limitation of which we are acutely conscious.

Not surprisingly, many of the contributors directly address the issue of differences and the ways in which bioethics is implicated in power, but nonetheless, the question remains as to why nonwestern voices are missing. In contradistinction to many academic fields, where, important though they are, the diverse ethnic origins of *western*-based and educated scholars appear sometimes to substitute for a global range of perspectives, the discussion of bioethics is by no means restricted to the West. This may be particularly true of feminist bioethics, where at least one influential umbrella organization, Feminist Approaches to Bioethics (FAB), attracts members and conference contributors from all over the world, with strong representation from South America and Asia.[4] Given that our initial call for papers was circulated not only through more western-identified sources but through FAB itself, and that later more targeted approaches failed to elicit a positive response, it seems likely that nonwestern bioethicists, perhaps even more than their western counterparts, may not see the analytical tools of postmodernism as useful to their purpose. Given that such a disengagement is not equally evident in other areas of study, such as postcoloniality, we wonder if there is something peculiar to ethics—or at least to bioethics—that might explain it. One tentative suggestion is that the discourses of legally recognized and enforced individual rights, and of personal autonomy (which are of course central to conventional bioethics), have been long established in western contexts, albeit often denied to specific groups.

In contrast, the experience elsewhere—and especially in those countries that have suffered colonial rule—is that while indigenous systems of ethics may have been overridden by the hegemonic and global sweep of western ideologies, historically there has been limited delivery of any perceived benefits. Could it be that the first concern in such situations is to ensure that what has been promised in the abstract is now applied, and that those directly engaged with bioethics see their immediate task as contributing to a more adequate and equitable practice?

One thing is certain; bioethics is no neutral abstraction but operates in the "real" world of lived-in bodies where the effects of power are tangible. It would be foolhardy in the extreme, or simply frivolous, to attempt to give any reductive account of the different concerns of others, but western power must surely play a significant part. Not only has the claim of conventional western morality to universal applicability been backed up by a material dominance, but the more recent insights of postmodernism relate back specifically, albeit critically, to that same intellectual system. It may be that the relative disinclination of nonwestern bioethicists to employ such paradigms reflects a mistrust of further developments of an ideology that has proved less than effective in securing benefits in the first place.

At the same time, a further difficulty arises in the perception that postconventional discourses, and more specifically postmodernism, are not entirely serious, that they are "playful" about issues that demand the utmost gravity. Postmodernists would willingly concede that there is a deliberate element of positive playfulness in their analyses, but not that it detracts from the significance and commitment of their perspective. It is after all an exercise in thinking differently, sometimes even thinking the unthinkable, that may, but may not, result in doing things differently, or at least in pointing the way to appropriate material changes. Nonetheless there is a suspicion that only those who already enjoy the advantages of intellectual and material dominance can afford to follow through such free-floating analyses. For many others without security or power, the substantive issues are always too urgent, the demand for action—in bioethics, the need for definitive decision—too pressing, to be delayed. There is certainly no implication that reluctance to utilize the insights of postmodernist thinking is limited to nonwestern circles, but it may be that those who must always struggle against the assumption of intellectual superiority by the West are particularly mistrustful. As the editors of this collection, one Canadian and one English, both white, we must acknowledge the limitations of our own perspective without presuming to fully understand their effects. Our hope is that skeptics from all academic and cultural backgrounds will take the risk of reading the essays in this volume and take from them insights that might be utilized in new and unforeseen ways. The focus of the volume is indeed western, but just as feminists have long reappropriated masculinist theory for their own ends, the invitation here is to read the material, not as definitive positional statements that close down their own application, but as a series of openings.

The division of any edited collection into user-friendly sections is more often than not arbitrary, but with a collection that is explicitly committed to an approach that questions divisions and boundaries, the difficulty of such an operation is instructive. Not one of the chapters has a finally fixed place, and we hope that the reader will make his or her own connections and think through the many shifts of perspective that the insights of any one essay can offer for another. The purpose is not to provide a text of easily assimilable and certain knowledge, but to provoke a critical openness that is excited by horizons that recede even as they are approached. That said, we have provided certain signposts.

Given the overriding importance of recognizing and acknowledging difference in any postconventional project, it is appropriate that part II should focus on critical differences. The section speaks to the notion of difference both in terms of the characteristic feminist focus on plural differences rather than on simple unified categories, and to the postmodernist project of dismantling binary oppositions in favor of a more dynamic crossing of boundaries. Philipa Rothfield uses an explicitly phenomenological approach that stresses the interdependence of lived bodies, but which at the very point of breaking down the oppositional difference between self and other, and between doctor and patient, has been accused of failing to fully acknowledge the diversities among bodies. Rothfield turns to some somatically oriented ethnographies to flesh out issues of multicultural differences within the medical setting, and asks how the phenomenological enterprise might be applied to a bioethics of difference. Where Rothfield focuses on the everyday problematics of the medical encounter, Jackie Leach Scully addresses issues given acute topicality by genetic research and the sequencing of the human genome. Her essay takes up the complexity of differences, and their relationship to the normative, in the context of genetic variation, specifically with regard to disability. As Scully observes, and other essays in the book indicate, the phenomenon of disability is too diverse to be encompassed by any single explanatory model. Her proposal is that a "pluralist postmodern methodology"—another form of critical difference—is best suited to the ethical task. Together the two chapters address the question of how difference, seen more properly as specificity, can escape the grip of normative thinking and feed into a more adequate model of bioethics.

In part III, "Thinking Through Crisis," the emphasis shifts to consideration of some specific issues of public and professional concern within biomedicine, which are especially evocative of moral anxiety. Unlike the practices of the new biotechnologies, the "conditions" seem to fit easily within existing paradigms, but each chapter argues that the conventional parameters of bioethics respond only to a rigid and oppositional notion of health and disease that fails to account for the fluidity of embodied selves. Through the medium of various categories—HIV (chapter 4), drug addiction (chapter 5), madness and especially borderline personality disorder (chapter 6) and cancer (chapter 7)—the essays raise fundamental challenges to the abstract organizing and normative principles that structure conventional bioethics. The mind–body binary, autonomy, beneficence, and rationality are all called into question, and the methods by which bioethical decisions are constructed, communicated, and evaluated are scrutinized and found wanting. Both Martha Rosengarten and Helen Keane call on their experiences of clinical research to contest the meanings attributed to their respective objects of study, and to suggest that the ethical issues are far more complex and fluid than models of normative embodiment can encompass. Each is acutely aware of the constructedness of both materiality and meaning. In Nancy Potter's contribution, attention is focused on the psychic elements of forms of embodiment, as she reflects on the marking and inscription of madness, particularly in women. Potter offers an illuminating exposition of how key postmodernist thinkers such as Derrida, Kristeva, Irigaray, and

Mouffe might contribute to a more responsive psychiatry, and she outlines what she calls an ethics of the in-between. In contrast to Potter's suspicion of narrative as therapy, Lisa Diedrich reclaims narrative—through the medium of two personal accounts of cancer—to suggest that it can be both postmodernist in tenor and explicate how the failure of the body and the failure of language can nonetheless ground an ethics.

The challenges and conundrums of recent biotechnologies move to center stage in part IV, where some of the most exemplary issues of postmodernity—the problematization of the parameters of both the "normal" body and the human self—are examined. Given their long-standing concern with the area of reproduction—where many advanced biotechnologies first evolved—feminist bioethicists have been in the forefront of addressing the new problematic. Where these essays carry the argument forward is in beginning to develop postconventional ethical models that answer the demands of a transformative bioscience. While subsequent chapters explore the limits of using the "natural" body as the arbiter of social relations and individual behavior, and reveal how new technologies invite a radical rethinking of ontological and epistemological categories, Sylvia Nagl first reminds us that what we accept as scientific facts and immutable aspects of the natural world are fabricated through rhetorical devices, in particular sites, by individuals following institutional agendas. As a member of the scientific community, Nagl is acutely aware of the professional constraints on, and yet responsibility to, "think otherwise." Like Nagl, Carol Bacchi and Chris Beasley look back to existing feminist bioethics and set out to critically review the ethics of care, in this instance within the context of biotechnology. As political scientists they are concerned with the test of political usefulness, and conclude that less normative and prescriptive approaches to ethics would better serve the users of biotechnologies. The following two essays, in contrast, are pitched right on the edge of current legal scholarship and project their analyses into the vexed issues of ontology and identity being raised by genetic technologies. Isabel Karpin argues that genetic research uncovers the transgressivity of all forms of embodiment, and like other contributors (Scully and Roen in particular), she reflects on aspects of the disabled subject. For Karpin, questions of the autonomy of the self are set against the implications of both genetic family and a community, rather than an abstractly human genome. In Karen O'Connell's chapter, the medium of genetics is used to investigate the limits of the "clean and proper body" in its Kristevan sense, and to reincorporate the abject in a space in which a new distinctive ethics might emerge.

A concern with the nature of embodiment in which the self is inseparable from its corporeality is the theme of part V, "Rethinking the Materiality of Embodiment," which turns once again to phenomenology and to some specifically anomalous forms of being-in-the-body. For many of the contributors, including myself, one highly significant breakthrough in thinking about a postconventional bioethics was provided by Ros Diprose's early 1990s essay "A Genethics that Makes Sense." That work is now out of print, but Diprose has provided a recent update that opens the final part of this volume. Again the disruptive power of genetics makes its appearance as the site that mobilizes a radical reconsideration of bioethics itself. In a piece that brings together many of the concerns of the collection, Diprose sets out a phenomenological approach to issues of biomedical knowledge, of limits and boundaries, and the construction of putative identities in the face of anomalies. That desire for sameness uncovered here takes on a highly material form in the essay by Katrina Roen. The question for Roen is how we are constituted as sexed and gendered subjects, which she addresses in the issue of intersex infants and children. By calling on feminist, poststructuralist, and queer theory, Roen outlines a bioethics that fully takes into account the discursive production and cultural inscription of all bodies, and that is both adequate for and open to the possibility of alternative ways of being. As in all the chapters here, the question returns to the status of difference, to the variability and contingency of embodiment, and to the insistence that an adequate bioethics can never center on abstract conceptions of well-being.

For all the evident intersections found in this text, it remains clear that there is no one theory of postmodernism, and no attempt is made to be comprehensive or to claim that all the points raised would find consensus. Nonetheless, there is wide agreement that both the body and the subject are unstable at best, provisional rather than fixed, and no longer the center of self-authorized meaning. Most important, there is a thoroughgoing deconstruction of the notion of discrete categories, of clear-cut distinctions that are marked by defensible and predictable boundaries. In particular, the material and conceptual separation of one body, and one embodied subject, from another—the basis on which a modernist morality of the autonomous self is founded—is shown to be fundamentally untenable. Some of these aspects are not limited to postmodernism, but appear in other postconventional theories, but what they all have in common is a commitment to a reconfiguration, rather than simple reform, of liberal humanist paradigms. In short, they demand a very different way of thinking about the issues at stake and the need for bioethics to go further in investigating the efficacy of new theoretical resources. Our purpose in this book is not to provide answers to moral conundrums, as conventional bioethics might endeavor to do, but to create an imaginative and fluid space in which to think about the ontological, epistemological, and ethical implications of not just diversifying the technical processes of biomedicine but also of materializing new forms of embodied relationships. To that end, we offer not a bioethics about the body, but an ethics of the body.

Notes

1. For a full account of the relation between Merleau-Ponty's phenomenology and Irigaray's rethinking of ethics, see Vasseleu (1998), and for an indication of Irigaray's potential for bioethics, see Rawlinson (2001).

2. Donna Haraway, for example, sees the task as one of "queering what counts as nature" (1992: 300), and she is unequivocal that natural order has always been a myth of humanism.

3. Although individual essays and many discrete references exist, any sustained development is harder to find. There have of course been some notable exceptions in book-length discussions, such as Diprose (1994) and Shildrick (1997, 2002), but despite plentiful postmodernist feminist work on the body (Butler 1993; Grosz 1994; Terry and Urla 1995; Shildrick and Price 1998), on bioscience (Lykke and Braidotti 1996; Haraway 1997; Waldby 1996, 2000), and on the law (Cornell 1991, 1992; Frug 1992), it has been brought together with ethics only peripherally.

4. See, for example, the FAB edited collections *Globalizing Feminist Bioethics* (Tong et al. 2000) and *Feminist Bioethics, Human Rights and the Developing World* (Tong et al. 2004).

References

Butler, Judith (1993) *Bodies that Matter: On the Discursive Limits of "Sex."* London: Routledge.

Cornell, Drucilla (1991) *Beyond Accommodation: Ethical Feminism, Deconstruction, and the Law*. London: Routledge.

Cornell, Drucilla (1992) *The Philosophy of the Limit*. London: Routledge.

Derrida, Jacques (1973) *Speech and Phenomena*, trans. David Allison. Evanston, Ill.: Northwestern University Press.

Derrida, Jacques (1992) *The Other Heading: Reflections on Today's Europe*. Bloomington: Indiana University Press.

Derrida, Jacques (2001) *On Cosmopolitanism and Forgiveness*, trans. Mark Dooley and Michael Hughes. London: Routledge.

Diprose, Rosalyn (1994) *The Bodies of Women: Ethics, Embodiment and Sexual Difference*. London: Routledge.

Foucault, Michel (1980) *Power/Knowledge: Selected Interviews and Other Writings, 1972–77*, ed. Colin Gordon. Brighton, UK: Harvester Press.

Frug, Mary Jo (1992) *Postmodern Legal Feminism*. New York: Routledge.

Gilligan, Carol (1982) *In a Different Voice: Psychological Theory and Women's Development*. Cambridge, Mass.: Harvard University Press.

Grosz, Elizabeth (1994) *Volatile Bodies: Toward a Corporeal Feminism*. Bloomington: Indiana University Press.

Haraway, Donna (1992) "The Promises of Monsters: A Regenerative Politics for Inappropriate/d Others" in Lawrence Grossberg et al. (eds.), *Cultural Studies*. London: Routledge.

Haraway, Donna (1997) *Modest_Witness@Second_Millennium.FemaleMan©_Meets_OncoMouse™*. New York: Routledge.

Irigaray, Luce (1985) *This Sex Which Is Not One*, trans. Catherine Porter. Ithaca, N.Y.: Cornell University Press.

Irigaray, Luce (1993) An Ethics of Sexual Difference, trans. Carolyn Burke and Gillian Gill. Ithaca, N.Y.: Cornell University Press.

Jones, Colin, and Porter, Roy (1994) *Reassessing Foucault: Power, Medicine and the Body*. London: Routledge.

Kristeva, Julia (1982) *The Powers of Horror. An Essay on Abjection*. New York: Columbia University Press.

Lykke, Nina, and Braidotti, Rosi (eds.) (1996) *Between Monster, Goddesses and Cyborgs: Feminist Confrontations with Science, Medicine and Cyberspace*. London: Zed Press.

Merleau-Ponty, Maurice (1962). *The Phenomenology of Perception*. London: Routledge.

Merleau-Ponty, Maurice (1968) *The Visible and the Invisible*. Evanston, Ill.: Northwestern University Press.

Rawlinson, Mary C. (2001) "The Concept of a Feminist Bioethics," *Journal of Medicine and Philosophy* 26, 4.

Sherwin, Susan (1992) *No Longer Patient: Feminist Ethics and Health Care*. Philadelphia, Pa.: Temple University Press.

Shildrick, Margrit (1997) *Leaky Bodies and Boundaries: Feminism, Postmodernism and (Bio)ethics*. London: Routledge.

Shildrick, Margrit (2001) "Reappraising Feminist Ethics: Developments and Debates," *Feminist Theory* 2, 2.

Shildrick, Margrit (2002) *Embodying the Monster: Encounters with the Vulnerable Self*. London: Sage.

Shildrick, Margrit, and Price, Janet (1998) *Vital Signs: Feminist Reconfigurations of the Bio/logical Body*. Edinburgh: Edinburgh University Press.

Singer, Linda (1993) *Erotic Welfare: Sexual Theory and Politics in the Age of Epidemic*. London: Routledge.

Terry, Jennifer, and Urla, Jacqueline (eds.) (1995) *Deviant Bodies: Critical Perspectives on Difference in Science and Popular Culture*. Bloomington: Indiana University Press.

Tong, Rosemarie (1997) *Feminist Approaches to Bioethics: Theoretical Reflections and Practical Applications*. Boulder, Col.: Westview Press.

Tong, Rosemarie, Anderson, Gwen, and Santos, Aida (eds.) (2000) *Globalizing Feminist Bioethics: Women's Health Concerns Worldwide*. Boulder, Col.: Westview Press.

Tong, Rosemarie, Donchin, Anne, and Dodds, Susan (eds.) (2004) *Feminist Bioethics, Human Rights and the Developing World: Integrating Global and Local Perspectives*. Lanham, Md.: Rowman and Littlefield.

Vasseleu, Cathryn (1998) *Textures of Light: Vision and Touch in Irigaray, Levinas and Merleau-Ponty*. London: Routledge.

Waldby, Catherine (1996) *AIDS and the Body Politic: Biomedicine and Sexual Difference*. London: Routledge.

Waldby, Catherine (2000) *The Visible Human Project: Informatic Bodies and Posthuman Medicine*. London: Routledge.

II

Critical Differences

2

Attending to Difference: Phenomenology and Bioethics

Philipa Rothfield

Although it has never dominated traditional bioethics, phenomenology has been quietly generating critical perspectives on medicine, while offering its own conceptual alternatives. Phenomenology has been at pains to establish that the patient's experience of illness is ethically paramount, and to suggest ways in which this recognition might be incorporated within medical practice. Its elucidation of the patient's experience within the biomedical setting is typically conducted at an abstract, formal level. According to such investigations, the particular merely serves to facilitate an understanding of the essential workings of subjectivity.

Judith Butler has criticized Merleau-Ponty, both for failing to specify the kinds of bodies and sexualities he was phenomenologically analyzing and for the unacknowledged intrusion of his own sexually specific understanding of the matter (Butler 1989). Butler's charge was that Merleau-Ponty did not consider *whose* bodies and *which* sexualities were at stake, nor did he acknowledge his own corporeal complicity in the way in which he viewed the subject. Thus, despite his intention to describe certain moments in the general structure of human, sexual being, Butler alleges that Merleau-Ponty's analysis was both partial and skewed.

Is it possible that phenomenological bioethics is similarly skewed? Should it too specify the kinds of bodies that it takes to participate within biomedical practice? And if it does, will this impact upon the character of its claims? To ask these questions is to critically review phenomenological bioethics in the light of postmodern sensitivities regarding difference. Phenomenology has a lot to offer in that it provides a philosophical commitment to everyday life as it is lived in corporeal terms. Yet, if difference is missing from the account, how is it possible to discern the diversity of bodily experience? Is it possible to generate a phenomenological bioethics that retains its formal validity while engaging with the differences that exist between bodies? This chapter pursues these questions by looking at cultural differences among bodies within medicine. It aims to ask of phenomenological bioethics whether it can deal with cultural differences as they occur within the medical setting.

Beginning with a brief account of phenomenology's approach to medical ethics, the challenges of cultural difference are introduced, then explored in relation to questions of corporeal specificity. Although there is little material on cultural difference in relation to phenomenological bioethics, medical anthropology looks at medical practice in a range of cultural settings. Set within this context, Thomas Csordas's work confronts the epistemological complexities of intercorporeal communication and interaction. Using a phenomenological framework of analysis, he highlights the problems that attend the effort to understand the corporeal specificity of another when that other is culturally different. Phenomenologists such as Zaner and Toombs recognize that the doctor-patient relation is not symmetrical. However, they do not dwell upon the effect that cultural difference has on this relationship. Their frameworks do not specify what sorts of bodies enter into the biomedical exchange. Csordas's work invites a response from phenomenology in regard to the bioethical dimensions of intercorporeal difference.

Phenomenological Bioethics

Although each approach has its nuances, phenomenology characteristically aims to analyze the structures of experience. In the case of biomedicine, it is the patient's experience of illness that is examined. Phenomenologists variously elucidate the impact of illness or injury on the subject, including the disruptions of everyday life, the experience of symptoms or discomfort, alien body sensations, or bodily distortions; in short, the existential dimensions of illness. They argue that doctors are not necessarily trained to recognize the centrality of the patient's experience in their work because the scientific paradigm tends toward a reductionist view of the person (Zaner 1988). Many phenomenologists trace the reductive tendencies of medicine to Descartes' mechanistic reading of the body. According to Leder:

> At the core of modern medical practice is the Cartesian revelation: the living body can be treated as essentially no different from a machine. Though any good clinician also engages the patient-*as-person*, the predominant thrust of modern medical therapeutics has been upon such mechanistic interventions. (Leder 1992: 23)

In contrast, phenomenological accounts of human subjectivity, especially arising from the work of Merleau-Ponty, understand the self as inextricably mind and body, thereby resisting both dualism and reductionism.

Phenomenology's remedy for the reductions of medicine is to propose a focus for medical practice that incorporates a closer attention to the vicissitudes of corporeal life, especially the patient's. Leder (1992) refers to the lived body and the existential dimensions of the medical setting, whereas Toombs (1992) emphasizes immediate experience and the meaning of illness. Shanner (1996) likewise draws attention to the experience of those patients who have lived through certain predicaments in order to stress what it was like for them. Both Zaner and Shanner refer to patient narratives as a means to understand and represent people's experiences. The thrust of these approaches is to make space for a fuller disclosure of the patient's experience of illness. Their aim is to highlight the importance and complexity of experience within medicine.

Given the divergence between the allegedly reductive views of biomedicine and the existential domain of the patient, it is not surprising that the medical encounter may fail to achieve a mutual understanding between the patient and the doctor. Toombs claims that there is a systematic distortion of meaning in the physician–patient relationship:

> [I]llness is experienced in significantly different ways by physician and patient. Consequently, rather than representing a shared "reality" between them, illness represents in effect two quite distinct "realities." (Toombs 1992: 10)

At present, it is the patient's experience of illness that is elided in the medical encounter, for the discourse of medicine prevails over the experiential lifeworld of the patient. This is understandable given the sense of therapeutic intervention that lies at the heart of medical practice. However, Toombs argues that physicians need to attend to the lived experiences of patients in order to set therapeutic goals (Toombs, 1992: xvi). She writes:

> As a first step towards achieving a shared understanding of the meaning of illness, physicians can learn to recognize and pay attention to, these typical characteristics of the human experience of illness. (Toombs 1992: 97)

Baron argues for a similar shift on the part of the doctor, toward an engagement with the patient's needs, desires, and demands (Baron 1992: 44).

This requires the construction of a shared world of meaning between doctor and patient, one that incorporates the patient's subjective experience of illness, a side of the equation systematically undervalued in relation to the scientific attitude embedded in the medical gaze. Despite structural differences between doctor and patient, both Baron and Toombs aim for a convergence of understanding within clinical practice. Such an understanding, they argue, needs to incorporate the experiential standpoint of the patient. Given that the scientific perspective of the physician does not conventionally incorporate patient experience, as distinct from patient diagnosis, the sort of epistemic shift required by the physician is significant.

How, then, is such a shift to be achieved? Toombs approaches the issue on the basis of that which is common among people—their lived corporeality. In her view, everyday experience can function as a basis for comprehending the disruptions of illness. One aspect of such everyday experience is the ambiguity of the lived body. According to Toombs, everyone has a sense of the ambiguity of lived corporeality: that I am my body but also separate from it (it is outside my control). I realize that I am my body because all my efforts involve physical activity, yet I realize that I cannot always control my body; I tire, I get sore, I get indigestion, I miss that backhand shot. For Toombs, illness confronts us with this not-unfamiliar state of affairs—on the one hand, I am this sick body, and on the other, its being ill is out of my control. There is also for Toombs a sense in which everyone experiences their bodies as alien; this is said to be the sense in which we all feel our bodies in terms of their limitations, as encumbrances.

All people, then, experience bodily ambiguity and the alien character of corporeality, although the experience may be more extreme in illness. These experiential facts are taken to indicate that the "lifeworlds of physician and patient do indeed provide for mutual understanding with regard to the illness experience" (Toombs 1992: 98). The lifeworld itself also enables the physician to understand particular bodily disorders

(Toombs 1992). Here, Toombs cites Engel and Engelhardt, who claim that the development of a scientific understanding of illness is built upon a more personal sense of one's own corporeal life processes. First, medical students draw upon their own bodily experience in order to develop a scientific understanding of bodily processes, and second, doctors relate the patient's experiences to elements of their own experience.

Cassell's work, written for doctors, also suggests that the lived body is a means toward effective communication:

> Because all of us have bowel movements, we all have a framework of reference to help us understand her. Persons taking histories should use themselves and their own experiences with their bodies and the world as a reference for what they hear. (Cassell 1985: 46)

In cases where the doctor has never had a particular experience, Cassell suggests that more questions need to be asked "so that when you are finished you have both acquired the diagnostic information and learned more about the world" (Cassell 1985: 46). There is a sense here that the gap between one corporeality and another is not that great.

In sum, Toombs argues that the humanity of physician and patient is a means to bridge perspectival, discursive, and lifeworld differences between the two parties. By emphasizing the utmost generalities of corporeal subjectivity, she asserts a common basis for the development of mutual understanding. Both Toombs and Cassell suggest that the doctor draw upon his or her own bodily experience and understanding in order to comprehend the experiential perspective of the patient. Even where that experience is lacking, it is thought that connections can be made. For Toombs, it may be possible to extend certain experiences of wellness into the domain of illness, while for Cassell, questioning can expand the doctor's understanding. In both cases, the doctor is potentially capable of reaching a corporeal understanding of the patient's lived body, one that incorporates elements from his or her own lived body.

Is it, could it, ever be the case that differences between the doctor and the patient stand in the way of that corporeal understanding? Rather than begin with universalist assumptions about human corporeality, what if we began with the difficulties that bodily specificity brings to the bioethical situation? What might this suggest to the project of phenomenological bioethics? In what follows, a number of cases have been selected that challenge the notion that a common corporeality underlies all parties to the medical encounter. These examples illustrate the ways in which racism and ethnocentrism in particular both enter into and trouble the biomedical scene.

Differential Treatment on Grounds of Color

Case 1

Although Cassell nowhere mentions skin color in his work on clinical technique for doctors, perceptions of color may well influence the way in which doctors approach their patients and vice versa. In her paper, "Reconstructing the Patient, Starting with Women of Color," Dorothy Roberts (1996) argues that doctors treat women of color differently than their white, female patients. She cites a number of studies which have found that women of color get worse treatment, less explanation, wait longer to be treated, and are told, not asked, what to do (Roberts 1996). Roberts claims that because of these negative experiences, these women are now thoroughly alienated from the medical establishment. As a consequence, reforming the ethics of the medical profession may not be enough to reverse the trend of poor treatment. The point is that it is not enough for white doctors to finally come to the party (were they to address their racism), for these women are skeptical, critical, and resistant to what they perceive to be "medical control." Roberts concludes by asking whether some other strategy of empowerment for these women might not be more effective, one where they have more control over the institutions that deliver health care (Roberts 1996: 136).[1]

Case 2

This example concerns the delivery of palliative care to the Pitjantjatjara people of central Australia. According to Jon Willis:

> [T]he issue is not simply to modify elements of palliative care so that cultural differences in belief and practice are accommodated, but to recognise that different cultures "do death" in different ways, and that institutions for the provision of palliative care are bound up in the "way of dying" of the culture in which they originated. (Willis 1999: 427)

Willis argues that it is not possible to provide for what he calls an "acceptable death," unless that care recognizes and accommodates the specific "way of dying" of Australian Pitjantjatjara Aborigines as a cultural aspect of these peoples' lives. He describes two elements of Pitjantjatjara culture that especially impact upon their dying. One is the importance of land, which relates to ancestral and dreamtime associations with land, and the second is the importance of being cared for by the mother's family rather than health care professionals. Given these factors, it could be argued that state-funded palliative care ought to reflect the Pitjantjatjara people's need to die in their homeland, under family care. Unfortunately, this contrasts with the fact that most palliative care in Australia is hospice or hospital-based, and that "patients in rural settings have typically been required to relocate to regional centres or even state capitals to access any structured form of palliation" (Willis 1999: 342). Furthermore, the costs associated with providing care to extremely remote locations would be high, taxing the scarce resources currently available in terms of district nursing staff. On the other hand, if patients are forced to relocate, this can provoke fear and isolation (Willis 1999: 425). A study of the experiences of indigenous patients on center-based dialysis for end-stage renal failure revealed the great social and cultural costs involved in removing patients from their homes in central Australia (Willis 1995). Moreover, once they were relocated, it was noted that race issues affected patient–carer interactions, a finding echoed by Preece, who cites one patient's remark:

> On average I take between 100 and 260 tablets a week. Pathology tests are performed monthly and the results are never discussed with me. Why am I having these tests done, and for what? There is no feedback from any of the hospital staff. . . . I feel the doctor is intimidated by me because I speak up if I am not happy with the service provision. I am also a spokesperson for the ATSI [Aboriginal and Torres Strait Islander] patients here on dialysis. *Sometimes I think the doctor wishes I would die so I would not be a problem.* (Preece, cited in Willis 1999: 428; my emphasis)

Cultural Factfiles

Case 3

From the late 1970s onward, a series of "cultural factfiles" were developed in the United Kingdom with a view to assisting health care professionals in the provision of culturally sensitive care. On the surface, these factfiles would seem to offer some educational grounding in cultural differences as it impacts upon service provision. However, according to Gunaratnam, these documents are simplistic and culturally reductive (Gunaratnam 1997). Smaje and Field make a similar point regarding the factfile approach:

> The implicit model of culture is an external modulation of some essentially stable "individual" whose behaviour, though perhaps culturally patterned in a distinctive way, is readily comprehensible as a response to the human universals of dying and death. Here "cultural difference" merely encodes "their way" of doing something in distinction to "our way" of doing it—the something in question being regarded as fixed. Such assumptions are questionable at best. (Smaje and Field 1997: 161)

In Gunaratnam's view, the codification and typification of cultural practice promotes a formulaic and essentializing conception of cultural difference.

Gunaratnam conducted focus group interviews with hospice staff on the ways in which ethnicity and death were handled in their workplace in order to explore the impact of health care workers' understanding of cultural difference. She found that although the cultural factfiles provided some information on cultural difference, they also provoked professional concerns about "getting it right" with respect to the information rather than attending to the particular situation. This led to the irony expressed by one worker:

> I have done my most miraculous stuff with cultures I know nothing about. If you don't know anything about a culture you are not tempted to come up with your own solutions for them. (cited in Gunaratnam 1997: 173)

A similar point was made by another health worker who pointed out the sense in which cultural factfiles can encourage workers to 'presume and act on those presumptions,' rather than think more carefully (cited in Gunaratnam 1997: 173). Gunaratnam also stresses the reductive implication of cultural factfiles, that individual subjectivities are wholly determined by cultural affiliation. In contrast to such a view, Gunaratnam maintains that people are not merely products of their cultural background (Gunaratnam 1997). However much generalized information is available, it cannot predict the complexities of any one person's predicament or the actions they will pursue. For example, Gunaratnam quotes a worker's recollection of the death of a young African woman who did not want her body sent to Africa because she wanted to preserve what monies she had for her children. This desire was at odds with the conventions of her cultural background, and a struggle ensued between the woman and the men of her family, who wanted to follow tradition in this respect (Gunaratnam 1997: 178). The hospice worker who was recounting the tale confessed:

> but I was thinking how it touches me as a worker . . . and I was thinking that's often a conflict . . . you know, is it that I only respect . . . other culture's attitudes so . . . long as it doesn't impinge on my own values, which are that, you know, that the kids are more important and they should benefit. (cited in Gunaratnam 1997: 178)

According to Gunaratnam, cultural sensitivity needs to be supplemented by a situational flexibility that includes listening to the particularities of the person beyond their cultural typification. The difficulty here is that the apprehension of particularities always occurs through the lived specificity of the health care worker, including the management values that determine what constitutes a "good" death. For example, the death of people from North Africa and Greece elicited a great deal of public grieving on the part of friends and family, threatening the order of the hospice as well as conflicting with the needs of the other patients for peace and quiet (Gunaratnam 1997). It was noted that the acceptability of the noise was filtered through the values and understandings of the hospice workers, which in turn related to the institutional norms around order and good management.

Implications for Phenomenology

Toombs's ideal convergence between doctor and patient is predicated upon a homogeneous cultural landscape. Although the doctor's perspective is scientistic and the patient's is not, the doctor him or herself has an existential grounding in a lived body that is fundamentally *like* that of the patient. Roberts, Willis, and Gunaratnam call this shared body into question. Writers such as Cassell suppose that not having an experience can be potentially remedied through careful questioning that aims to provide the doctor with a greater understanding, enhancing the doctor's own worldly understanding. But experience does not always add up. Ceres Victora conducted an ethnographic study of working-class women in Porto Alegre, Brazil. In particular, she listened to their accounts and explanations of their pregnancies. These accounts revealed, among other things, the embodied experience of an organ—called by these women, the "body's mother"—that does not exist according to biomedicine. How to explain a bodily experience that does not tally with biomedical knowledge? Rather than view the experience as simply nonmedical, lay, or folk lore, Victora's explanation refers to the organization of space and time within the everyday lives of these women. She takes this to include:

> The ways their families are organised, the way they relate to other people, the way they raise their children, the way they cook, the way they love, the way they look after the ill. . . . I have discussed elsewhere how the shantytown groups' experience of a more fluid space organization in the households is coherent with a more fluid notion of body organs and systems. I suggest that this differs from the biomedical images of the body that rely on a much more rigid structure. (Victora 1997: 171)

Victora understands and explains the lived body according to its own social and cultural setting. Bodily facts do not exist outside this setting, but only make sense within the social and cultural practices that constitute everyday life. When one apprehends the diversity of cultures in the world, it becomes possible to appreciate the view that "people know their bodily facts in different ways" (Victora 1997: 170). In other words, bodily experience is a specific sociocultural event that cannot be extracted from the setting of the experience and ascribed to some universal body.

What does the multiplicity of lived bodies suggest for phenomenological bioethics? First of all, it disrupts the process by which Toombs, Cassell, Baron, and others imagine the ideal doctor–patient scene, for it suggests a heterogeneity that cannot be overcome by reference to a common body. Second, it calls into question the neutrality of those phenomenologists who, through the phenomenological reduction, seek to set aside all presuppositions concerning the nature of the world (Toombs 1992: xiii). According to phenomenological doctrine, the phenomenologist him or herself aspires to a perspectival neutrality. For instance, Shanner describes a process by which the bioethicist comes to a refined and general understanding of "what it is like" to experience a particular condition. She aims to produce a typical characterization (a Weberian ideal-type) framed from the point of view of the patient. As a means to finding the "shared meanings" and "patterns" of a certain state, Shanner suggests that the investigator brackets his or her own life-world and enters that of the patient. She advocates drawing upon narratives from a multiplicity of sources in order to extend the experiential reach of the bioethicist. She uses the term "triangulation" as a methodological metaphor to represent the cross-checking that aims to iron out the distortions and differences between the various perspectives (Shanner 1996: 125).

Although articulated differently, the phenomenological approaches of Toombs, Zaner, and Shanner all aspire to extract the common, shared, invariant features of experience. In methodological terms, it is thought that the phenomenologist him or herself can transcend his or her own lived specificity in order to apprehend those transcendental features of the patient's experience, which in turn can be apprehended by the doctor, who also transcends his or her own corporeal specificity. This presumes that all differences come later, after the phenomenologist has done his or her work.

It is ironic that phenomenology both enables specific attention to the lived body and effaces its specificity. Perhaps the phenomenological reduction has the matter the wrong way around. Perhaps we might relinquish the erasure of difference according to some conception of universal corporeality and approach the meeting of bodies within the medical exchange as a potential negotiation of difference. What would we find if we started with the corporeal specificities of the relevant parties?

Corporeal Spectatorship and the Cultural Other

Ethnographer and cultural phenomenologist, Thomas Csordas, focuses upon the means by which one bodily subjectivity, typically that of the ethnographer, might understand and apprehend another, typically that of a cultural other. Like his fellow phenomenologists, Csordas writes of the lived body and embodiment as the field within which other subjectivities are articulated. But—and here lies the difference—as an ethnographer, he recognizes the cultural character of lived corporeality. Csordas takes the field of embodiment to signify the inextricability of culture and experience. Cultural phenomenology is likewise supposed to synthesize "the immediacy of embodied experience with the multiplicity of cultural meaning in which we are always and inevitably immersed" (Csordas 1999: 143). The point is that the field of "immediate" experience is neither prior to nor outside of culture, but is articulated within and according to a heterogeneity of cultural meanings and practices. To this extent, any understanding of self and body is necessarily "unstable and culturally variable" (Csordas 1999: 143). There is no universal, invariant bodily self. As Victora has put it, "people know their bodily facts in different ways" (Victora 1997: 170).

The recognition that bodily subjects are always culturally specific does not merely apply to the cultural other as an object of knowledge but also extends to the knowing subject. It pertains to the corporeal means by which the knowing subject apprehends the specificity of the other, via what Csordas calls the exercise of somatic attention. Somatic attention is characterized by Csordas as those "culturally elaborated ways of attending to and with one's body in surroundings that include the embodied presence of others" (Csordas 1993: 138). There are two salient features of somatic attention. First, we attend with or through the body, and second, this mode of attention is culturally and socially informed. In other words, "neither attending to nor attending with the body can be taken for granted but must be formulated as culturally constituted somatic modes of attention" (Csordas 1993: 140).

In a sense, we are returned to Cassell and Toombs—the doctor understands the patient's condition by reference to his or her own corporeality. However, the difference lies in the fact that for Csordas, having a culturally specific body means also that one perceives and understands the world in a culturally specific manner. I understand what is happening in my own and other's bodies through my own body. The culturally specific body is not just a cultural artefact, it is our means of experiencing the world. Csordas's point is that experience itself involves the exercise of certain kinds of sense and sensibility, and that these embodied faculties are permeated by culture and cultural values (Csordas 1999: 155). The concept of somatic attention as a cultural, corporeal mode of apprehension signals lived corporeality as the manner by which one person engages with another. The tendency for phenomenological bioethics to emphasize the universal aspects of experience renders the cultural specificity of the body epiphenomenal, whereas Csordas sees the body (embodied subjectivity) as the lynchpin of intersubjective communication and apprehension.

To return to the medical setting, and in light of Csordas's analysis, we might say that the doctor's comprehension of the existential situation of his or her patient occurs according to an act of corporeal spectatorship. Where the doctor hails from a different cultural setting than his or her patient, he or she is somewhat like Csordas's ethnographer attempting to understand a form of cultural alterity. By way of comparison, the doctor, like the ethnographer, can only comprehend the patient through the specificity of his or her own lived corporeality. The ethical difficulty is that the doctor's specificity could well act as a filter for the experiential reality of the cultural other. In such a case, difference might be effaced, distorted, or disregarded in favor of some projection on the doctor's part. Perhaps the doctor has read a pile of cultural factfiles and now feels qualified to make culturally sensitive diagnoses. Csordas refers to an ethnographer's adapting to the everyday practices of a Nepalese community in order to understand the bodily metaphors inscribed within its spiritual and religious rituals (Csordas 1999: 155). This is the point at which the analogy between doctor and ethnographer fails, for the doctor is not going to go anywhere in order to be able to apprehend the corporeality of a cultural other. Rather than adapt to the patient, there is a greater likelihood that the doctor will impose the familiar, where otherness is misrecognized as sameness. Remember the hospice worker in Gunaratnam's study, who was worried that she might only respect those cultural attitudes that did not impinge on her own values (Gunaratnam 1997: 178)? Here the question has to do with whether cultural and corporeal values are perceived at all, and whether they are misrecognized as like one's own values or, alternatively, are taken to be foreign to the point of alienation (as in the exoticism of Orientalism, for example). It also concerns the invisibility of whiteness; who "oneself" is. If a "woman of color" is cited as a possible other, who is she other to? If she is perceived as the same, who functions as the norm of sameness?

It is in light of these difficulties that we might consider Smaje and Field's assertion that some thought should be given to employing people with ethnic backgrounds similar to those of patients:

> One important step might be to encourage greater recruitment of palliative care staff from minority ethnic groups. No data are available on current levels of employment, but certainly hospices are often regarded as fairly "white" institutions. (Smaje and Field 1997: 159)

We might likewise consider Roberts and Nossall's point regarding empowering people to set up and run their own community health care centers. Multicultural medical clinics conceived along similar lines would have to deal with the signature ethnicities of their community, instituting mechanisms by which client needs could be recognized and accommodated.

The clinical setting contributes to the kind of sensibility that is deployed in the medical encounter. Roberts depicts this in regard to the public hospital settings where women of color get a good dose of racism along with their medical treatment. The point is that institutional protocols condition the subjectivity and sensibility of its professionals. The somatic attentions of a hospice worker in multicultural Britain or Aboriginal Australia derive in part from the values enshrined in the management of death. Although not apparent, management protocols are liable to be predicated upon particular cultural and, no doubt other forms of dominance. Thus we encounter the indigenous Australian patient who feels his doctor sometimes wishes he would die, and the "noisy" Greek and North African mourners in the English hospice. The perception of these sick and grieving peoples is based on the deployment of a certain sensibility that ensues in part from the cultural values embedded in institutional sites and discourses.

Csordas's work on somatic attention produces the insight that the doctor–patient exchange is always refracted through the cultural and corporeal sensibilities of its participants. While Leder, Baron, Toombs, and others lead us into the clinical encounter, and encourage us to value the patient's experience, they do not see corporeal differences as impacting upon the doctor's means of understanding, or the phenomenologist's for that matter. Cultural difference is envisaged as having something to do with the patient, but not particularly the doctor. Although Toombs admits that "cultural meanings are an important determinant in the manner in which illness is apprehended" (Toombs 1992: 36), these meanings are taken to form an interpretative layer that coats a prereflective universality of experience. She thus writes of the meanings assigned to bodily sensations as if the sensation itself has an integrity that preexists its cultural interpretation. Similarly, pain is taken to be a universal experience whose significance is all that varies from culture to culture. Toombs's solution to the problem of cultural difference is, like Cassell's, for the doctor "to ask the patient" in order to reveal the underlying experience that is common to all (Toombs 1992: 45).

Cultural difference for such theorists is information, whereas for Csordas it goes to the heart of intercorporeal communication, implicating both doctor and patient. Inasmuch as the doctor endeavors to comprehend the patient's predicament, his or her corporeality is brought to the fore, for it is the means by which the other can be understood. The doctor's attempt to understand is an act of corporeal spectatorship. Although not emphasized in Csordas's framework, corporeal spectatorship occurs within a discursive and institutional setting. The protocols of these settings both embrace cultural values and authorize the use of perceptual sensibilities that embody these values. In the medical setting, this means that the doctor might well impose certain norms in making perceptual and diagnostic judgments. It also means that the apprehension of people's behavior reflects as much upon the perceiver and the site from which the perception ensues as it does upon its object.

The obstacle medicine faces that ethnography does not is its presumed universalism. Phenomenological bioethics at its best draws our attention to the concrete lived bodies that participate in the medical encounter. It also speaks to the tendency for the doctor to diagnose rather than apprehend the lived corporeality of the patient. Having transported us to the space inhabited by the doctor and patient, however, Csordas alerts us to the cultural specificity of corporeal spectatorship. Henceforth it becomes impossible to give a culturally neutral reading of the somatic interchange. The doctor's ability to perceive the patient is formed according to a number of factors relating to his or her cultural milieu.

Were phenomenological bioethics to address this state of affairs, it would concern itself with the kinds of ethical complications that arise because of such differences between doctor and patient. These include the degree to which cultural factors are also embedded in the institutional settings in which doctor and patient are found. The issue is not merely one of difference but concerns the relative status of the players and the prevalence of certain values over others. It also concerns the relations of power embedded in the physician's subject-position and professional setting, and relates in turn to the patient's perception of the doctor.

To speak of cultural difference is often to identify the cultural other without identifying the one who is culturally the same, that is, whose privilege renders their cultural status invisible. Aileen Moreton-Robinson has shown the many ways in which whiteness remains invisible within Australian feminism, despite the attempt to represent difference (Moreton-Robinson 2000). The point is that white privilege allows whiteness to remain unmarked, even where color and cultural difference are on the table:

> The representation of "difference" in feminism was first articulated as gender, culture and class differences between white men and women. . . . As the foregoing literature review shows, whiteness as subject position, "race," privilege and dominance are not marked as a difference in the early literature. . . . Nor is whiteness made visible in the later literature, which focuses on differences between white women and women who are "Other." (Moreton-Robinson 2000: 69)

By highlighting the cultural constitution of the corporeal spectator—the one who deploys a very particular sensibility in exercising somatic attention—Csordas reveals one of the means by which racism and ethnocentrism occur, for the bodily experience of the doctor is the perceptual filter by which the situation of the patient is apprehended. Although Csordas writes that in principle neither party has any a priori rights to objectivity, in practice, the doctor's perception and his or her institutional norms have historically determined what counts as objectivity.

Csordas has depicted the ethnographer's attempt to adapt to the culture of the other in order to understand its rituals (Csordas 1999). This strategy is not available however to the doctor. Moreover, as Moreton-Robinson points out:

> Indigenous women as embodiments of racial difference can never know what it is like to experience the world as a white woman, just as white women can never know what it is like to experience the world as an Indigenous woman. *To know* an Indigenous constructed social world you must experience it from

> within; to *know about* such a world means you are imposing a conceptual framework from the outside. These two ways of knowing inform us that there are limits to knowing an "Other" be they black or white and these restrictions impact on intersubjective relations and the exercising of power. (Moreton-Robinson 2000: 185)

These remarks raise questions about the possibility of intercorporeal knowledge and understanding where the parties embody very different sensibilities. To "know about" another's subjectivity is seen to be conceptual rather than experiential. If the conceptual knowledge of difference has its limits, what ethical considerations follow? Power is a crucial term here; ignorance is one thing, socially sanctioned ignorance another, and imposition another. Given the limits to "knowing an 'Other'," perhaps empowerment and control over health care arise as necessary strategies by which to address cultural difference and racism, in that the apprehending sensibilities of the institution would reflect those of its clientele.

Concluding Remarks

Phenomenological bioethics, coupled with Csordas's cultural, corporeal insights, enable the doctor's body and sensibility to emerge as an important element in the apprehension of the patient's situation. As Toombs and others have argued, in its current incarnation, biomedicine does not typically require the doctor to comprehend the existential character of the patient's predicament. Although Toombs argues that the doctor should comprehend the patient's experience, she assumes that a common experience of corporeality will suffice to support the intersubjective endeavor. The notion of somatic attention as a culturally elaborated activity casts serious doubt upon that idea. Moreton-Robinson's work indicates the extent to which theory is often predicated upon an unacknowledged whiteness. The phenomenological bioethicist is liable to silently locate herself and her whiteness at the center of the work; for, who is deemed to be other?

In view of these arguments regarding corporeal spectatorship, phenomenological bioethics might well do more than "attempt to uncover the invariant features of phenomena" (Toombs 1992: xiii), looking down from the detached perspective of the phenomenological reduction, shedding all presupposition along with the natural attitude. While it is perhaps possible to articulate the bare bones of the medical encounter, ethical and political issues of substance emerge once the concrete specificity of its participants, and their discursive and institutional settings, are revealed. What phenomenology offers to the analysis is the recognition that the matter is both experiential and corporeal; that the lived body is the site of sickness as well as its means of apprehension. What Csordas offers to the analysis is the recognition that the matter is also cultural and epistemological; that the lived body reflects a methodology of apprehension that is thoroughly marked by its cultural affiliations and origins. It seems a small thing to say that people know their bodily facts in different ways, but it appears that acknowledging such a state of affairs would have a significant impact on the ways in which the medical encounter might be approached.

In this chapter I have critically reviewed phenomenological bioethics by contrasting the view of a universal lived body with the concrete differences that obtain among bodies. Culture and, to a lesser extent, "race" were the two registers of difference used to examine the phenomenological approach. Despite certain problems in its elaboration, phenomenology draws attention to lived corporeality as the place and space of human existence. Csordas's work on somatic attention extends this insight into the realm of the concrete, rather than the abstract, body. Adapting his thought to the medical encounter, the doctor's bodily experience emerges as an important means by which the patient's lived corporeality is apprehended.

Attention to the concrete makes visible the institutional, discursive, and corporeal powers of doctors (and other health care workers) to identify and understand their patients. When confronting issues of racial inequality and ethnocentrism, it becomes evident that the doctor represents a site of partiality and potential oppression. At its best, phenomenological bioethics can expose the interests and partialities at work in the medical setting. The next step is to challenge those formations of privilege that support that partiality in order to achieve a more equitable distribution of health care. As argued by Roberts, this may well require more than unilateral work on the part of doctors, leading instead to a focus upon that which might bring about more community empowerment, autonomy, and control.

Note

1. The issue of control, and therefore empowerment, appears quite central. Sir Gustav Nossall recently commented on national radio (3RN, September 5, 2001) that improvements in Australia with regard to indigenous health care have been significantly greater in local, small clinics run and largely staffed by indigenous people. Roberts similarly refers to the National Black Women's Health Project, which aims to facilitate black women taking control over their own health. In policy terms this is to recognize that "a feminist reconstruction of the patient should not encompass solely the physician's understanding of the patient, but also the patient's understanding of the physician" (Roberts 1996: 136).

References

Baron, Richard (1992) "Why Aren't More Doctors Phenomenologists?" in *The Body in Medical Thought and Practice,* Drew Leder (ed.) Dordrecht: Kluwer Academic, pp. 37–47.

Butler, Judith (1989) "Sexual Ideology and Phenomenological Description, A Feminist Critique of Merleau-Ponty's *Phenomenology of Perception,*" in *The Thinking Muse, Feminism and Modern French Philosophy,* Jeffner Allen and Iris Marion Young (eds.). Indianapolis: Indiana University Press, pp. 85–99.

Cassell, Eric (1985) *Talking with Patients,* vol. 2. Cambridge, Mass. MIT Press.

Csordas, Thomas (1993) "Somatic Modes of Attention," *Cultural Anthropology* 8, 135–156.

Csordas, Thomas (1999) "Embodiment and Cultural Phenomenology," in *Perspectives on Embodiment, The Intersections of Nature and Culture,* Gail Weiss and Honi Fern Haber (eds.) New York and London: Routledge, pp. 143–162.

Gunaratnam, Yasmin (1997) "Culture Is Not Enough, A Critique of Multi-Culturalism in Palliative Care," in *Death, Gender and Ethnicity,* David Field, Jenny Hockey, and Neil Small (eds.) London and New York: Routledge, pp. 166–185.

Leder, Drew (1992) "A Tale of Two Bodies, The Cartesian Corpse and the Lived Body," in *The Body in Medical Thought and Practice,* Drew Leder (ed.) Dordrecht: Kluwer Academic, pp. 17–35.

Moreton-Robinson, Aileen (2000) *Talkin' Up to the White Woman: Indigenous Women and Feminism.* Brisbane, Australia: Queensland University Press.

Roberts, Dorothy (1996) "Reconstructing the Patient: Starting with Women of Color," in *Feminism and Bioethics, Beyond Reproduction,* Susan Wolf (ed.) New York and Oxford: Oxford University Press, pp. 116–143.

Shanner, Laura (1996) "Bioethics through the Back Door: Phenomenology, Narratives and Insights into Infertility," in *Philosophical Perspectives on*

Bioethics, L. W. Sumner and J. Boyle (eds.) Toronto: University of Toronto Press, pp. 115–142.

Smaje, Chris and Field, David (1997) "Absent Minorities? Ethnicity and the Use of Palliative Care Services," in *Death, Gender and Ethnicity,* David Field, Jenny Hockey, and Neil Small (eds.) London and New York: Routledge, pp. 142–165.

Toombs, Kay (1992) *The Meaning of Illness, A Phenomenological Account of the Different Perspectives of Physician and Patient.* Dordrecht: Kluwer Academic.

Victora, Ceres (1997) "Inside the Mother's Body, Pregnancy and the 'Emic' Organ 'the Body's Mother'," *Curare* 12, 169–175.

Willis, Jon (1995) "Fatal Attraction, Do High Technology Treatments for End-Stage Renal Disease Benefit Aboriginal Patients in Central Australia?" *Australian Journal of Public Health* 19(6), 603–609.

Willis, Jon (1999) "Dying in Country, Implications of Culture in the Delivery of Palliative Care in Indigenous Australian Communities," *Anthropology and Medicine* 6(3), 423–435.

Zaner, Richard (1988) *Ethics and the Clinical Encounter.* Englewood Cliffs, N.J.: Prentice-Hall.

3

Admitting All Variations? Postmodernism and Genetic Normality

Jackie Leach Scully

Biomedicine and Bioethics

Contemporary biomedicine is probably our major source of expressed notions about the limits to what human beings and bodies are. Inevitably, biomedical assumptions about normality affect bioethics and what bioethics itself has to say about normality, especially with regard to health care. In its turn, bioethics has tended to accept biomedicine's set of assumptions about the meaning of normality and the parameters of the human body: for example, that we know what the normal limits are for a human body at each stage of its life cycle; that a normal human body is healthy and a sick body is abnormal; and that when a human body is not normal, it is the job of biomedicine to make it so. Most notably in its genetic manifestations, biomedicine has become a technology offering the potential transformation of the limits to human existence through various kinds of intervention. Given that this technology exists and is becoming daily more powerful, the current attention paid to ethical questions in biology and medicine is, on one level, reassuring. It shows that the issues are being taken seriously and effort is being put into generating an acceptable resolution of some of them. The positioning of bioethics as a new discipline that acts as the regulatory arm of medical technology, nevertheless, reinforces the idea that biomedicine itself has no limits, whether these are limits of possibility (it might not be possible to keep on making better and better bodies), or moral limits imposed by the actors within biomedicine itself.

Biomedicine is not just a technology. It is also an interpretive framework and an ideology, and from these perspectives it reflects and shapes our attitudes to human diversity, normality, and abnormality in rather more complex ways.

Bioethics can therefore no longer avoid questioning the meaning of terms like "normality" and "abnormality" as they are used within biomedicine and bioethical debate. The need to do so has become more acute, especially in terms of biomedicine's ideological function, because recent advances in genetic medicine and the implementation of the Human Genome Project (HGP) have shifted the perspective from which the relationship between genomes and identity is considered. The coordinated attempt to sequence the entire human genome, and the genomes of other species, began in the early 1990s, and a number of writers have traced these developments (see, for example, Watson and Cook-Deegan 1991; Kevles 1992; Judson 1992). The motivation behind the HGP was complex and rhetorically linked to increasing biomedical knowledge with the promise of medical and other benefits to come. Genetic mapping and sequencing were techniques that had been applied in molecular biology for some time, but earlier efforts were ad hoc; research into the genetic aspects of a condition would eventually require the isolation and characterization of the gene sequences involved. Thus the investigative train of thought started from the observation of embodied human variation presenting as some form of pathology. An attempt was then made to track the expression of pathological symptoms back to genetic alterations. The starting point was an observed change in phenotype,[1] which made no assumptions about the biological mechanisms through which this change had occurred: by choosing to look for associated genetic alterations, it was clearly hypothesized that the difference was genetically associated, but not that it was genetically defined or that a genetic association excluded any other causative factors. Neither was any associated genetic change necessarily thought of as a deviation from a norm. I want to emphasize this because this assumption has since become so automatic it is hard to remember that earlier, it was the *association of phenotype with genotype* that was of interest and not the detection of genotypic deviation.[2] In this respect, therefore, early genetics was outside the mainstream of medicine, which since the nineteenth century has been predominantly concerned with defining abnormality as deviation from a quantitative norm rather than as the subjective experience of disease (Feinstein 1975; Helman 1990; Scully and Rehmann-Sutter 2001).

When the coordinated effort of the Human Genome Project was first proposed to replace the ad hoc mapping and sequencing of interesting bits of the genome, objections were raised both inside and outside the research community. At the time, these objections were largely about the diversion of limited research resources to a single project. Another objection that was not mentioned at the time was how the shift in methodology also entailed a shift in the way we (researchers and everyone downstream of them) look at the relationship between the genomes of individuals and the identity of the human species. The sequencing of "the" human genome has also changed the way we consider biological and medical norms. It makes a clear statement that there is "a" normal human genome rather than numerous normalities, that the norm is equivalent to the canonical gene sequence, and that once we have it, we will be able to read off directly from this genetic text (Wilson 2001) what is normal for human embodiment and what is not. Abnormality becomes deviation from the canonical genomic norm and is taken to be the same as the possession of a defective genome. In other words, the nonmaterial genomic body has become a surrogate marker for the norms of material embodiment, reflecting and reinforcing the "certain attitude about difference" (Diprose 1991: 69) illustrated by genetic screening and testing. Even before any selective practices are enacted, the model of identity derived from deterministic gene processes supports the notion that normality can be distinguished from abnormality with facility, because the normal genome can be clearly distinguished from the abnormal, and the genome necessarily gives rise in a linear and deterministic fashion to identity (Scully, forthcoming).

Disability

Contemporary biomedicine therefore manages the rather neat trick of being both unlimited and rigidly bounded. In its technological manifestation it remains resolutely modernist in its faith in progress toward human perfectibility, the limitless ability of humans to be transformed into something better. What remains strictly limited—in fact, as we will see, is increasingly rigidly delimited—is what kind of human embodiment biomedicine should make efforts to bring into being. This issue becomes acute now because biomedicine has changed the set of ethical questions we face about variant human embodiments. Until very recently, biomedical interventions that attempted to modify or extend human capabilities were extremely limited. What biomedicine could and did do was intervene extensively in the existence of what it considered to be "substandard" people through treatment, amelioration, or rehabilitation. Since the advent of prenatal screening, a further interventional option has been termination. The question then is, is it better not to exist than to exist with a specific disability? Many disabled people, including some who recognize disadvantages in disability and in impairment, claim that this is very rarely true, and that the unreflexive assumption that it is true is an expression of discrimination against disabled people (Parens and Asch 2000). Even those who would not go that far would acknowledge that the moral gravity of taking away life, even from a fetus, is such that the disadvantage of the impairment must be severe enough to justify it. This means that in many cases although a predicted variation from the norm, a disability, might not be wanted, it is not of such gravity that termination is a morally acceptable option.

But techniques such as preimplantation genetic diagnosis, which allows in vitro screening and selection of embryos before implantation into the uterus, and gene therapy with its potential to remove a genetic trait from an individual or a lineage, means we are asking a different question. Given that a person can exist in state A, without detectable disabilities, or state B, with a disability, which is preferable? The issue here is the choice about the kind of people we want to have (raising the question of who "we" are in this context), irrespective of other, important questions about the right to life or the moral status of the fetus or embryo. More directly than before, we are confronted with our evaluation of variations in embodiment and our ideas about disability.

Models of Disability

Understanding disability poses some profound problems. Until recently, the dominant model for understanding disability, and therefore imagining what to do about it, was provided by the medical model. Within this framework, disability is configured as a nominative pathology: a disease, degeneration, defect, or deficit located in an individual. What is defined as disease, degeneration, defect, or deficit is determined by reference to a norm elaborated through the statements of quantitative medicine. Although biomedicine is concerned with the identification of a multiplicity of abnormalities, the actual mode of operation of the medical model—reinforced by the "genomic body" described earlier—is a binary one in which the standard of normative embodiment is opposed against the "chaotic residue" (M. Griffiths 1995: 171) of everything else, all the various embodiments that cannot be made to correspond to the normative one. The medical model has been severely criticized for maintaining this binary opposition.

More recently proposed alternative models to the medical one come under the broad heading of the social model or models of disability (Abberley 1987; Oliver 1990, 1996; Barnes 1998; Linton 1998; Marks 1999). This originated within disability activism, where disabled people were dissatisfied with the limitations of a purely medical perspective for comprehending the experiential reality of disability, especially the way that such a perspective neglects the social and economic factors that construct disability. Since the social model was developed within an explicitly political context of the disability movement, it has also been concerned about the ease with which the medical model lends itself to the support of oppressive forms of sociomedical regulation (Foucault 1973; Zola 1975; Turner 1995; Wilkerson 1998). The social model's most fundamental critique of the medical model, however, is that it wrongly locates the "problem" of disability in the phenotypic crossing of a biological limit. By contrast, a social model finds that social, economic (and sometimes environmental) factors are at least as important as biological ones in the construction of disability, which is "socially constituted by the interaction of individuals with their environments when particular conditions, either physical or mental, become social impediments" (Wilson 2001: 170). The earliest forms of disability theory thus established a sharp distinction between impairment—an individual biological manifestation such as hearing loss; and disability—the collective experience of oppression resulting from a disabling society that, for example, considers television subtitling to be an optional extra. Some disability theorists, focusing exclusively on the material basis of a disabling environment, therefore appear to be arguing that disability could be eradicated if the appropriate modifications were made to modes of production, architecture, transport, information provision, and education.

Parallels in Feminist Thought

Some parallels with disability theory can be found in feminist thought and ethics. From the point of view of gender, feminism has questioned the assumption that the male physical form embodies normality, implicitly calling into question the general validity of physical norms. It has disrupted many notions about the universality of phenomena associated with men, and questioned whether phenomena associated with women should be seen as abnormal variants of the male version. Like the social model of disability, it has challenged the medicalization of some embodied attributes; in feminism's case, specifically female attributes such as menstruation and menopause. In its necessary focus on gender differences, however, mainstream feminism has largely assumed that there is a pattern of corporeal normality to which normal men and women correspond and from which normal men and women deviate. Beyond a consideration of the dual oppression of disabled women (e.g., Morris 1993) and of women as carers of disabled people (e.g., Kittay 2001), feminist thought has therefore had little to say directly about disability (with some notable exceptions, e.g., Silvers 1998; Wendell 1996; Thomas 1999). Nevertheless, an examination of where the parallel between two marginalized groups stops being useful can itself be helpful in clarifying what exactly the problem of disability is and how it differs from the problem of gender.

A basic methodological principle of feminist thought is the inclusion of different experiences into any plausible theory; experience, because feminism is grounded in and concerns itself with the lived lives of women, and different experience, because feminist thought presumes that the lives of women are, in detectable ways, different from those of men. Again, this has parallels with the epistemology of disability theory and activism. Here the claim is that any theory of disability should be based on the subjective experience of disabled people (rather than the experience or, worse, projections of those who treat them or care for them).

It is interesting to compare this not entirely revolutionary notion with the processes of identifying and categorizing impairment. We can ask what enables us to know that having only one arm is an impairment. I want to emphasize that questioning this equation between a particular phenotypic variation and an impaired being does not demand that the real difficulties and disablements associated with certain impairments be ignored or trivialized. Both the social model of disability and more recent postmodern versions (see later discussion) have been criticized for doing so. The equation, however, allows impairment to be evaluated by criteria that are only partially and only indirectly connected with what we claim to find negative about it, that is, the subjective experience of difficulty or disadvantage. The criteria we use are only partially connected with experienced disadvantage because a choice about which difficulties are seen as impairments and which are not has already been made. We "know" that having only one arm rather than two in a world of shoelaces is definitely impairing; but we also do not "know" that having only two arms rather than three is a severe impairment, even though we live in a world where small children and shopping have to be carried at the same time as the front door opened. Here, impaired is used to mean "limited in a way that is unfamiliar and therefore unacceptable to most of us." The concept of biological impairment slides in as a kind of surrogate (or surrogate marker, as it would be termed in medicine) for the familiar and acceptable limits of biological variation. This may be an administratively useful thing to do, but it allows us to evade the questions of how the criteria for acceptability are generated from familiarity, and by whom. Often, for example, they are not generated by those with an impairment.

Moreover, the criteria for identifying impairment are only indirectly connected with the lived experience of difficulty, because the judgment of impairment is made before (or, frequently, instead of) assessing how the biological variation actually affects a person's ability to carry out her or his life projects. What we evaluate as impairment is not the experience of limitation, whether familiar or not, but the individual's match to the human phenotypic norm. Here, a phenotypic dissonance is being used as a surrogate marker for impairment, and by extension for the experience of difficulty. The advent of the genomic body mentioned previously introduces yet another layer of surrogacy.

A different parallel with feminist theory is provided by attempts to understand "disability" as a category of characteristic, equivalent to categories such as gender, ethnicity, age, or sexuality. In many ways this seems a plausible way of analyzing one set of the many characteristics that constitute identity. As embodied subjects, people identify themselves and others as belonging to these categories. We are familiar with the idea that within each category there exists a ranking of its various possible manifestations. Within the category of gender, for instance, men rank higher than women in most societies. Social survival generally demands a minimum of ambiguity about the manifestation a person presents. With the possible exception of class,[3] it is generally recognized that these categories have a biological component or aspect but are not determined by biology, and that, for most of the categories, the consequences of membership have more to do with cultural appraisals than with biology per se. For disability to be regarded as a category equivalent to gender, then, being disabled must be a characteristic with biological elements that is also socially constructed. From the previous discussion, this would seem uncontroversial. Regarding disability as an ontological or even social characteristic like gender may therefore be justified, and may be especially useful in a political context to challenge discrimination against disabled people by analogy with discrimination on the grounds of gender or race.

The comparison also reveals a significant conceptual difference between disability and gender, class, ethnicity, or sexuality, whether these are considered to be ontological or socially constructed categories. This is significant because it means that some of the ways in which these other categories are used analytically and politically are not appropriate for disability. Unlike the others, it is possible to be outside the category of disability. It is possible not to be disabled in a way in which it is not possible not to be gendered, for example. It could be argued that "disability" is not equivalent to "gender" as a category but to "women." It is a subcategory, as women are a subcategory of the wider concept of gender, and just as it is possible for some people not to be women, it is possible not to be disabled. In that case, what term is available to signify the same sort of thing for being disabled that "gender" signifies in relation to being a woman? It is revealing that our language lacks a word for "the general category of things we are talking about when we talk about disability." "Ability" is not a satisfactory alternative, partly because it is uselessly broad, and also because it negates, rather than includes, disability. It is the equivalent of "being a man," not of "gender."

This lack is more than a linguistic inconvenience. It holds a number of messages, yet to be explored in bioethics, about our attitudes toward difference, our apparent need to make it as difficult as possible to talk about what it is that is different in disability, and the functions that the concept of disability serves for us, as individuals and as cultures. I want to look now at only one of the possible ramifications: that in using the term "disability" we are making a different kind of judgment than when we use the terms "gender" or "race," and that this is often an a priori moral judgment.

"Disability" as Moral Evaluation

The terminology we have available makes the word "disability" a value judgment in a way that other categories, including gender and race, are not. While these categories make judgments of value through the internal ranking of their members, for disability the category is an evaluation. There is a real difficulty, however, in determining in any case what kind of evaluation it is. One kind that it can be is moral. For some people, categorization under "disability" may be used as a marker for the inferior moral status of disabled persons, or for their inferior capacities as moral agents. I have argued elsewhere that seeing phenotypic variation as a pathological state "pathologizes the identity of persons embodying that state, and renders it in need of restoration if their claim to moral agency is to be equivalent to that of 'normal' people. . . . The treatment of disabled people as less than full subjects, incapable of genuine moral agency, is manifest in taken-for-granted processes of social exclusion and oppression" (Scully, forthcoming).

It may be uncommon for the moral worth of disabled persons to be questioned overtly today, but history and the contemporary experience of disabled people include enough examples of marginalization and abuse to indicate that disabled people, as a group, matter less to some people; and there are enough examples of disabled people's choices being overridden "for their own good" to indicate that some people consider disabled people, as a group,[4] less able to exercise moral agency. Perhaps a more widespread consequence is that the connotations of inadequacy, deficit, and dependency associated with the category of disability define the social roles to be taken by, and therefore the kind of moral relationship that will exist between, members of that category and those outside. As feminist care ethics has shown (Tronto 1993; Kittay 1998), this is strongly marked by the negative connotations of inadequacy and dependency in our culture.

Note that I am not suggesting that categorization under "disabled" is only ever a moral evaluation, or that it is always the same kind of evaluation, or even that it is always wrong to make such an evaluation. However, if the category of disability is used, under certain circumstances or by some people, as a moral evaluation, then the concept is morally as well as biologically, socially, and discursively constructed, and this needs to be taken into account in any attempt to theorize disability.

Postmodern Approaches

Is there any way of evaluating phenotypic variation that does not make a preemptive moral judgment? One approach is indicated by the postmodern turn recently taken by some disability theorists, where postmodernism is broadly understood as rejecting the possibility of ultimate grand truths, or metanarratives, acknowledging the socially and discursively constructed nature of meaning, and decentering authority to a diversity of subject standpoints that we recognize as inseparable from the historical and social processes that constructed them. Ultimately, postmodernism's diffraction of subjectivity into multiple standpoints rules out the sort of critical theory that can make use of essentializing categories like gender, race, or class. Again, feminist theory has already found this in its encounters with postmodernist thought, and influenced by it, has moved toward replacing "unitary notions of 'woman' and 'feminine gender identity' with plural complexly constructed conceptions of social identity" (Fraser and Nicholson 1988: 101). Fragmentation has occurred both top-down from theory, and bottom-up as the voices of working-class, black, or lesbian women increasingly challenge the central position of white, educated, and heterosexual women.

From the outset, the social model had a decidedly postmodern flavor in its perception of disability as socially constructed rather than ontologically or biologically grounded. However, its materialist focus has made adherents of the social model unsympathetic to suggestions that disability or impairment has much to do with discourse. Other disability theorists, however, have argued that the removal of structural barriers alone would leave intact the attitudinal and discursive dimensions of social relations and that these dimensions are equally problematic for both the academic and the political goals of disability studies. A discursive paradigm would emphasize that "disability is *produced* in the relationships between impairment and oppression" (Corker 1999: 640; my italics) rather than being the experience of oppression through disabling practices.

The discursive model also criticizes the social model for perpetuating false dichotomies. The challenge to the distinction between impairment and disability has already been noted. It has also been suggested that to serve the political aims of the disability movement, the social model must artificially create an internal coherence within the category of disability that homogenizes the real experience of disabled people, and also inadvertently reinforces the existence of a stable and oppositional category of "normality," even though disabled people themselves "often allude to a complex existence that occupies the space between health and illness, disability and 'normality,' impairment and empowerment and nature and culture" (Corker 1999: 633). There is a growing awareness of the complexity of individual subjective experience and standpoints, how disabled people understand themselves as selves in the world and how nondisabled people understand them, and how individuals stand at the intersection of many different identities, with gender, ethnicity, age, sexuality, and class all having their own complex interactions with disability within a person's life (e.g., Clare 1999).

While welcoming a postmodern cultural perspective on diversity, including its skepticism toward centralized authority, and the opening up of nonstandard self-understandings, disability theory—like feminist theory before it—has been more dubious about the political and ethical consequences of the postmodern view of the world. Hardcore postmodernism holds to a belief in the exhaustion of all metanarratives, and rejects any form of universalisability. Thus a postmodern approach presents a substantial threat to the political aims of any emancipatory movement, including the disability movement. The postmodern removal of the authority of metanarratives means that our moral and epistemological representations are not supported by anything more "meta" than existing social and political structures. Feminism has welcomed an interpretation of this that includes abandoning narratives that automatically disadvantage women, and disability theory would do the same for those that assume inferiority or automatically devalue disabled people. Less comfortable is the realization that the loss of recourse to universal moral norms means that "a meaningful argument in support of the equal right to coexistence of all everyday cultures cannot be constructed" (Honneth 1985: 155), and can just as well lead to the renunciation of narratives that consider equality for disabled people to be a desirable goal. If "the postmodern celebration of plurality and multiplicity . . . refuses to privilege any general recipe or any social group" (Best and Kellner 1991: 286), then it can be difficult to make a plausible case for the general recipe of justice for oppressed minorities. It is for reasons like this that Hartsock concluded that "postmodernism represents a dangerous approach for any marginalised group to adopt" (Hartsock 1990: 160).

Some feminist thinkers have proposed steering the delicate course of retaining ideals of Enlightenment emancipation while simultaneously jettisoning the assumptions about authority, the self, and knowledge that usually go with it. Nevertheless, the effort that this requires makes it tempting to agree with Pattison that "non-realistic, postmodern theories offer little that is tangible to those seeking social change . . . although they do provide amusement for what is left of the academic classes, and government appears to find them inoffensive" (1997: viii).

Beyond the political difficulty, postmodern thought presents disability theory with another problem, rooted, paradoxically, in its celebration of diversity. It might seem self-evident that a multiplicity of subject positions is more accommodating of the existence of variation, including varied embodiment. Refining our moral engagement with difference is, I would argue, necessary and valuable. It is much more questionable whether "strong" postmodernism in fact does this. (Note that this does not hold true for all strands within postmodernism. It is less of a problem for those that consciously focus their attention on the way meaning is constructed by binary opposition within *différence*; I am alluding here to postmodern thinking that starts from the assumption that these dichotomies can be disposed of.) The problem is how to maintain sensitivity to difference while rejecting ontological or other categorization, or the privileging of one category over another.

In practice it is not possible to direct one's evenly suspended attention everywhere at once; the desire to analyze, investigate, or simply perceive something implies favoring it, at least temporarily, over other things. What postmodernism calls a radical decentering of agency may be no more than a replacement of a central norm with whatever was at the margins. This may well be both timely and just for the marginalized. What it does not do is subvert existing ideas about how we construct and maintain norms and margins. On the strong postmodern horizon, the refusal to privilege any one position has less to do with celebration of diversity than being symptomatic of a refusal to engage with otherness. It is hard to see how this effacement of difference differs significantly from the much-criticized tendency of modernist universalization to "smother . . . the alterity of the Other" (Bauman 1995: 29). We seem unable to escape the conviction that difference is always, in some sense, deficit; and we defend ourselves against the knowledge that difference surrounds us and *is* us, all the time, either through the universalist claim that everything is really the same, or conversely, with the postmodern perception that everything is so uncategorizably diverse that all aspects of otherness become insignificant.

For disability, this otherness is manifested in an embodied reality of variation. It includes (but is not limited to) the problems of pain, frustration, and physical degeneration. Variant human embodiment is not always straightforwardly a matter of joyful performativity and corporeal transgression. Some of the time, biological variation—for reasons that are not reducible to the biological—goes beyond being compatible with human existence, and other times it goes beyond the limits of human flourishing. However, theories of the social or discursive construction of disability may fail to take seriously the embodied reality of physical variation that extends toward impairment. Liz Crow suggests that this failure stems from the fear that "admitting there could be a difficult side to impairment" (Crow 1996: 208) might compromise the will of the nondisabled world, which is not great at the best of times, to make the necessary social modifications to remove disabling barriers.

Within the category of disability there are at least some embodiments where there is a disadvantage intrinsic to the biology, which is not removable by the engineering of social or attitudinal constructions. This provides another contrast with other ontological categories. For at least some of those other categories, we can say that there is nothing intrinsically undesirable about being black or being a women, and we can imagine worlds without the associated disadvantages (they might not exist outside the kingdom of heaven, but we can imagine them), but "for many disabled people personal struggle related to impairment will remain even when disabling barriers no longer exist" (Crow 1996: 209).

Moving Forward

The medical model of disability has been so thoroughly criticized within disability studies for its totalizing and oppressive role that it may be hard to accept a need to revisit the biomedical construction of disability. Nevertheless, molecular biology, which provides one of the most extensive contemporary metanarratives about human nature and the structure of progress, also provides material for a deeper questioning of the norms of embodiment. In considering the biomedical contribution, there is a need to focus on information and themes generated by molecular biology and not on the abnormal/normal dichotomy that structures the social activity of medicine. It is important to recognize that biomedical and biogenetic models of human variation can be used without necessarily setting up such a binary opposition between normal and abnormal.

Thus variations in embodiments may be characterized solely by medical or even genetic criteria, but could still be part of a hermeneutic that interprets them as variations on a theme, or on several themes, rather than deviations from a standard. Understanding genetic data as deviation from a canonical genomic norm is an interpretive choice, connected as we saw earlier, with the methodological shift after the sequencing of the human genome was established as a coordinated project. It is not intrinsic to the information provided by molecular biology.

Sequence information tells us about quantitative and structural differences in DNA. It is clear that the current model of the relationship between genes and phenotype is linear and deterministic. In the program model of gene action, the meaning of the genetic material is constructed by an inflexible, causal relationship between the genetic sequence and the phenotype. In the program concept of gene action, the DNA sequences of an organism are responsible for what the organism will become and therefore for differences among human beings. Thus the ultimate meaning of disability is also to be found encoded in the gene sequences that give rise to a particular disabling variation, and the information encoded within gene sequences is given unprecedented significance. Postmodernists such as Jameson and Baudrillard, who have characterized postmodernity in terms of the commodification of cultural forms, have identified information as the most important of contemporary commodities. This characterization can incorporate genetic information, possibly too neatly, as yet another tradable cultural form, locating it within the familiar story of commodification and global capitalist exchange. However, this misses the subversive potential of the genetic model.

Within molecular and developmental biology there exist other models that relate gene expression to the organism as a whole, to processes of organismic development and maintenance. Even within the field of biomedicine, then, there are ways of seeing that do not necessitate conferring sole causal power to the genome. In recent years experimental data have demonstrated that the classical molecular gene concept (Griffiths and Neumann-Held 1999) in which a gene is defined as an uninterrupted stretch of DNA coding for a single polypeptide chain, has had to be revised to incorporate the evidence of sequences that regulate gene expression; alternative splicing of transcripts; overlapping genes; and the context dependence of many transcriptional, editing, or translation processes. The process concept (Neumann-Held 2000) defines a gene as a recurring process in the context of which particular DNA sequences are given meaning. In the systemic approaches or systems theories, the significance of DNA lies in the interrelation of parts and processes in the morphologically structured system, which includes the cell and its components as well as features of the environment. Gene action "is no longer restricted to something inherited from the ancestors with their gift of DNA but has its reality in the interaction of the cell *living* with this DNA" (Rehmann-Sutter 2002: 28). The systemic view breaks down the dichotomy between information and embodiment: "Embodiment is an autonomous developmental process which is not separate from psychic and mental and social development" (Rehmann-Sutter, 2002: 46).

Molecular genetics provides a way of questioning norms of embodiment—through revised ideas about individual and community relatedness, the diffuse boundaries between categories of people, genetic stability and flux, and phenotypes arising out of transactions between genes and other factors. It is true that the medical, social, and discursive models retain at some level an ideal of normality. In the medical model as it currently exists, this ideal is unambiguously encoded in physiological parameters and is also unambiguously a preferred state; it is medicine's task to sustain it and to retain deviations from it. Social models have a pragmatic image of normality as whatever it is that the disabling environment or prejudicial social attitudes are tailored to favor, and discursive models see it as constructed by language.

The genetic model, however, can be used to destabilize the ideal of normality. First, it has space to see variation as morally neutral. Difference is always a divergence from something, but the original something need not be afforded greater value than any other form. Developed within a methodological tradition of collecting deviation for its own sake, the genetic model may be better able than others to maintain a balance in making difference the focus of attention while avoiding using it to shore up a norm. If comparison with a genomic norm is resisted, the collection of individual sequence data offers a way of talking about variation that might change the way we think about genotypic and phenotypic differences and eventually modify the preemptive value judgment that is made with placement into the category of disability. As we have seen, molecular genetics has acquired a substantial amount of data supporting a more contextual understanding of the connection between genetic information and embodiment, including models of gene action in which the genetic development of human identity is not separable from environmental, psychological, and social development.

Since more than one genetic model of normality and abnormality is available, the meaning of genetics for concepts of human identity and its diversities can be interpreted in more than one way, and there can be more than one way of using genetic data to create or reinforce particular metaphysical and ethical stances toward these concepts. Thus the choice of genetic model will be morally informed and have ethical consequences. It will be influenced by our preexisting self-image and image of the world and relationships, and will also reinforce these preconceptions in our language and acts. An important question then becomes how to determine the criteria for good models, and their good uses, for ethical and political purposes. This responsibility for the choice of self-image and world image provides a fundamental link between the political and biomedical programs in disability.

A move toward using a genetic model of disability does not entail a straightforward return to a univocal medical model. The phenomenon of disability is complex enough that no single approach currently available is capable of explaining it. Biomedically based models, including genetic ones, are able to catalogue developmental differences and provide biological mechanisms for them; social models are placed to understand collective practices; and discursive approaches focus on the linguistic construction of difference in general and disability in particular. The methodology I propose here is to exploit each theoretical (and empirical) approach for what it does best, taking note of biological, social, discursive, phenomenological, and moral perspectives while remaining aware that none of these perspectives is "complete in itself nor accessible independent of the others" (Shildrick 1997: 178), and knowing that it may prove impossible to harmonize all approaches within one narrative. This would be a pluralist postmodern methodology, buffered from the loss of moral vision through being used in an explicitly ethical task. Since bioethics is (or should be) less concerned with the truth of a theory than with the implications of the theory for living a good life, we might see the bioethics of the future able to mediate among different interpretations of human variation.

Notes

1. The phenotype of an organism is constituted by its physical characteristics, including its structure, biochemistry, and behavior.

2. In some fields of biology there was substantial skepticism about genetic norms; as a student, I was told that the wild type, or norm for the species, was by definition "the one nearest the road," i.e., whatever a collector came across first.

3. I say "possible," to point to the way that the physical effects of class membership, for example the results of malnutrition, can recursively influence class identity.

4. The argument is complicated because there are cognitively disabled people who genuinely are less able to exercise full moral agency. Here I am referring to the attitude toward disabled people as a group.

References

Abberley, Paul (1987) "The Concept of Oppression and the Development of a Social Theory of Disability," *Disability, Handicap and Society* 2, 5–21.

Barnes, Colin (1998) "The Social Model of Disability: A Sociological Phenomenon Ignored By Sociologists?" in Tom Shakespeare (ed.), *The Disability Reader: Social Science Perspectives*. London and New York: Cassell, pp. 65–78.

Bauman, Zygmunt (1995) *Life in Fragments: Essays in Postmodern Morality*. Oxford: Blackwell.

Best, Steven, and Kellner, Douglas (1991) *Postmodern Theory: Critical Interrogations*. New York: Guilford Press.

Clare, Eli (1999) *Exile and Pride: Disability, Queerness and Liberation*. Cambridge, Mass.: South End Press.

Corker, Mairian (1999) "Differences, Conflations and Foundations: The Limits to 'Accurate' Theoretical Representations of Disabled People's Experience," *Disability and Society* 14, 627–642.

Crow, Liz (1996) "Including All of Our Lives: Renewing the Social Model of Disability," in Jenny Morris (ed.), *Encounters with Strangers: Feminism and Disability*. London: Women's Press, pp. 206–226.

Diprose, Rosalyn (1991). "A 'Genethics' that Makes Sense," in Rosalyn Diprose and Robyn Ferrell (eds.), *Cartographies: Poststructuralism and the Mapping of Bodies and Spaces*. Sydney: Allen & Unwin, pp. 65–76.

Feinstein, A. R. (1975) "Science, Clinical Medicine and the Spectrum of Disease," in P. B. Beeson and W. McDermott (eds.), *Textbook of Medicine*. Philadelphia, Pa.: Saunders, pp. 3–6.

Foucault, Michel (1973) *The Birth of the Clinic*. London: Tavistock.

Fraser, Nancy, and Nicholson, Linda (1988) "Social Criticism without Philosophy: An Encounter between Feminism and Postmodernism," *Theory, Culture and Society* 5, 373–394.

Griffiths M. (1995) *Feminisms and the Self: The Web of Identity*. London: Routledge.

Griffiths, Paul E., and Neumann-Held, Eva M. (1999) "The Many Faces of the Gene," *BioScience* 49, 656–662.

Hartsock, Nancy (1990) "Foucault on Power: A Theory for Women?" in Linda J. Nicholson (ed.), *Feminism/Postmodernism*. New York and London: Routledge, pp. 157–176.

Helman, C. (1990) *Culture, Health and Illness: An Introduction for Health Professionals*. London: Wright.

Honneth, Axel (1985) "An Aversion Against the Universal: A Commentary on Lyotard's Postmodern Condition," *Theory, Culture and Society* 2, 147–157.

Judson, Horace Freeland (1992) "A History of the Science and Technology Behind Gene Mapping and Sequencing," in Daniel J. Kevles and Leroy Hood (eds.), *The Code of Codes: Scientific and Social Issues in the Human Genome Project*. Cambridge, Mass.: Harvard University Press, pp. 37–82.

Kevles, Daniel J. (1992) "Out of Eugenics: The Historical Politics of the Human Genome," in Daniel J. Kevles and Leroy Hood (eds.), *The Code of Codes: Scientific and Social Issues in the Human Genome Project*. Cambridge, Mass.: Harvard University Press, pp. 3–36.

Kittay, Eva Feder (1998) *Love's Labor; Essays on Women, Equality and Dependency*. New York: Routledge.

Kittay, Eva Feder (2001) "When Caring Is Just and Justice Is Caring: Justice and Mental Retardation," *Public Culture* 13, 557–579.

Linton, Simi (1998) *Claiming Disability: Knowledge and Identity*. New York: New York University Press.

Marks, Deborah (1999) *Disability: Controversial Debates and Psychosocial Perspectives*. London: Routledge.

Morris, Jenny (1993) "Feminism and Disability," *Feminist Review* 43, 57–72.

Neumann-Held, Eva M. (2000) "Let's Talk About Genes: The Process Molecular Gene Concept and its Context," in S. Oyama, P. Griffiths, and R. Gray (eds.), *Cycles of Contingencies*. Cambridge, Mass.: MIT Press, pp. 69–84.

Oliver, Mike (1990) *The Politics of Disablement*. Basingstoke, UK: Macmillan.

Oliver, Mike (1996) *Understanding Disability: From Theory to Practice*. Basingstoke, UK: Macmillan.

Parens, Erik, and Asch, Adrienne (2000) *Prenatal Testing and Disability Rights*. Washington D.C.: Georgetown University Press.

Pattison, Steven (1997) *Pastoral Care and Liberation Theology*. London: SPCK.

Rehmann-Sutter, Christoph. "Genetics, Embodiment and Identity," in Armin Grunwald, Matthias Gutmann and Eva Neumann-Held (eds.), *On Human Nature: Anthropological, Biological and Philosophical Foundations*. Berlin: Springer (2002).

Scully, Jackie Leach "Nothing Like a Gene," in Christoph Rehmann-Sutter and Eva Neumann-Held (eds.), *Genes in Development: Rereading the Molecular Paradigm*. Durham, N.C.: Duke University Press (forthcoming).

Scully, Jackie Leach, and Rehmann-Sutter, Christoph (2001) "When Norms Normalize: The Case of Gene Therapy," *Human Gene Therapy* 12, 87–95.

Shildrick, Margrit (1997) *Leaky Bodies and Boundaries: Feminism, Postmodernism and (Bio)Ethics*. London and New York: Routledge.

Silvers, Anita (1998) "On Not Iterating Women's Disabilities: A Crossover Perspective on Genetic Dilemmas," in Anne Donchin and Laura Purdy (eds.), *Embodying Bioethics: Feminist Advances*. Lanham, Md.: Rowman & Littlefield, pp. 177–202.

Thomas, Carol (1999) *Female Forms: Experiencing and Understanding Disability*. Buckingham, UK: Open University Press.

Tronto, Joan (1993) *Moral Boundaries: A Political Argument for an Ethic of Care*. New York: Routledge.

Turner, Brian S. (1995) *Medical Power and Social Knowledge*. London: Sage.

Watson, James D., and Cook-Deegan, R. M. (1991) "Origins of the Human Genome Project," *FASEB Journal* 5, 8–11.

Wendell, Susan (1996) *The Rejected Body: Feminist Philosophical Reflections on Disability*. New York: Routledge.

Wilkerson, Abby L. (1998) *Diagnosis: Difference. The Moral Authority of Medicine*. Ithaca, N.Y.: Cornell University Press.

Wilson, James C. (2001) "Disability and the Genome: Resisting the Standardized Genomic Text," *Disability Studies Quarterly* 21, 166–179.

Zola, Irving (1975) "In the Name of Health and Illness," *Social Science and Medicine* 9, 83–87.

III

Thinking Through Crisis

4

The Measure of HIV as a Matter of Bioethics

Marsha Rosengarten

This chapter is intended to go some way toward addressing a dilemma I have grappled with while undertaking *social* research into the HIV epidemic. For some years I have welcomed the contributions of feminist poststructural theory in defining my approach. Yet, almost equivalent to my commitment to the ethical and political significance of such contributions is my frustration with where their accent on social constructionism leaves me when trying to address the question of medical intervention. While I would describe my work as informed by the view that the objects of medical science are materialized and delimited by the means by which they are made known, at times my location within a large London-based HIV clinic made this view seem almost ethically preposterous. This is not, I hasten to add, because I have mistakenly understood the poststructural critique to mean that matter is merely an effect of language. Nor is it because I hold the view that whatever the substance of matter is, it is inconsequential to how it is known. Rather, the difficulty I experience in my uncertain relation to the matter of HIV has precisely to do with the consequences of how it is known.

In place of a more conventional approach to bioethics which, within the field of HIV, could address questions such as patient consent, treatment access, doctor–patient power relations, and the rather more nebulous matter of quality of life issues, my interest is in an interrogation of the very objects on which such a conventional style of bioethics might proceed, namely, virus, body, embodied sexual subject, embodied virus, and infectivity. The motivation for this interest can be attributed to my concern with the limits and effects of HIV biomedicine. It can also be attributed to the feminist project—evidenced by this volume—of challenging the naturalness and thus limiting force of scientific definitions of the body. However, in acknowledging the importance of such a challenge, as I indicated in my opening paragraph, I do hold reservations about a culturalist critique within the HIV arena at this time. How is it possible to query the object(s) of matter while contributing to materially necessary interventions? Is it possible to contribute to arresting the virus by *not* furthering its conceptual stability?

A Question of Purchase

While there is a substantial field of work on how the body is an effect of the cultural matter of concepts, metaphors, narratives, and more (see, for example, Haraway 1991; Martin 1990; Treichler 1999), a debate is currently taking place on how this style of analysis can engage *with* biological accounts *of* the body (see, for example, Wilson 1999; Keane and Rosengarten 2002; Fraser 2002). Inherent to many culturalist critiques is a tendency to foreclose what can be said about the matter of the body or the biological. Ironically, the foreclosure may be implict in the intention of inquiry. As my friend and colleague Helen Keane so aptly captures when reflecting on her and others' work in this field: "It seems that any account of the body is vulnerable to the criticism that it is somehow not fleshy enough" (Keane and Rosengarten 2002: 262). Conversely, a move away from the nonfleshiness of social constructionism, as Keane characterizes it, returns us to the constraints of biological reductionism. Her insights more than resonate when trying to come to grips with what might constitute an ethical relation to the investigation of HIV matter.

For Vicki Kirby (1999) this difficulty requires no less than a reexamination of the premises of both science and its cultural critiques. Taking up Derrida's claim that "there is no outside of text," she reveals a fallacy on which much social constructionism proceeds—an unquestioned distinction between nature and culture. For if culture is that which can be claimed inherently about language, biology can also be recognized as such. The exemplar is DNA, the basic building block of human and other animate matter. Its four molecular bases—each given a letter from the alphabet—enable the necessary work of making (and destroying) matter and, in this sense, evidence highly sophisticated literacy and numeracy skills. In other words, the identified characteristics of the object that is known as DNA are, like the matter of culture, dynamic and interpretative in being so. While Kirby's querying of matter offers a valuable insight to those situated on the social constructionist side, the ground matter on which the argument relies may not come as news to those involved in the realms of science, for Kirby takes her example from the theoretical and empirical matter *of* science. What Kirby does not address is how this may be of major significance to both sides of the envisaged impasse. The question is critical, though, to someone, such as myself, situated *in* the physical as well as intellectual space of the clinic.

Although I do not by any means propose to overcome the sort of difficulties now illuminated by feminist work on the question of the body, I do want to attempt a type of strategic negotiation of the dilemma in-(my)-situ. My hunch is that at this point in the debate and in response to an increasingly medicalized HIV epidemic, the effectiveness of any strategy will depend on holding the empirical of science in some sort of tension with a set of epistemiological and ontological concerns about its conceptual and conceptual-material stability. In order to proceed with this dilemma, posed at the interface of feminist critique and HIV medical science, I will look at an inadequate yet highly productive scientific model of embodied subject and embodied virus. The inadequate part of the science is well known. For those living and/or working with HIV, the model has not achieved "the magic bullet" necessary for fully arresting the virus. The productive aspect is not so evident or, perhaps I should say, so easy to grasp. To speak of it requires a language able to capture a dynamic conceptual–material relationship and yet resistant to the pitfall of either reductionism or constructionism. Within the scope of inquiry focused on HIV, it requires a language cognizant of the effects of molecular-based diagnostic technologies as well as pharmaceutical interventions in the transformation of bodies and viruses. Contrary to the assumption by science that conceptual work is distinct from observational work and that both in turn remain distinct from the materialization of biological matter, this essay shows that the observational is part of the conceptual. Furthermore, it will show that these more usually distinct areas are implicated in what is lived as matter. HIV medical science participates in the materialization of objects while presuming these objects to be external to its operations. Drugs and tests are not just technologies for the management of HIV, they are part of a productive terrain that takes its form from their conceptual and conceptual–material reapplication. It is within this space that I propose that HIV be seen as a matter of bioethics.

Medical HIV

With the introduction of HIV antiretroviral combination therapy in 1996, here referred to as antiretroviral therapies (ART), the epidemic can be seen to have altered radically in numerous ways. Foremost in a conventional evaluation of the inroads made by science is the statistical decline in the number of people with HIV going on to develop AIDS (Palella et al. 1998). The arrested progression of the virus is most usually considered as powerful evidence of the efficacy of ART and the model on which it proceeds. Given this important advance in HIV suppression, it is necessary to consider carefully what may be gained from a style of interrogation that queries the very means by which this outcome has been achieved. To those living and/or working in HIV, and whose experience of living with HIV has been radically altered as a consequence of HIV treatments, the argument that the objects of "body," "virus," and "infectivity" are effects of the means by which they are known may seem at best irrelevant. Nevertheless, there is ample evidence within HIV medicine to show that the scientific understanding that has produced ART continues to require more investigation, if not a radical rethinking.

The desired effects of the drug therapy for viral suppression are accompanied by a varied and complex array of unwanted effects. Some are already known to be potentially lethal and others are so severely damaging that they can be disabling and/or disfiguring.[1] Added to these is the almost unmanageable nature of some dosing regimens that can require taking up to seven pills three times a day and at specified periods, including before food, with food, and after food. "Poor adherence" to difficult dosing regimens is often held responsible for insufficient drug absorption which in turn can enable strains of the virus to replicate and mutate (BHIVA 2001). Within the clinic, a series of complicated and uncertain decisions must be made on the basis of such limitations and risks: when to commence combination therapy, given the damaging effects of the drugs; what combination of drugs should be used, given the difficulty of adhering to strict dosing regimes and possible development of drug resistance; and, also, how to negotiate individual and gender-identified physiological differences that may influence test results, drug absorption, and the manifestation of side effects. Outside, although not entirely distinct from the clinic, there are concerns about cultural shifts incurred by the drugs. These concerns include debate on whether the treatments are increasing the practice of unprotected intercourse (see, for example, International Collaboration on HIV Optimism 2003; Kippax and Race 2003); debate about the provision of an HIV postexposure prophylaxis (Kalichman 1998); and debate on whether the increased practice of unprotected anal intercourse increases the risk of the transmission of drug-resistant HIV (Little 2001).

The Measure of HIV

In order to illustrate the field of HIV as a site for potential reworking, I focus on the research and diagnostic technology of the HIV viral load test. This test is used to measure virus particles within a given sample of bodily fluid, such as blood or seminal fluid (Mortimer and Loveday 2001). It is a standard feature of HIV clinical management in a context of ART. Its productive role in the epidemic is recognized by science and the HIV field in general, but only partially. From the perspective of the HIV scientist or the medical clinician, the test has provided a form of access to the virus in vitro that was previously unavailable. Prior to the test, knowledge of the presence of the virus relied on the detection of antibodies to the virus, not on the detection of the actual virus. Knowledge of viral activity relied on the detection of visible disease symptoms. In the absence of a "sighted" virus and visible disease symptoms, a latent stage in viral activity was believed to take place after initial infection. The detection of the virus made apparent by the test, dispensed with this belief-cum-theory and made new strategies feasible. In place of monotherapy (one drug), combination therapy (two or three drugs in unison) came to dominate treatment (Race 2001b). "Hit hard, hit early" became the slogan of clinical practice because it advocated that treatment start at the time of infection and involve a considerable onslaught of drugs (Ho 1995). However, toxic drug effects and the development of drug resistance has since brought it under review.

The test is now understood to not only reveal the presence of the virus and its level of replication, it also functions as an indicator of the likelihood of disease progression and the possible level of infectivity to another. Further, it is also used to determine the sensitivity, or lack thereof, of the virus to pharmaceutical interventions. In these ways the test can assist in determining an individual patient's prognosis. Test results, operating within a scientific gaze, involve carefully calibrated amounts of virus and the body's CD4 T-cells.[2] The measure of these two substances acquires specific significance in a relational scenario. High viral load may not be such a concern if the CD4 T cell count (a measure of immune system cells) is also high. However, if the CD4 T cell count falls below a certain level, any identifiable amount of virus will be a consideration for introducing or varying drug therapy. In some contexts, the relational nature of the two measures is mediated by other factors. For instance, the British HIV Association (BHIVA 2001: 4) states: "In late disease, the CD4 cell count is of greater prognostic significance than viral load, whereas in early disease the reverse is true." The complex means of visibilizing, measuring, and relational weighing provides guidance on deciding how and when to intervene, given what can be regarded as a growth area in knowledge—drug design and evidence.

From the perspective of a bioethical account of matter, the test might also be held accountable for its more productive role in the materialization of new wanted and unwanted biological and social phenomena. While it is not my intention to question the gains achieved in viral suppression as a result of the test, I am interested in how it might provide a starting point for rethinking the self-evidency of the current HIV medical terrain. For this reason, I will discuss a series of examples of the viral load test at work in the transformation of virus and bodies.

The Materialization and Transformation of Bodies and Virus

"The virus you get this year is not the virus you got 10 years ago" (Flynn 2001: 38, 39).

This statement was made by a leading London-based HIV specialist clinician. It emphasizes current medical concern with the transmission of a drug-resistant virus and how newly infected persons may not be sensitive to the drugs currently available. I will return later to this area of concern. First, though, I want to look at the multifaceted role of the viral load test in Flynn's claim. Within the HIV field, it is generally acknowledged that the development of this test brought about a turning point in scientific knowledge of the workings of the virus. As mentioned earlier, knowledge obtained from the test has provided new understanding of how the virus replicates, and this has been critical in the design and ongoing modification of delivery therapies. What is not included in the new understanding are the effects of this, that is, new knowledge of the virus is not usually acknowledged as directly implicated in the materialization of the matter of the virus. Here I shall argue otherwise.

For Karen Barad, the viral load test might be termed a site of discursive-material activity and as such, a site of agential realism. In her account of how ultrasound technology is an implicit part of the performativity of the materialization of gender, Barad draws attention to the way in which technological hardware reflects discursive presuppositions about identity and acts to materialize these (1998: 88, 89). Further, the ultrasound technology intra-acts with the matter of the body to materialize the latter in a manner that appears apart from the technology, yet is already a bearer of this coextensive engagement (1998: 89, 90). Similarly, the viral load test can be regarded as technology shaped by knowledge of the virus and, in turn, active in the materialization of the virus or what has come to be known—in science—as the virus. The test reflects some preconceptions of the virus and, following from this, enables further so-called observations and transformations. In this way, like the mediating effects of language on the objects that we might presume are outside or external to language, material technologies such as the viral test give shape to what appears to be self-evident or, external to, the test. Barad's critical insights into the role of material technologies extends Judith Butler's concept of performativity and by doing so also highlights the way in which science is ethically implicated in the materialization of matter. It also makes apparent in a more comprehensive manner how the virus, no longer the same as 10 years ago, has changed as a result of the forces of scientific intervention.

From the perspective of the cultural critic of science, the test works to remake the body, the body with the virus, and, as Flynn implies, the virus itself. For instance, a type of conceptual remaking of the body and virus could be said to take place through the mapping of the virus and through the antiviral drugs intended to penetrate its locales. The careful balancing act played out in measures of virus and CD4 T-cells is one example of how the body with HIV is now categorized according to three stages: (1) patients with primary HIV infection having been diagnosed at the time or soon after infection and possibly showing signs of what is read as seroconversion illness; (2) patients with asymptomatic HIV infection who have been infected some time back and do not experience any detectable effects of the presence of the virus; (3) patients with symptomatic HIV disease or AIDS, which could encompass some or many documented visible signs. The first group are recommended to start treatment straight away; the second are recommended to defer treatment until their CD4 T-cells drop below a certain measure; and the third are recommended to begin treatment (see BHIVA 2001). These different treatment strategies, which may also involve different types of drug combinations according to early- or late-stage infection, no doubt produce different sorts of bodies. A later case scenario derived from this might anticipate finding those from categories (1) and (3) having to deal with damage to the body brought about by toxic drug effects, in contrast to those from (2) requiring different medical care that is not based on such damage but perhaps on viral damage.

The viral load test is also integral to a more complex materialization of the body as a site of possible risk to another. The test has enabled a theory of compartmentalism whereby the presence of the virus can be mapped according to preidentified "compartments" within the body. This has led to claims that drug design should be modified to prioritize penetration of the male genital tract as a public health strategy against risk of transmission of resistant virus (Eron et al. 1998). Particularly revealing here is the configuring of the body as a risk to another according to a model of pharmacological penetration. It is one of the more explicit examples of how the matter of the body and that of risk are made in science, rather than being wholly prior to it and awaiting a correctly devised intervention. It also demonstrates how certain cultural concerns, informed by biological understandings of the transfer of matter from one body to another, may influence drug design such that the genital tract can be nominated as a priority for targeting on the grounds of public interest. Furthermore, as certain body parts or compartments come to be known, new sites of surveillance and possible intervention enter the field. Within this activity—a mix of conceptual and material intervention—a reshaped body inevitably appears. In both of these examples the body, already constituted by existing scientific paradigms and specific technologies, is available to alteration by the pharmacological effects of drug penetration and absorption measured in terms of arresting viral replication and/or inducing side effects. Restructured by these activities, the body with the virus is then available for new readings and refashionings to occur yet again and possibly again and again. It is on the basis of this activity that the claim that the virus is not the same as it was 10 years ago could be understood within the scientific imaginary as a direct reference to conceptual change as much as to material change.

Normative Modeling and Multiple Bodies

The test is extensive in the materialization of HIV and bodies with HIV and, I would argue, ripe for question as a site bioethical concern. Yet the manner in which those within the field represent the test conceals the need for scrutiny. Indeed, many accounts understand and thereby construct HIV medicine as a field of overall progress, making it even more difficult to come to grips with the unwanted iatrogenic effects of medical science. For instance, at the level of clinical management of the virus, the viral load test has been claimed to allow a more custom-made approach to treatment. According to one prominent and highly respected UK-based voluntary sector organization: "Viral load testing made possible the beginning of an era of 'individualised therapy,' in which patients would no longer be prescribed drugs according to the results of a clinical trial . . . [but, rather] tailored to the individual viral load of a patient, and to their previous treatment history" (Alcorn and Fieldhouse 2000: 24). Presumably the statement refers to the use of individual test results to determine when and how to introduce or change the prescription of ART. But this tailoring is not based on self markers. Although the test is conducted on an individual's blood sample, the reading is understood as a surrogate marker only. The meaning of the marker is in fact based on data drawn from clinical trials. Furthermore, the bodies that make up clinical trials may not be an appropriate measure against which to assess a particular individual's results. In the terms of science, these bodies might be understood as genetically different.

Emphasis on the statistical achievement of HIV management and the contribution of the viral load test to this scenario may provide some explanation for the paucity of work on the question of difference recently highlighted by Epstein (2004). Viral suppression by ART relies on the appropriate metabolizing of the drugs, yet metabolic activity is recognized as differing among individuals (as well as within an individual). For instance, women as a category have been found to have lower levels of virus than men when they have the same number of CD4 T-cells (Gandhi et al. 2002). In other words, it could be deduced that it takes a smaller amount of virus to create damage in women that is equivalent to that in men. The reason for gender differences in viral load is not known. In response to the possibility that it may be a concern, there is debate based on contradictory or inconsistent trial findings. One explanation offered is that variations in different studies may be due to differences in trial design (BHIVA 2001: 5). Other explanations include the effect of interactions between female hormones and viral load (Gandhi et al. 2002). Social explanations are also speculated on, such as disproportional access to welfare and social care, which may also explain the variations observed in injecting drug users and nonwhite people (Alcorn 2000). While debate continues about the comparability of studies in terms of their design, use of methods, and even sample composition, there is no question within this debate that the concept of sex difference itself might be inadequate (for further discussion of the problematic of sex difference as a stable concept, see, for example, Keane and Rosengarten 2002).

An alternative approach might situate the apparency of difference as contingent on the way in which "difference" is conceptualized. For instance, the earlier noted empirical findings of sex differences in the measurement of viral load and CD4 T cell counts might be used to suggest that either the category of sex difference is inadequate to the task of conceptualizing bodies for intervention or the intervention is inadequately conceived (because it cannot be consistently matched across bodies). A brief reflection on the historical deployment of the binary of male and female difference in structuring clinical trials gives weight to the suggestion that bodies are constructed through practice rather than a given basis of inquiry. If it were not for a certain style of differentially designating sexual difference, those categorized as "woman" would not have been historically excluded from early research (Epstein 1996). Without this exclusion current pharmacological interventions might be very different. Even now though, it is important to add that although the inclusion criteria for clinical trials has since been extended, the problematic conceptualization of difference pervades scientific research. As one specialist HIV clinician stated in a recent study of the field:

> I think we have to acknowledge that there is an immense diversity amongst human beings and I don't think that clinical trials address that diversity at all. At one end you're saying "oh, but they're all being conducted on White gay men, and isn't that shocking and why aren't there some more Black African women in that group"? Well actually the next question is "do you want Black African women in that group or do you actually want trials on Black African women"? Because they may be different. And so, without being racist or stigmatising, I think you have to say to yourself "are we seeing metabolic differences and differences of handling of drugs that actually require certain people to have more intensive studies done on them"? Because what worries me is that if you just say "oh, you know, we're not being representative, we must get Black Africans into clinical trials," you will muddy the waters so that you don't know what's going on. You almost need to say "are there significant differences here? And, if there are, how do we best explore that? (HIV clinical specialist)[3]

Materializing Viral Resistance

The viral load test is also potent in the constitution of a responsibilized socially embodied subject expected to take a critical role in preventing the progression of his or her own disease. Within the social research field, considerable attention has been given to the issue of adherence to dosage (see, for example, Chesney et al. 2000; Wagner 2003). Such studies attempt to identify ways of ensuring better adherence in order to maintain the drug levels necessary to prevent viral replication and, as a result, possible viral resistance. But implicit in their design is an underlying assumption that "perfect" dosing is possible and positively effective. In response to these studies, Race (2001a) has provided an incisive critique pointing out how the specific technology of measuring viral load, working in tandem with the delivery of the drugs, institutes a highly individualized experience of HIV infection in which the person becomes responsible for keeping his or her *own* viral levels down. Moreover, this has implications for the way in which HIV is now perceived in the gay community imaginary. Race explains that the test, in association with ART, has altered public perception of HIV as well as the response of the gay community: "For many gay men with HIV, it becomes visible as a private responsibility, as a chronic manageable illness, as something about which it would be shameful to make too much of a fuss about" (Race, 2001a: 178). Race bases his argument on an account of a prior cultural moment invested heavily with the sense of a community sharing the burden of a public experience of HIV and AIDS, evidenced by death notices in the gay press and the visibility of AIDS among its constituents.

Assumptions about dosing leave its incorporation as a necessary activity relatively unquestioned. Yet it is important to note that while viral resistance can result from what is often referred to by doctors as poor adherence, this may have to do with the difficulty (even impossibility, perhaps) of perfect dosing adherence and the now demonstrated occasional ineffectiveness of even perfect dosing. Paul Flowers argues: "the responsibility of adherence and indeed culpability rests with people taking complex drug regimens and rarely, for example, with the drug companies who fail to develop drugs that are easier to take, or alternatively, the medics and pharmacists who prescribe and deliver these drugs" (Flowers 2001: 64). It is important to note that the responsibility for adherence is an effect of a prior constituting of the individual *in possession of* a body with virus, which, in turn, makes it possible for the onus for the effects of pharmacological design to be folded back into the individual. In light of the effects of what Flowers points to as a responsibilizing of the person with HIV, I want to suggest that "the failed individual" be reinverted to undermine its scientific maker. The "failed individual" depends on the presumption that viral suppression is achieved through deliberate conscious pill-taking and, conversely, that the development of viral resistance is the result of missed doses. However, it is not difficult to find other explanations for the development of viral resistance.

By giving attention to the complexity of the biological, as evidenced by science, the simply applied yet politically and ethically fraught notion of a failed individual casts doubt on the interpretative work of science. There are also substantial data in the HIV scientific and social scientific literature that confound the presupposition that adherence necessarily achieves suppression. For example, there are individuals who report missing doses without change to their viral load. Also, despite good adherence, viral resistance can occur. In the scientific literature this is attributed to a variety of reasons. These include possible different drug absorption rates in individuals and/or the presence of other drugs, dietary conditions, extra vitamin intakes, or genetics (Schapiro, 2001; Alcorn, 2000). According to the field of pharmacogenetics, this may not be surprising. The relationship between drugs and bodies is infinitely more complex than implied by the assumption that bodies and drugs are two universally stable distinct entities across a population.

Living with HIV and Envisioning Its Bodily Containment

In this final section, I discuss the role of the viral load test in the materialization of the transmission of drug-resistant virus. In the course of doing this, I reintroduce the problematic of biological reductionism. The intention to avoid this problematic has most recently shaped HIV prevention strategies. But more recently, the intent has had the effect of foreclosing on a more dynamic mode of thinking matter. The following quote attempts to capture a potent mix of biological and social phenomena now giving rise to a new concern in the HIV field:

> Recent studies on the reduction of viral shedding [virus in seminal fluid] produced by HAART [highly active antiretroviral therapy] are encouraging. . . . whether this will lead to reduction in sexual transmission is largely unknown. . . . Ironically, the more widespread use of antiretrovirals . . . may paradoxically increase the sexual transmission of drug-resistant HIV. (Taylor and Drake, 2000: 23)

This quote forms the conclusion of a leading article in an issue of the *Journal of HIV Therapy*. The article addresses the question of whether HIV in semen may be reduced to the point of nil infectivity by anti-HIV drugs and how this may connect with changes in sexual behavior. The connection is suggested as arising from an improved sense of well-being provided by the treatments. While it is not clear what the authors themselves mean by the term "sense of well-being," the array of toxic side effects makes it difficult to accept that treatments necessarily lead people to say they *feel* better physically. Indeed, according to a study by Race, those on anti-HIV drugs may feel sicker than their tests suggest. As one of the participants in the study stated: "My feeling of well-being is shithouse. Really bad. Um, actual health—like going to the doctor—is fabulous. There's a nice contradiction for you. I feel awful but my actual health is very, very good" (Race, 2001b: 183). However, it is feasible to consider that attitudes and understandings are changing in the debate about infectivity. For readers who are not familiar with HIV clinical practice, it may be helpful to know that the results of a viral load test are usually made available to the individual concerned. Some individuals report that this knowledge informs their assessment of their likely infectivity to another (Davis et al., 2002; Rosengarten et al., 2000). It is therefore more likely that it is the knowledge of possible reduced infectivity that creates an improved sense of well-being based on the knowledge of not being infectious to another.

Despite its limitations, the article by Taylor and Drake (2000), cited above, might be considered an important attempt within the field to give necessary consideration to the presence of a subject with virus, in contrast to a more usual science focus on an objectified biological body. More usually, the field remains divided according to the disciplinary division of science and social science. The respective objects of each—the biological body and the social subject in possession of a virus-infected body—are available to be examined independently and exclusively within the respective areas of science and social science. As Race (2001a) indicated, this can result in the muddled and ethically fraught accounts of a responsibilized patient. It can also be shown to produce limited and therefore ethically impoverished social research and subsequently education about prevention.

For social scientists and educators in the HIV field, questions concerning the presumed biological matter of the body are now largely left to science. This has not always been the case, but the shift away from direct engagement with the subject matter of science may also say something about the way in which pharmaceuticals have all but dissolved a prior activist style of engagement (see Epstein 1996). But it may also have something to do with an intention to avoid the risks of biological reductionism that has been noted in much feminist work on the body (Wilson 1999). In the past, HIV prevention education focused on promoting a set of practices to deal with the biological effects, the main one being "use a condom every time." While condom use was advocated on the basis of the biological difference of HIV seropositive or seronegative status, it also sought to dissolve the distinction in the minds of its target audience. Undermining and thus foreclosing the distinction between bodies designated by HIV status was regarded as crucial to preventing discrimination against those of positive status.

In the current context, the intent to foreclose may be misplaced. The serodivide—a distinction that can be read at the level of the biological and at the social—is now indicative of bodies differentiated not so much by the presence or absence of the virus, but by the measure of it among those infected. Those who are coming to know their HIV status according to a barrage of tests are experiencing different meanings of HIV—including the likelihood of infectivity—than those who have very little or no engagement with the medicalization of HIV. This may have important implications for future prevention education strategies. Moreover, it may be an important area of consideration with regard to the potential transmission of viral resistance. The knowledge that I am referring to is not merely a scientific report of viral load, however. It is a knowledge that involves a prior conception of the matter of self—a form of embodiment that may well involve some conception of wholeness with regard to HIV infection and not according to a more recent and specialized scientific conception of bodily compartments. In the past, HIV positive status was perceived to be a state of the entire body, at least in the public imaginary. Now, in HIV medical science, it is more specific and limited in that the locale of the virus may be different than that which is tested, for example, blood versus semen. In this sense, blood and semen or vaginal fluids occupy an unstable equivalence in the assessment of viral presence. However, it is likely that this different conception of the body as more fragmented has not penetrated the thinking of those living with HIV. Consequently, measure of virus or nil virus *in blood* may be read, by the tested subject, into the entirety of his or her body.

Conclusion

If an impasse has been reached between science and cultural studies arising from their opposing commitments—science to an external and absolutely knowable referent[4] and social constructionist critiques to the dismissal of this presumption—there may be strategic value in examining more closely where and how they are played out. Here I have sought to engage with a mode of analysis that invites recognition of how the more unsettling effects of science may be of value to the social analyst. Of course it goes without saying that the matter was already active, in Kirby's terms, prior to the intervention that made the conceptual material. What continues to require articulation is that the interventions and their material effects are the result of a coextensive relation of knowledge and matter (Butler, 1993), however difficult this is to pinpoint for either the cultural analyst or, somewhat differently, the scientist. The most obvious illustration of this relation is in the very "fleshy" act of performing either role. It is perhaps one of the most telling aspects of cultural work that the matter that makes it possible is often forgotten. As Rosalyn Diprose reminds us, "the word is always *of* a body, written in blood, sweat and tears" (2002: 279).

The virus acquires form at the intersection of bodies, knowledges, treatments and associated tests, and social practices (Haraway, 1991), but it also does so within the constituted lived experience of having the virus. Perhaps most ironical and worrisome, in the sort of rigidity that currently sets the biological and cultural as absolutely distinct and thus distributes effects accordingly, is that posed by the territory that comprises the experience of actively negotiating *having* HIV. The matter of HIV is not just thought differently, it is materially different at the site of an individual as an effect of the interventions following its reconceptualization. In putting forward such a proposition I am reminded of Foucault's (1984) account of power as everywhere and invariably inducing resistances. While the area of viral resistance is one pertinent example, the entire field of material activity requires this recognition. If the objects that comprise the epidemic have changed—as indicated by the empirical of science—there is ample reason for a further review of the presumed biological and for assisting in a "culturalist" and ethical engagement in and with it.

Acknowledgments

Research for this paper was undertaken as part of a social research study titled "Transitions in HIV Management" funded by the Innovative Health Technologies Programme, UK Economic & Social Research Council. I am also grateful for feedback I received during its writing from Cath Le Couteur, Carla Drago, Helen Keane, and Kane Race.

Notes

1. The range of known possible side effects is extensive. They can result from an allergic reaction to the drug(s) or from the toxicity of the drug itself. For a comprehensive listing, see HIV i-Base (2001).
2. CD4 T-cells are known as cells within the body's own immune system that are crucial to the function of immunity to disease and yet are highly susceptible to cooption and destruction by HIV. Significant measures of these cells are currently understood to indicate that an individual with HIV is unlikely to become ill as a result of the virus.
3. This extract is from an interview with an HIV specialist clinician. See Rosengarten et al. (2004) for details of the study and other published accounts.
4. This is my interpretation and adaption of Kirby's claim (1999), which in the article cited, alludes to the role of humanism in constituting the gaze of science.

References

Alcorn, K. (ed.) (2000) *HIV & AIDS Treatments Directory,* National AIDS Manual. London: NAM Publications, pp. 157, 56.

Alcorn, K., and Fieldhouse, R. (2000) *AIDS Reference Manual.* London: NAM Publications.

Barad, K. (1998) "Getting real: Technoscientific practices and the materialization of reality," *differences: A Journal of Feminist Cultural Studies* 10, no. 2: 87–128.

BHIVA (British HIV Association) (2001) *Guidelines for the Treatment of HIV-Infected Adults with Antiretroviral Therapy.* BHIVA Writing Committee on behalf of the BHIVA Executive Committee UK. Available at http://www.bhiva.org.

Butler, J. (1993) *Bodies That Matter.* London and New York: Routledge.

Chesney, M. A, Ickovics, J. R., Chambers, D. B., Gifford, A. L., et al. (2000) "Self-reported adherence to antiretroviral medications among participants in HIV clinical trials: The AACTG adherence instruments," *AIDS Care* 12, no. 3: 255–266.

Davis, M. D., Hart, G. J., Imrie, J., Davidson, O., Williams, I., and Stephenson, J. M., (2002) "'HIV is HIV to me': The meanings of treatment, viral load and reinfection for gay men living with HIV," *Health Risk and Society* 4, no 1: 31–43.

Diprose R. (2002) "'Response' to Helen Keane and Marsha Rosengarten, 'On the biology of sexed subjects'," *Australian Feminist Studies* 17, no. 29: 279–282.

Epstein, S. (1996) *Impure Science.* Berkeley: University of California Press.

Epstein, S. (2004) "Bodily differences and collective identities: The politics of gender and race in biomedical research in the United States," *Body & Society,* 10, no. 2-3: 183–203.

Eron J. J., Vernazza, P. L., Johnston, D. M., Seillier-Moiseiwitsch, F., Alcorn, T. M., Fiscus, S. A., and Cohen, M. S. (1998) "Resistance of HIV–1 to antiretroviral agents in blood and seminal plasma: Implications for transmission," *AIDS* 12, no. 15: 181–189.

Flowers, P. (2001) "Gay men and HIV/AIDS risk management," *Health* 5: 50–75.

Flynn, M. (2001) "Resistance unrest," An interview with Dr. Mike Youle, director of HIV research at London's Royal Free Hospital, *Positive Nation* 67 (June): 38, 39.

Foucault, M. (1984) *History of Sexuality,* Harmondsworth: Peregrine Books.

Fraser, M. (2002) "What is the Matter of Feminist Criticism," *Economy & Society* 31, no. 4: 606–625.

Gandhi, M., Bacchetti, P., Miotti, P., Quinn, T. C., Veronese, F., and Greenblatt, R. M. (2002) "Does patient gender affect human immunodeficiency virus levels?" *Clinical Infectious Diseases* 35: 313–322.

Haraway, D. (1991) "The Biopolitics of postmodern bodies: Determinations of self in immune system discourse," *Simians, Cyborgs, and Women*. London: Free Association Books, pp. 203–230.

HIV i-Base (2001) *Avoiding and Managing Side Effects*. London: HIV i-Base Publications.

Ho, D. D. (1995) "Time to hit HIV, early and hard," *New England Journal of Medicine* 333, no. 7: 450–451.

International Collaboration on HIV Optimism (2003) "HIV treatments optimism among gay men: An international perspective," *Journal of Acquired Immune Deficiency Syndromes* 32(5): 545–550.

Kalichman, S. (1998) "Post exposure prophylaxis for HIV infection in gay and bisexual men. Implications for the future of HIV prevention," *American Journal of Preventive Medicine*, 15, no. 2: 120–127.

Keane, H., and Rosengarten, M. (2002) "On the biology of sexed subjects," *Australian Feminist Studies* 17, no. 29: 261–276.

Kippax, S., and Race, K. (2003) "Sustaining safe practice: twenty years on," *Social Science & Medicine*, 57: 1–12.

Kirby, V. (1999) "Human nature," *Australian Feminist Studies* 14, no. 29: 19–29.

Little, S. (2001) "Is transmitted drug resistance in HIV on the rise?" *British Medical Journal* 322: 1074–1075.

Martin, E. (1990) "Toward an anthropology of immunology: The body as nation state," *Medical Anthropology Quarterly* 4:4: 410–426.

Mortimer, P. P., and Loveday, C. (2001) "The virus and the tests," in *ABC of AIDS* (5th ed.) Michael W. Adler (ed.), London: BMJ Books.

Palella, F. J., Dalaney, K. M., Moorman, A. C., et al. (1998) "Declining morbidity and mortality among patients with advanced human immunodeficiency virus infection," *New England Journal of Medicine* 338:853–860.

Race, K. (2001a) "The undetectable crisis: Changing technologies of risk," *Sexualities* 4, no. 2: 167–189.

Race, K. (2001b) "Incorporating clinical authority: A new test for people with HIV," in N. Watson and S. Cunningham-Burley (eds.), *Reframing the Body*. Hampshire, UK and New York: Palgrave, pp. 81–95.

Rosengarten, M., Race, K., and Kippax, S. (2000) "'Touch wood, everything will be OK': Gay men's understandings of clinical markers in sexual practise," Monograph 7/2000 Sydney: National Centre in HIV Social Research.

Rosengarten, M., Imrie, J., Flowers, P., Davis, M., Hart, G. J. (2004) "After the euphoria: HIV medical technologies from the perspective of clinicians," *Sociology of Health and Illness* 26, no. 5: 575–596.

Schapiro, J. (2001) "Understanding protease inhibitor potency: The intersection of exposure, efficacy, and resistance," *The AIDS Reader* 11, no. 6: 311–315.

Taylor S., and Drake S. (2000) "HIV in semen: Clinical implications," *Journal of HIV Therapy,* 5: 18–25.

Treichler, P. (1999) *How to Have Theory in an Epidemic.* Durham: Duke University Press.

Wagner, G. (2003) "Does discontinuing the use of pill boxes to facilitate electronic monitoring impede adherence?" *International Journal of STD & AIDS* 14, no. 1 (January): 64–65.

Wilson, E. (1999) "Introduction: Somatic compliance—Feminism, biology and science," *Australian Feminist Studies* 14 (29): 7–18.

5

Addiction and the Bioethics of Difference

Helen Keane

If there is a difference between ethics and morals, it is clearly that morality is concerned with statements like "must one," or "must one not," whereas ethics must, above all else, ask the question, "Who am I to say to the other 'you must,' or 'you must not,' and how will this statement define my relation to this other?"

—Isabelle Stengers (1997)

The moral consensus that drugs are bad is based in large part on their ability to cause addiction. Addiction, understood as a unique condition in which the individual has lost the power to control his or her drug use and therefore behavior, is described in the globalizing shorthand of news reports, popular psychology, and politicians' speeches as a meaningless life of degradation. Among the most familiar drug stories told in the media are those that feature formerly exemplary young people who fall into the trap of addiction after taking some ecstasy at a party or trying one shot of heroin. In these stories, the dramatic contrast between the individual's happy and privileged nonaddicted life and the lows of addiction reveals the transformative power of drugs.

In the dense rhetorical and moral landscape of "the drug problem," the addict appears as an unstable although always transgressive figure, both a victim of drugs who requires help and treatment, and the criminal perpetrator of drug-related harm who must be punished. But as both victims and perpetrators, the addicted are situated as subjects about whom the truth is known, and who cannot speak their own truth. What is also clear is that the body and psyche of the addict must be normalized in order to normalize the social body. A currently dominant strategy of normalization is to approach the addict as a medical case requiring diagnosis and treatment. The view that addicts suffer from a disease or disorder is widely accepted in medical, psychological, and popular arenas, and the treatment of drugs and addiction as health issues is promoted as the way to overcome the inhumane and unscientific policies of the past.[1]

However, medical and therapeutic approaches currently coexist with the legal structures and rhetoric of "the war on drugs," and it seems quite possible for a government to endorse the view that addiction is a disease while simultaneously supporting increased criminalization of addicts. Moreover, medical models of addiction do not necessarily undermine visions of the addict as a uniquely compromised subject who requires surveillance, management, and control. In fact, an emphasis on the physiological transformation of addiction can justify a wide range of responses in which assumptions are made about what such people need and how they should change.

This chapter explores some of the troubling ethical consequences of contemporary understandings of the addict as a certain type of morally and physiologically disordered person. It argues that a particular formulation of difference is crucial to discourses of addiction. The addict is understood in terms of a moral *and* physiological difference from the normal subject, and this difference is posited as a deviation from an unmarked and unproblematic norm. Alterity is equated with deficiency. This is a not-unfamiliar formulation of difference; a similar hierarchical opposition organizes dominant notions of sexual difference and a field of connected binaries. More specifically, however, the difference of addiction is constituted as the result of a process of pollution and corruption, in which foreign substances have disrupted the original balance and self-sufficiency of the body. This understanding of the addicted body is examined in relation to withdrawal and craving, two widely discussed and researched symptoms of substance dependence.

These concerns are largely outside the traditional framework of bioethics, which has tended to downplay the significance of embodiment to ethical relations. As Rosalyn Diprose has observed, it is assumed that biomedical ethics regulates relations between "self-present, autonomous, disembodied individuals" rather than bodies (1994: 1). This constricted notion of ethics itself acts to exclude those identified as addicted (and therefore trapped by their bodily desires) from having their voices heard.

Against the view of the addicted body as corrupted, the final part of the chapter explores the drug–body encounter in terms of the body's affinity for drugs. Drawing on the work of Gilles Deleuze, it offers a different way of approaching the differences of the drug-affected and drug-addicted body. It is hoped that it also suggests the possibilities of an ethics based on relations among bodies that are dependent and vulnerable to change, whether addicted or not. Instead of judging the drugged body against a fixed moral and physiological code based on self-control and independence, such an approach accepts the openness of bodies. It enables an ethical response to addiction that respects the freedom of others to choose their own way of life, while recognizing the limits to their freedom. First, however, I examine the production of addiction as a particular kind of moral disorder.

The Moral Differences of Addiction

In the dominant discourse of western ethics, moral agency is grounded in the individual's capacity to choose and act freely and rationally. Indeed, autonomy and rationality are privileged as the necessary attributes of full subjectivity. Margrit Shildrick (1997) has argued that the demands of moral agency require the agent to act on the calculations of some given utility; or in accordance with the rules of a preexisting hypothetical contract with other members of the moral community; or according to the dictates of virtue. On each of these grounds, the addict fails to attain the standard. The addict's conduct is presumed to be determined by his or her need for drugs, one that is not naturally occurring but created through the repetition of freely chosen acts. Or as an article in the *Lancet* puts it:

> At some point after continued repetition of voluntary drug-taking, the drug user loses the voluntary ability to control its use. At that point the drug misuser becomes drug addicted and there is a compulsive, often overwhelming involuntary aspect to continuing drug use and to relapse after a period of abstinence. (Nutt 1996: 31)

Despite this involuntariness, however, and unlike most other sufferers of chronic conditions, the addict is always presumed to be capable of a return to normality, if he or she *really* wants to. In both the lack of control over behavior and the dependence on others to save him or her from this situation, the addict is infantalized and placed outside the realm of normative adulthood, but the potential for redemption provokes continued intervention.

As a number of critics have outlined, the notion of a disease characterized by loss of control relies on a presumption and expectation of personal self-control that is historically and culturally specific (Room 1985). Harry Levine has argued that the understanding of alcoholism as a disease of the will emerged in early nineteenth-century America because of the rise of bourgeois society in which social stability and individual success depended on self-discipline: "The idea of addiction 'made sense' not only to drunkards, who came to understand themselves as individuals with overwhelming desires they could not control, but also to great numbers of middle-class people who were struggling to keep their desires in check—desires that at times seemed 'irresistible'" (Levine 1978: 165). Almost two centuries later, the addict is still the threatening shadow of the rational self-regulating citizen. He or she is also disturbing because of his or her proximity to the modern experience of ourselves as avid consumers, desiring unnecessary objects and short-lived pleasures, even if (or perhaps because) their price is excessive. The disorder of addiction makes sense both because of a belief in the possibility and importance of self-control but also because of a recognition of the tenuousness and burden of that self-control. What marks the difference between the compulsive shopper and the drug addict is the particular potency, both cultural and physiological, of drugs.

Taking into account the full range of symptoms officially identified for substance dependence, it appears that the diagnosis of the medical disorder is inseparable from judgments about what a normal and healthy life should look like and the way time and priorities should be organized. A defining feature of addiction is continued drug use despite harmful consequences such as job loss, relationship conflicts, and health problems. This takes for granted a certain level and style of social functioning, assuming that in the absence of drug use the subject would not be facing problems such as unemployment and poverty. It also, as Mariana Valverde (1998) points out, assumes norms of social respectability: for a bartender or sex worker for instance, heavy drinking and drug use could aid rather than hinder occupational functioning. Drug use can also facilitate relationships and time management; for many people it is quitting that brings loneliness and loss of daily structure. The simple picture of a life with drugs as bad (filled with harms), and a life without drugs as good (free of harms) overlooks the fact that drug use, as a social practice, is linked in complex ways to the other elements of people's lives and cannot be straightforwardly isolated from or contrasted to "important social, occupational or recreational activities" (American Psychiatric Association 1994: 181). It also disavows the possibility that for some, continuing drug use may make more sense than trying to give up, and that therefore persistence is not simply a sign of pathology.

The reading of social harms as symptoms of dependence can easily lead to a circular chain of attribution whereby the existence of problems with work and family determines addiction, and addiction implies there must be serious work and family problems (caused by the substance use). This can result in a constellation of negative attributes being almost automatically attached to members of negatively valued social categories, such as unemployed youth or welfare moms. For example a recent U.S. report on substance-abusing parents warns that parents who abuse substances are likely to neglect and abuse their children, and it also urges that every investigation of child abuse and neglect should include screening for parental substance abuse (National Center on Addiction and Substance Abuse 1999: ii). The use of the term "parental" notwithstanding, the targeted individuals are the poor women of color whose practices of motherhood are most likely to come under the scrutiny of child welfare authorities. These women are presented as antimothers; they are "second and third generation addicts," with "violent and troubled relationships with men who encourage drug use"; their social skills and emotional maturity are "stunted"; they have little education and were "born into poverty" (1999: 20). In addition, these problems of violence, poverty, and lack of resources are not presented as conditions affecting women's welfare; rather, they are regarded as harms visited on a child by its mother because they diminish her capacity to be a responsible parent.

Twelve-step models of addiction, promoted through the publications and programs of the highly profitable recovery industry, also produce a highly moralized and totalizing vision of the addict's difference from the normal individual.[2] In the twelve-step model, alcoholism and addiction are diseases whose symptoms are nourished by a profound moral bankruptcy. In these programs, recovery from addiction demands not only abstinence but extensive work on the self, leading to spiritual transformation. Addiction operates here as an identity rather than a type of conduct. An addict who has been abstinent for years must still accept that they are an addict, otherwise complacency and relapse will follow (Nowinski and Baker 1992: xvi). Both the past and the future are contained by the truth of addiction. In the personal stories told at meetings and reprinted in recovery literature, addiction explains "what we used to be like, what happened and where we are now" (Alcoholics Anonymous 1976: 158). All misbehavior, errors of judgment, disappointments, and losses are interpreted as the fruits of the disease, even if they seem unrelated to drinking or drug taking.

In more medicalized discourse, moral bankruptcy and spiritual transformation are not often mentioned, but the framework of addiction nevertheless constitutes the sufferer as a certain type of person by linking physical, psychological, and social signs and reading them as symptoms of an underlying fixed and unified pathology. One aspect of this pathology that has significant impact on the ethical status of the addict is the cognitive impairment that is regarded as fundamental to the addictive disease. Denial, the central form of distorted thinking attributed to addiction, has long had a prominent place in self-help discourse, where it is presented as the most damaging and insidious symptom of the disease. The concept has now been incorporated into medical discourse and treatment practices, at least in the United States. It is described as "an unconscious, irrational defense mechanism in which the individual fails to perceive and acknowledge an important objective truth that is obvious and apparent to others" (Landry 1993: 196). Denial perpetuates the addiction by keeping the addict in a state of delusion, unable to recognize the true cause of his or her problems. In the words of a popular guide to drug abuse:

> Most people when they come down with a disease, will set about trying to find treatment for it. . . . Here is where chemical dependence distinguishes itself as

a disease unlike any other. *The people who have it generally do not seek treatment of their own volition because they are not aware they have it.* (Johnson 1990: 20; emphasis in original)

Because denial is a symptom of a disease, and the person in denial is unable to see the truth, the addict's expressed wishes and version of reality must be ignored in order to respect his or her genuine needs and desires. And the stronger the addict's insistence that he or she does not need treatment or that the problem is other than addiction, the stronger the proof that the disease has him or her in its grip and that coercion is justified. The addict is unable to speak the truth of his or her condition, although his or her words and actions are taken to reveal this truth. The flaw in the addict's being is not merely dishonesty but a more profound state of inauthenticity, an inability to be true to oneself (Keane 2002: 73).

When notions of impairment and inauthenticity combine with other hierarchies of social value such as gender, race, and class, already vulnerable and disadvantaged people are denied a voice in decisions about their lives. In the case of the substance-using mothers discussed earlier, the focus is on their physical, social, and psychological incapacities, particularly their inability to recognize the nature of their disorder. The possibility that their reluctance to enter treatment may be due to reasonable concerns such as lack of child care, fear of losing their children, distrust of treatment providers, or skepticism about the treatment process is easily discounted because of the overriding concern with their cognitive failings.

The Physiological Differences of Addiction

Substance dependence is commonly described in medical accounts as a "biopsychosocial" condition. The clumsy omnibus term is employed to demonstrate awareness of the complexity of addiction and the significant role played by nonpharmacological factors. However, in its simple additive construction the term reveals an assumption that the elements of addiction can be divided into easily distinguishable categories, and that a clear boundary exists between individuals and the world they inhabit. Moreover, the biological and pharmacological are given primacy.

Psychological and social factors are seen as influencing or providing the context for the underlying biochemical process of addiction. Drugs and their unique chemical properties are seen as initiating and driving the addictive process, causing the bodily changes that result in dependence and producing a compulsion beyond individual control.

In contrast to the everyday usage of the term, medical definitions of drug describe a broad category of chemical agents with no explicit reference to questions of harmfulness, legality, or social acceptability. These issues are regarded as irrelevant, or even inimical, to the accurate and scientific description of a natural category of substances called drugs. However, the belief that use of the words "chemical" and "substance" are a way of avoiding the morally loaded cultural category of drugs is misguided. Drugs are commonly viewed as chemical others to the natural substances of the human body, toxic pollutants of the body's organic innocence. The corruption of the natural body by intruding and alien chemicals represents both physiological and moral breakdown. In such constructions, the dichotomy of natural and chemical can be viewed as a substitute for the displaced moral dichotomy of good and evil.

Defining drugs as substances other than those required for normal health is a way of finessing this attribution of unnaturalness (Johns 1990: 5). As I have argued elsewhere, it puts in place a distinction between therapeutic substances like insulin, which work to restore health in cases of disease, and recreational drugs. However, identifying normal health and normal biology, and assessing whether a drug is being used to restore or disrupt function, is based on normative judgments about proper and improper bodies as well as proper and improper substances (Keane 2002: 18–19). Is a body in pain functioning normally or in a disrupted state? Is pain relief a disruption of normality or a restoration of normal functioning? Does it depend on whether the analgesic is aspirin or heroin and whether it has been medically prescribed or self-prescribed? How are drug therapies for conditions like social anxiety different from the routine use of alcohol and cocaine to deal with lack of self-esteem and confidence? "Normal" in medicine is an ambiguous term that refers both to the habitual state of an individual body and to an ideal type of organic structure. As Georges Canguilhem (1989) argues, individuals set their own bodily norms through their habits of living, and therefore normality and pathology can never be objectively, universally, or precisely defined. The maintenance of a normal state of health, meaning the capacity to continue one's usual activities, can often require the regular intake of externally produced chemicals such as insulin, Prozac, or heroin, undermining the idea of a group of substances that can be universally and objectively defined as drugs.

Nevertheless, the notion of an addicted body as one that is uniquely dependent on an external and artificial substance for its continued functioning remains prominent. The addict's transgression of physiological norms and moral norms merges in this notion of a dependent and contaminated body, a body that is locked in a prison of repetition. The addict's physiological dependence on drugs mirrors his or her failure to achieve a mature way of life that follows a trajectory of progress and growth that is founded on self-discipline and autonomy. In this way, medical discourses of addiction not only reinforce the ideals of self-control discussed in the previous section, but also a moral norm of independence. The ethical value placed on the impossible ideal of a self-sufficient body, and its connection to norms of development, is particularly clear in discussions of withdrawal symptoms.

Despite the official unshackling of physical dependence from addiction in diagnostic criteria, withdrawal symptoms and tolerance still appear in medical discourse as important elements in the charting of the addictive process within the body, providing visible and sometimes dramatic signs of deviation from the physiologically normal. The explanatory narrative is that over time, drug use causes the brain (and thus the body) to adapt to the presence of the drug, often reducing the production of neurochemicals that are similar to the drug. Suddenly stopping or reducing drug intake causes decompensation symptoms as the nervous system readjusts to the absence of the drug (Schuckit 1995: 16).

The concept of withdrawal constitutes the normal body as a complete and perfect unit that exists in nature in a finely tuned and dynamic state of balance. In its original state, before being polluted by drugs, the body is imagined as uncontaminated by foreign matter and effortlessly maintaining equilibrium. The repeated introduction of an extraneous chemical disrupts the delicate operation of the system, but the system eventually adapts to its presence and indeed comes to need it. The concept of withdrawal symbolizes the conflict between the artificial substance and the natural body. If the drug is suddenly removed from the organism, it has to readjust. Unpleasant symptoms are experienced, but ultimately the capacity of the body to right itself prevails and balance is restored. The body is imagined as a self-healing entity which, even after years of abuse, retains the ability to detoxify and rebalance itself. Withdrawal then becomes not only a physiological readjustment but a profoundly meaningful process of purification and restitution.

The simple logic of adaptation and readaptation is muddied, however, by the inconsistencies and unpredictable elements of what one author carefully calls drug cessation phenomena or the events that occur when chronic drug use is halted. He categorizes these events into "true" withdrawal symptoms that "reflect the attempt of the body to maintain pharmacodynamic and pharmacokinetic homeostasis" (Leccese 1991: 61); rebound symptoms from a preexisting disorder that become worse when medications are suddenly ceased; and the feelings of frustration, anxiety, and longing that are experienced when a habitual and rewarding activity is abruptly halted. But how confidently can symptoms be attributed to one sort of cessation response and not another? Both depression and stomach pains could be explained as either the result of neurotransmitter adjustment or feelings of "frustrated nonreward" (Leccese 1991: 61). This seems to suggest that judgments about the presence or absence of physical dependence cannot easily be made. The sensitivity of withdrawal symptoms to factors such as memory, experience, anticipation, and environment is evidence of the enmeshment of the pharmacological, the psychological, and social contexts and processes. Rats show greater signs of withdrawal when kept in the same cage in which they were dosed with drugs, and less marked signs when in an unfamiliar cage (Davies 1992: 53). The symptoms arising from neuroadaptation and decompensation cannot be separated from the experience of remembering and longing for a past pleasure or comfort.

The solidity and reliability of withdrawal symptoms as markers that directly correspond to a disordered physiological or neurological state is at least in part illusory. They are more like complex signs that are inevitably subject to interpretation: by the clinical observer, by the individual experiencing them, and by the public commentator on drug problems. This interpretation is easily influenced by already existing views about good and bad drugs. In a widely published article, the former director of the (United States) National Institute of Drug Abuse, Alan Leshner, states that although opiates are addictive in most circumstances, the physical dependence that can result from medical treatment for pain can be easily managed and therefore does not represent addiction. In contrast, marijuana users do not usually experience withdrawal symptoms, yet this drug is highly addictive for many people who suffer from "uncontrollable marijuana craving, seeking and use" (Leshner 1997b: 2). Leshner's comparison between morphine and marijuana inverts the usual association between withdrawal symptoms and addiction, allowing him to reiterate the safety of medical drugs and the danger of illicit drugs. My point is not that genuine addiction requires physical dependence, but that the attribution of both physical dependence and addiction is a process of semiotic interpretation and decoding. And because the existence of the referent, the addicted body, is inferred from the signs, the final truth of dependence remains elusive.

The biology of dependence is also linked to the addict's moral and ethical flaws because of its role in producing and maintaining the repetition, circularity, and habitual action that are regarded as characteristic of the addict's mode of existence. The fear of withdrawal and the need to maintain the fragile homeostasis of the physically dependent body is regarded as locking the addict into a rigid pattern of behavior. The contrast between the socially influenced fluidity of normal consumptive behavior and the inflexible routine of addiction is highlighted by psychiatrists Griffith Edwards and Milton Gross in their classic description of the alcohol dependence syndrome. They observe that:

> The ordinary drinker's consumption and beverage will vary from day to day and from week to week: he may have beer at luncheon one day, nothing to drink on another, share a bottle of wine at dinner one night, then go to a party on a Saturday and have a lot to drink. His drinking is patterned by varying internal cues and external circumstances. (Edwards and Gross 1976: 1058).

They then state that as dependence develops, the drinking repertoire becomes increasingly narrowed because the desire or, in fact, the need for alcohol, is generated internally, rather than as a response to social factors. The alcoholic "begins to drink the same whether it is work day, weekend or holiday: the nature of the company or his own mood makes less and less difference" (1976: 1058). The drinking behavior is regular and rigid because it is following an unvarying physiological schedule of required dose to maintain a certain level of alcohol in the blood and avoid the pain of withdrawal, rather than a fluid pattern of social events or psychological moods.

Here addiction is produced as consumptive behavior that has been robbed of its mobility, the normal flexibility that is expected of human social behavior. It is a compulsive and physiologically driven attachment to the repetition of the same. This is another aspect of the addict's ethical impoverishment and exclusion from the ideal of the autonomous subject. As Rita Felski has argued, modernity is marked by disdain for repetition and horror of the imprisoning forces of unthinking habit and routine because "repetition is seen as a threat to the modern project of self-determination, subordinating individual will to the demands of an imposed pattern" (2000: 84). Moreover, the addict is not attached to his or her habits as a result of commitment to a noble ideal, or because he or she is serving others, or even as a result of a love of pleasure. Rather he or she is a subject of fear, his or her will subordinated or even destroyed by the need for drugs.

The intense attachment of the addict to his or her drug habit also removes the addict from the narrative of progress and growth that is taken to describe the normal life cycle in standard psychological accounts of human development. Although the term "life cycle" is conventional in this literature, the process of development described (and prescribed) is in fact a trajectory in which the individual passes through set chronological stages, based on the resolution of particular "socio-emotional tasks" (Wallen 1993: 2). According to Jacqueline Wallen, author of a textbook on developmental psychology for substance abuse professionals, the failure to resolve developmental issues is both a cause and a result of drug problems. She presents a typical case of a couple in their thirties whose history of drug and alcohol use has left them still struggling with the developmental tasks of late adolescence. They have two children but are not providing adequate parenting or a stable home; there is unresolved conflict with their own parents; and their existence as a couple depends largely on the pseudointimacy generated by partying together (1993: 6–7). They are frozen in time because the repetitious cycle of addiction that dominates their days prevents them from following the challenging but rewarding path of growth and maturity.[3]

Ultimately, however, it is the addict's intense desire for the drug that is at the heart of the disorder. The production of addictive desire as both quantitatively and qualitatively distinct from normal desires is central to the production of dependence as a pathological state. The disorder is defined by the compulsion of the addict to continue his or her drug use, even if he or she desperately wants to stop and even if the costs are severe. The terms "craving," "compulsion," and "loss of control" are employed to signify the strength of the forces directing the addict's behavior. They reinforce the idea that drug dependence is a different order of thing from attachment to daily routines and habits and normal preoccupation with certain activities. By suggesting a will that has been compromised, they explain the addict's seeming irrationality and indifference to the high price of his or her habit.

The notion of craving has a double meaning that renders it highly productive in addiction discourses. It refers both to a specific level of desire (intense), and to desires for particular objects (drugs). The term thus constitutes the desire for drugs as unique and out of the ordinary, both in its intensity and its aim. The slippage between the two meanings has the effect of suggesting that all urges for drugs, even if mild, are pathological. In particular, the connection made between addictive desire and the physiology of addiction highlights the distance between craving and ordinary wanting.

Underlying the notion of craving is the assumption that biological needs can be distinguished from mere wants, and that the former are harder to resist than the latter. But the reality of desire is surely more messy than this. We know we are in love when the desire to hear the voice of the beloved is overwhelming, while the need for food and sleep are faint and easily ignored sensations. As psychologist John Booth Davies has observed, even within pharmacological accounts, craving often emerges as "a 'want' deriving from the normal everyday pharmacology of memory; not a 'have to' underlaid by some alien drug-induced pharmacology" (1992: 52). That is, people remember that an experience was pleasurable and this is coupled with the hope that it will happen again. Craving can then be understood as an intense and specific longing, an experience certainly not confined to drug addiction.

In its production of dependence and the concomitant production of normal and abnormal bodies and normal and abnormal desires, medical discourse is involved in setting norms and judging bodies against these norms. All bodies interact with the environment, adapt to it, and come to depend on various inputs and stimuli, but this openness to and reliance on the external is easily made into a pathology when already devalued bodies and suspect substances are involved.

Rereading Drugs and Bodies

While medical discourses of addiction often produce the addicted body as "other" to the normal, drug-free body, pharmacology also provides material for an alternative reading of the drug–body encounter. A standard pharmacology text begins with a chapter on principles of drug action, which is divided into pharmacokinetics, the movement of drugs through the body, and pharmacodynamics, the interactions between drugs and receptors (Julien 1998). In both modes of action, the openness of the body to drugs and its affinity for drugs is clearly what enables drug effects and the potential intensity of the drug experience. It is not just that drugs affect the body, but that the body welcomes drugs. Drugs can be absorbed into the bloodstream through the stomach and intestine, through the mucous membranes of the mouth, nasal passages, rectum and vagina, through the lungs, through the skin, and through muscles. Once in the bloodstream, the drug is distributed throughout the body by circulating blood, and because the entire blood volume circulates in the body about once every minute, the distribution of molecules is rapid. They are then transmitted through the capillaries to body tissues, enabling them to reach their sites of action, the receptors (Julien 1998: 8). Receptors are specialized to respond to one endogenous neurotransmitter molecule with great sensitivity and selectivity, and thus they respond equally avidly to similar drug molecules. Therefore, as the text states, a drug does not create any new effects, it "merely modulates normal neuronal functioning, mimicking or antagonizing the actions of a specific endogenous neurotransmitter" (Julein 1998: 30).

This simple description of drug–body interaction suggests that the body can be conceived of as a machine for the absorption and circulation of drugs. Drugs are not so much a foreign outsider, but a familiar neighbor, working with the body's existing repertoire of effects. Even more provocatively, such a reading encourages a conception of the body that is not coincident with what is usually identified as the material and organic attributes of a single human being. Instead, the body emerges as an assemblage of molecules, both endogenous and exogenous, an entity that blurs the distinction between not only inside and outside but also self and other. Moreover, because most people ingest some sort of substance every day, this is not a deviant or unusual state, but rather the norm of embodiment. As well as destabilizing oppositional distinctions between normality and pathology, the chemical interaction of drugs, blood, and tissue challenges fictions of the body as a naturally complete and closed system. As Avital Ronell states, "the body of the addict, engendering dependency and the possibility of a *chemical prosthesis,* withdraws from the nostalgia of the body's naturalistic/organic self-sufficiency" (Ronell 1993: 70–71, emphasis in original). This model of the addicted body is not defined by lack or loss; rather, it describes a body that has fabricated "a supplementary organ (that) requires absolute attention in the mode of care" (Ronell 1993: 70–7).

The brain in particular emerges as an organ that cannot be contained in the narratives of purity and pollution and innocence and corruption that structure dominant accounts of drug use. Rather, it has a natural affinity for drugs, for pleasure, and thus for addiction. In neuroscience, the distinction between the natural and the chemical cannot serve to identify threatening substances because the brain is itself chemical. Here the power of drugs is not so much their artificiality, but their proximity to the natural. A drug is something that is not the body interacting with the body on false pretenses, in fact mimicking the body's natural substances. It is, however, not subject to the same control and regulation that endogenous substances are, and its effects are therefore marked by destructive excess and escalation.

The theme of neurochemical mimicry often found in neurological explanations of drug use leads to a distinction between true and false pleasures. When we satisfy hunger by eating, dopamine is released, which gives us a feeling of well-being. Drugs provide a similar dopamine-related pleasure without meeting any needs, but the brain nevertheless registers pleasure. And because the illusory pleasure of drugs is more rapid, predictable, and powerful than the genuine well-being gained from daily life and fulfillment of responsibilities, the addict eventually loses interest in the real in favor of the simulation.[4] As I argued earlier, the idea of addiction as a state of alienation from truth is central to contemporary discourses of drug use. What the neurological discourse of addiction provides is a scientific basis for the division of pleasures into true and false. The inauthenticity of the addict is constituted as a chemically produced and objectively verifiable state, rather than an ethical judgment about a way of being. By using artificial means to feel artificial pleasure, the addict is already in the realm of untruth, even before any evaluation of his or her interior being. But while positing a distinction between natural needs and unnatural addictions, these explanations also suggest that for the brain the two are easily, perhaps naturally, substitutable.

As this discussion has indicated, a reformulation of drugs and their relation to the body requires an understanding of corporeality that moves away from the conceptualization of bodies as organic and unified entities. It also needs to be an approach that views bodily difference in positive terms, rather than seeing only loss, lack, or perversion in any departure from or modification of the norm. One promising conceptualization of the body for this project is found in the work of Gilles Deleuze. As Rosi Braidotti (2000) has argued, Deleuze's account of the body as a dynamic, discontinuous, and nontotalizable assemblage is highly attuned to the realities of the technological era, including the prevalence of pharmacological experimentation. For Deleuze, a body is not an expression or representation of an inner truth nor is it confined to the bounded physical space of the individual. Embodied subjectivity is instead conceived of as the result of a folding in of external influences, and a folding outward of affects (Braidotti 2000).

Drawing on Spinoza, Deleuze (1992) famously defines the body by what it can do rather than what it is. His concentration on the capacities of a body, more specifically its capacity to affect and be affected by other bodies, allows a mode of individualization to be envisaged that is not dependent on the existence of a subject considered morally exemplary for its self-control and independence. The affective capacity of a body comprises its power, which can be either decreased or increased when it connects with another body. A body in this schema is anything that has the capacity to affect or be affected, including human, animal, textual, social, and physical bodies. In the Deleuzian model, there is no ontological essence or stable subject behind a body's actions. A body is essentially active; it cannot be separated from what it can do, how it can be affected, the linkages it can make, and these capacities are always changing, giving rise to a body that is always in a state of becoming rather than being. As a "becoming" rather than a being it cannot be defined in terms of substance, organs, form, or functions. As Claire Colebrook suggests, the ethics of this body asks "not 'what does this body mean—what is its intent, condition or genesis?' but 'how does this body work?'" (2000: 124). This entails a technical rather than a moral approach to the diversity in embodied existence found in cultures that embrace drugs and other biotechnologies. The value of the technical frame is that it brings to light not only the multiple differences and distinctions among bodies but also the surprising similarities among different bodies, without assuming in advance what a good body is.[5] It recognizes that bodies all have a particular sex, race, and morphology, and that these specificities encode bodies and subjects, their conduct and habits, with meaning and value.

Writing with Felix Guattari, Deleuze develops a complex model of the body as assemblage created and connected by flows of desire and intensity. The elusive notion of the "body without organs" (BwO) forms the limit point of the body as assemblage; it acts as a powerful reminder that we need not think of our bodies in terms of their biological organization.[6] The BwO is not opposed to the organs but to the organic organization of the organs. The body without organs is also opposed to the articulation and interpretation of meaning and the formation of the subject. Deleuze and Guattari (1987) emphatically state that becoming a BwO is not an ideal state, but something we do every day, at least to some extent.

The BwO is of particular interest in relation to addiction because Deleuze and Guattari identify the drugged body as one of a "dreary parade" of "sucked-dry" and empty BwOs, along with the masochist body, the paranoid or schizo body, and the hypochondriac body (1987: 150). The empty BwO is a body that has been evacuated of intensities and flows, but emptiness does not in fact capture its condition. As Elizabeth Grosz explains: "This body does not lack; its problem is the opposite: it fills itself to the point where nothing further can circulate. It is empty only in the sense that if a body is made up of proliferations, connections and linkages, the empty BwO has ceased to flow" (1994: 170–171).

The empty BwO with its frozen circulation resonates with the image of addictive desire and addicted subjectivity discussed earlier. However, the description of the empty BwO is not a moral or medical judgment; it does not view the addict body in terms of a pathological ontology or a singular disease. Rather, it is an ethological account of a specific arrangement of forces. The addicted body has forged a link that has become frozen and fixed, and that is therefore regulatory and limiting in its effects. To understand difference as positivity does not demand that we view all forms of existence as equally productive of positive effects such as joy or freedom. The addict may be marked by frozen intensities (and a dreary life), depending on his or her circumstances, but a *recovering* addict body could be viewed as equally frozen, stuck in repetition of a singular truth and closed to the circulation and proliferation of intensities.

Deleuze and Guattari's use of the drugged body as a model of the empty BwO can be distinguished from an attempt to refigure drug use and addiction by using their account of corporeality. A body that indulges in excess and depends on certain substances and patterns of behavior to function can still allow the circulation of intensities and remain open to connections with other bodies. Indeed, there is no reason to believe that an addicted body has necessarily ceased to flow apart from a prior assumption that addiction is a totalized condition that determines all the actions and affective capacities of the body.

It is possible to argue that for the "becoming" body, having abandoned the nostalgic mythology of organic origins, drugs would not be encountered as radically other and inherently damaging. Rather than alien substances invading a space of innocence, the relationship would be between two bodies each made up of forces, energies, and intensities. Although each body–drug encounter could be judged as positive, negative, or neutral, depending on its specific effects, the encounter between the two bodies itself would not be assumed to be intrinsically bad. Instead of a moral distinction between substances as either good or evil, healthy or unhealthy, the question would be one of either bad or good encounters. Again utilizing Spinozan ethics, Deleuze argues that for us the good is when an encounter increases our power, such as when food is consumed, the bad is when "a body decomposes our body's relation," as when a poison breaks down our blood (1988: 22).

An encounter between a body and a drug could be either a bad poisonlike or a good foodlike encounter, depending on the specific body, the specific drug, and the specific situation. Decomposition is always a possibility when two bodies combine. The challenge is to increase the good encounters and limit the bad, just as we do in other relationships. An ethics of drug use conceived in these terms suggests that this challenge includes not only an individual responsibility but a social and political imperative to support effective forms of "harm reduction."[7] More generally, a Deleuzian ethics of bodily practice offers a means of thinking seriously about the demands of a corporeal existence that depends on attachments to other bodies, both human and nonhuman. The intense relationships that can emerge from our needs for connection can go terribly wrong. Even when joyful and enhancing, they are difficult to manage, given the weight placed in the contemporary West on ideals of bodily and psychic independence. When faced with demanding and troubling manifestations of the need for connection, an ethological approach to the body can replace moral rhetoric with a careful articulation and account of specific encounters, capacities, and activities.

Notes

1. See, for example, Leshner (1997a).

2. Here I am not referring to the fellowship of Alcoholics Anonymous, but rather the extensive literature and theories of addiction that have developed from its twelve steps. There are significant differences between the contemporary recovery movement and the work of its expert authors and therapists, and the more egalitarian and pragmatic approach of Alcoholics Anonymous (Rapping 1996; Valverde 1998; Miller and Kurtz 1994).

3. Significantly, denial, discussed earlier as the characteristic cognitive state of the addict, is the most "primitive" form of psychological defense in developmental terms. Infants who cannot yet perform complex mental operations can still employ denial to repress unpleasant realities (Wallen 1993).

4. See Concar (1994) for a discussion of dopamine, drugs, and pleasure.

5. For a brilliant discussion of the value of positioning social problems as technical questions, see Stengers (1997).

6. Ian Buchanan (1997) usefully describes the BwO as a proposed solution rather than a primary term or even a problem.

7. Harm reduction refers to drug policies and programs such as needle and syringe exchanges, which primarily aim to reduce drug-related harms rather than drug use per se.

References

Alcoholics Anonymous (1976) *The Big Book* (3rd ed.) New York: Alcoholics Anonymous World Services.

American Psychiatric Association (1994) *The Diagnostic and Statistical Manual of Mental Disorders,* 4th ed.: *DSM-IV*. Washington DC: American Psychiatric Press.

Braidotti, R. (2000) "Teratologies," in I. Buchanan and C. Colebrook (eds.), *Deleuze and Feminist Theory*. Edinburgh: Edinburgh University Press, pp. 156–173.

Buchanan, I. (1997) "The Problem of the Body in Deleuze and Guattari, Or, What Can a Body Do?" *Body and Society* 3(3): 73–91.

Canguilhem, G. (1989) *The Normal and the Pathological,* trans. C. Fawcett. New York: Zone Books.

Colebrook, C. (2000) "Is Sexual Difference a Problem?" in I. Buchanan and C. Colebrook (eds.), *Deleuze and Feminist Theory*. Edinburgh: Edinburgh University Press, pp. 110–128.

Concar, D. (1994) "Prisoners of Pleasure," *New Scientist* 1945 (Oct. 1): 26–31.

Davies, J. B. (1992) *The Myth of Addiction: An Application of the Psychological Theory of Attribution to Illicit Drug Use*. Chur, Switzerland: Harwood.

Deleuze, G. (1988) *Spinoza: Practical Philosophy,* trans. R. Hurley. San Francisco: City Lights Books.

Deleuze, G. (1992) "Ethology: Spinoza and Us," in J. Crary and S. Kwinter (eds.), *Incorporations*. New York: Zone Books, pp. 625–633.

Deleuze, G., and Guattari, F. (1987) *A Thousand Plateaus: Capitalism and Schizophrenia,* trans. B. Massumi. Minneapolis: University of Minnesota Press.

Diprose, R. (1994) *The Bodies of Women: Ethics, Embodiment and Sexual Difference*. London: Routledge.

Edwards, G., and Gross, M. (1976) "Alcohol Dependence: Provisional Description of a Clinical Syndrome," *British Medical Journal* 1: 1058–1061.

Felski, R. (2000) *Doing Time: Feminist Theory and Postmodern Culture.* New York: New York University Press.

Grosz, E. (1994) *Volatile Bodies: Towards a Corporeal Feminism.* St. Leonards, N.S.W.: Allen & Unwin.

Johns, A. (1990) "What is Dependence?" in H. Ghodse and D. Maxwell (eds.), *Substance Abuse and Dependence: An Introduction for the Caring Professions.* Basingstoke, UK: Macmillan, pp. 5–29.

Johnson, V. E. (1990) *Everything You Need to Know About Chemical Dependence.* Minneapolis: Johnson Institute.

Julien, R. (1998) *A Primer of Drug Action.* (8th ed.) New York: W. H. Freeman.

Keane, H. (2002) *What's Wrong with Addiction?* New York: New York University Press.

Landry, M. (1993) *Understanding Drugs of Abuse.* Washington D.C.: American Psychiatric Press.

Leccese, A. (1991) *Drugs and Society: Behavioral Medicines and Abusable Drugs.* Englewood Cliffs, N.J.: Prentice-Hall.

Leshner, A. (1997a) "Addiction Is a Brain Disease, and It Matters," *Science,* 278 (5335): 45–46.

Leshner, A., (1997b) "The Essence of Drug Addiction," National Institute on Drug Abuse. Available at www.drugabuse.gov/Published_Articles/Essence.html (accessed September 12, 2003).

Levine, H. G. (1978) "The Discovery of Addiction: Changing Conceptions of Habitual Drunkenness in America," *Journal of Studies on Alcohol* 39 (1): 143–174.

Miller, W. R., and Kurtz, E. (1994) "Models of Alcoholism Used in Treatment: Contrasting AA and Other Perspectives with which It Is Often Confused," *Journal of Studies on Alcohol* 55: 159–166.

National Center on Addiction and Substance Abuse at Columbia University (1999) *No Safe Haven: Children of Substance-Abusing Parents.* New York: National Center on Addiction and Substance Abuse at Columbia University.

Nowinski, J., and Baker, S. (1992) *The Twelve-Step Facilitation Handbook.* New York: Lexington Books.

Nutt, D. (1996) "Addiction: Brain Mechanisms and their Treatment Implications," *Lancet* 347: 31–36.

Rapping, E. (1996) *The Culture of Recovery: Making Sense of the Self-Help Movement in Women's Lives.* Boston: Beacon Press.

Ronell, A. (1993) "Our Narcotic Modernity," in V. A. Conley (ed.), *Rethinking Technologies.* Minneapolis: University of Minnesota Press. pp. 70–71.

Room, R. (1985) "Dependence and Society," *British Journal of Addiction* 80: 133–139.

Schuckit, M. (1995) *Drug and Alcohol Abuse: A Clinical Guide to Diagnosis and Treatment* (4th ed.) New York: Plenum.

Shildrick, M. (1997) *Leaky Bodies and Boundaries: Feminism, Postmodernism and (Bio)ethics*. London: Routledge.

Stengers, I. (1997) "Drugs: Ethical Choice or Moral Consensus" (with Olivier Ralet) in *Power and Invention: Situating Science*, trans. Paul Bains. Minneapolis: University of Minnesota Press.

Valverde, M. (1998). *Diseases of the Will: Alcohol and the Dilemmas of Freedom*. Cambridge: Cambridge University Press.

Wallen, J. (1993) *Addiction in Human Development: Developmental Perspectives on Addiction and Recovery*. New York: Haworth Press.

6

Liberatory Psychiatry and an Ethics of the In-Between

Nancy Potter

The equation of women with madness is nothing new. But can a postmodernist framework for understanding the inscription of madness on certain bodies (those already marked with difference) help to decolonize the mentally ill subject? I argue that postmodernist claims about instability within order, and madness within reason, are epistemologically and politically significant for psychiatrists and offer a feminist approach to therapy that I call an ethics of the in-between.

A feminist postmodernist ethics for psychiatry deliberately takes on the metaphysics of the medical model; it plays with ambiguities and antimonies without being goal oriented; yet it explicitly and uncomfortably dances in and out of modernity just enough to circulate memories of oppression and subjugation. While this chapter does not offer a full-fledged theory for ethics in psychiatry, it ends on a note of cautious optimism for a postmodernist-informed messiness that can coexist with modernity's order and subjugation.

There are many forms of postmodernism; this chapter maps a particular trajectory of a collision with modernity. The first section outlines a view of madness taken from Derrida and Lacan, after which I turn to feminist concerns.

Logos and Madness

According to the American Psychiatric Association's *Diagnostic and Statistical Manual of Mental Disorders*, a mental disorder is a psychological syndrome that "occurs in" an individual, is exhibited in behavior, and is accompanied by distress or functional impairment or increased risk of suffering. Deviant behavior and conflicts between an individual and society do not, in themselves, constitute mental disorders—"unless the deviance or conflict is a symptom of a dysfunction in the individual" (American Psychiatric Association 2000: xxxi). As criticisms mount up that "mental health" is an industry that constructs madness in the interests of order and normativity and that in particular it pathologizes those who fail to conform to dominant norms, psychiatry faces fundamental challenges to its theory and practice. Furthermore, as critiques of foundationalism have taken hold in the late twentieth century, the notion of justification has become increasingly suspect. This is especially the case with psychiatry, which deals in the diagnosis and treatment of mental disorders. Psychiatry is particularly vulnerable to charges of ontological confusion because it has not been possible to point definitively to natural kinds of diseases or concrete causes of symptoms.

The challenge to psychiatry, however, is much deeper than an assault on its justificatory status. "What Michel Foucault teaches us to think is that there are crises of reason in strange complicity with what the world calls crises of madness" (Derrida 1978: 63). Thus ends Derrida's famous critique of Foucault's analysis of Descartes' *cogito* in *Madness and Civilization*. But what can Derrida mean by this complicity of reason with madness?

Derrida argues that any syntactical usage makes a possible meaning and hence carries normality (that is, *sense*) with it. "In its most impoverished syntax, *logos* is reason . . . madness is indeed, essentially and generally, silence, stifled speech . . . silence plays the irreducible role of that which bears and haunts language, outside and *against* which alone language can emerge" (Derrida 1978: 54; italics in original). Language and meaning, then, are acts of force that reassure against madness—not by banishing it, but rather because the reassurance of reason is valid *even if* it contains madness (Derrida 1978: 61). The crisis that the postmodern period marks is, in a sense then, always already haunting us—threat and deferment.

Postmodernist thinkers argue that *logos* dominates but that its subjugating role is paradoxical. Because making meaning requires that we treat signs as stable yet cannot stabilize them, we experience an irresolvable shift or alternation between perspectives—an alternation that Derrida calls *différance.*[1] There is no fixed meaning that underlies the flow of differences, yet there is a desire for a center or some fastening point. The psychiatric diagnosis is an effort to stabilize, where reason and order are imposed by the boundaries that mark them off from chaos and madness. *Différance* is the space in between the madness and reason—or the spilling over from one to another. Leakiness leads the modern psychiatrist to impose reasoned order more firmly; hence the use of electroshock therapy, physical restraints, and drug treatments.

Lacan, too, theorizes a longing for stability that cannot be realized. As Lacan argues, we are born into language, so we must use the terms available to us to construct a subject. The signifier of subjectivity (the "I") is inherently unstable because its meaning is purely a function of the moment of utterance, but that doesn't shake our conviction that somewhere there is a point of certainty, of knowledge, and of truth. For Lacan, the Other then becomes the site of fantasied knowledge and certainty (Rose 1982).

Lacan terms language "the symbolic order," which, in this theory, is phallic.[2] For Lacan and Derrida, discourse is that system where the central signified is continually deferred, "never absolutely present outside a system of differences" (Derrida 1978: 280). Subject positions are constituted by and through difference and hence subjectivity is the site of struggles—for example, through normalizing discourse that decenters some subjects and through resistances to subjugation. Since marking off differences is never totalizing and signification never fully present, subjectivity is never a stable entity but rather a fluidity where resistances, contestations, and struggles for power are exerted.

Discourse, in order to function, must escape madness, and this is a necessity (Derrida 1978: 53). The madman teeters precariously at the edges of sense, of reason, of subjectivity: *logos* is not present, the words escape him, and he glances into the depths of madness. Yet we may see him pull himself back after flirting with madness; it's the language of reason that tells us that words are unstable and arbitrary. According to Derrida, the language of reason is simultaneously the language of the universal rationality of which psychiatry wishes to be the expression, and the language of the body politic—the right to citizenship. However, where Foucault claims that the psychiatrist is the delegate of societal and governmental reason, Derrida argues that psychiatry has opened itself up and that madness as unreason has dislocated itself. A Derridean analysis suggests that psychiatry can be a source of liberation and not only a source of subjugation. Liberation from what, one might ask—from modernity's fictive metaphysics? or from real oppression, to which women of all classes and colors are particularly susceptible?

If we take seriously the claims of Derrida, nosology, diagnosis, and treatment look different. For example, once the metaphysics of time as linear is called into question, the clinical practice of " taking a history" is revealed as a way to impose order while disguising authorship. Furthermore, as Sally Swartz argues, practitioners who operate from a modernist perspective are committed to a metaphysics that necessarily creates those who deviate from that metaphysics as mad: "[T]he elisions, erasures and contradictions which constitute our experience of our past become narrative coherence and explanation of illness, foreclosing and interrupting lived actuality" (1996: 7). The purpose of the intake is not mere "fact gathering"; its purpose, Swartz points out, is to position patients as in need of intervention and the clinician as able to help. These issues are particularly salient for members of disenfranchised groups who are vulnerable to being marked and medicated or incarcerated by psychiatry. It is these concerns, then, that the remainder of this chapter addresses. What, in postmodernist views of madness, is feminist?

Madness and Subjugated Others

This section articulates ways in which postmodernist theory might illuminate a feminist vision of madness. Drawing initially on the work of Irigaray and Kristeva, I focus on two thematic issues: femininity as inscribed within the symbolic order, and notions of subjectivity and unity as they are spelled out in psychiatry. I then remark on the need for a feminist postmodernist psychiatry that considers intersections of raced, classed, sexualized, and gendered subjectivity rather than the more prevalent privileging of gendered subjectivity alone, before discussing current diagnostic and therapeutic practices for one of the personality disorders most commonly associated with women: borderline personality disorder (BPD).

Feminist Uses of Lacanian Theory

Many feminist postmodernists focus on ways that discursive practices inscribe the subject as male. Luce Irigaray (1985), following what she takes to be Lacan's position, argues that discourse, in its circulation of power through the (phallic) erection of the symbolic order, is utterly male. Within the symbolic order, woman is wholly Other. The implications of this claim cannot be overemphasized. According to Irigaray, woman's otherness cannot even be spoken, described, or characterized outside the symbolic order.

In Irigaray's view, "the feminine" is the sign of unrepresentability except in reference to the symbolic (phallic) order. Females do not speak the "I" from the same place as do males, so their demand for co-subjectivity is contested (Whitford 1991). As Whitford explains, Irigaray is pointing to a monosexual structuration of subjectivity that is overarching.

> In this structure, to be a subject is to take up the male position in the Oedipus complex, to identify with the Father (the Law), and thus, for women, to find themselves in conflict, potentially at odds with their mother, other women, and their self, for lack of an identificatory support in the symbolic order that would confirm them as female subjects. (Whitford 1991: 38)

Irigaray's approach as analyst is to listen for the unconscious and to effect interventions in the interpretations. Her ultimate vision is the emergence or development of a feminine syntax. Julia Kristeva, too, claims that women need to write the feminine, but Irigaray and Kristeva differ in their understanding of Lacan's view of sexual signification for men and hence differ in the degree to which they view women as having a specific (and specifically difficult) task. There are similarities between the two, however. Kristeva, like Irigaray, views the semiotic as the psychic grounding that makes signification possible. Moreover, Kristeva also sees psychoanalysis as a place from which to make disruption of the symbolic order possible (Zulick 1991). Through psychotherapy, the semiotic can be drawn out so that the subject has a voice.

Kristeva, although criticized for presenting the semiotic voice as too privatized and internalized, seems to leave the door open to theorizing the development of subjugated subjectivity other than gender. But both Irigaray and Kristeva, to varying degrees, treat gender as the primary axis of domination and subordination.

Erasure of Racial Subject Formation

Irigaray and Kristeva are not alone in this mistake. A disturbing feature of many feminist critiques of madness is that they privilege gendered subjectivity and neglect the role of racialized constructions of subjectivity in the formation of madness. Although racism and ethnocentrism are increasingly attended to in psychiatric literature, that is not the same as considering how the symbolic order constructs subjectivity that is raced. As Jean Walton puts it,

> [A] racial subtext informs this [psychoanalytic] developmental model, in which maturity also implies the full (or again, classically flawed) assumption of a heterosexualized, *raced* adulthood; according to this model, one must be fully "white" (or perhaps fully one's "race," however that might locally be constructed) in order to fully become a subject, or more to the point, one's subjectivity will inevitably be marked by the way in which one fails to be fully white. (Walton 2001: 5; emphasis in original)

Franz Fanon, of course, set out a resoundingly clear explanation of the process of becoming a racialized subject in *Black Skin, White Mask* (1967). And Ann Pellegrini carefully attends to this topic in her *Performance Anxieties: Staging Psychoanalysis, Staging Race* (1997), but theorizing about racial subject formation is certainly a weak link in postmodernist discourses on mental health and illness.

When not overlooked or suppressed, racialized subjectivity is pathologized. Sander Gilman gives an historical account illustrating that stereotypes of madness are often simultaneously racialized (1985). Yet discourses in mental illness persist either in uncritically accepting the trope of madness-as-black or the black-as-mad, or in subsuming the function of "race" as a sign. As an example of subsuming race, consider Walton's (1997) analysis of Joan Riviere's "Womanliness as a Masquerade." Walton suggests that some white women in therapy introduce a third term into the gender binary—a racialized Other—as a way to distance themselves from the unattractive "choices" of exhibiting either femininity or masculinity (1997: 234). Yet, Walton argues, racial difference in the fantasy of a white patient is transmogrified into a familiar story of gender struggles and, furthermore, feminists continue to elide the theme of race: "Riviere's indifference to the racialized components of her patient's fantasies is reproduced with a striking monotony by her feminist successors. It would seem, thus, that a peculiar readiness of Riviere's essay as a 'usable' text lies to a great extent in the permission it gives to invoke, only to ignore, the cultural constructions of race that inform it" (Walton 1997: 243).

The neglect of racial content in the fantasies of white female patients' is only a part of the overall problem in psychiatric literature of giving short shrift to the discursive positioning of racial subjectivity. A larger problem is the prevailing assumption that the central struggle for subjectivity is one that concerns white folks (both as practitioners and as patients). This assumption is mirrored by some black feminists who view psychological problems as secondary to material struggles for living. Elizabeth Abel points out that "the de-essentialization of race among black feminists (in contrast to both white feminists and male Afro-Americanists) has occurred primarily through the intervention of material rather than textual differences and under the aegis of Marxism and cultural studies rather than deconstruction" (Abel 1997: 114). Some writers reject the metaphorical spin that postmodernist thinkers give to race, arguing that race (and gender) are literally embodied and cannot be cast as figurative [see Homans (1997) for a discussion of tensions between "race" literalists and metaphorists]. For patients with ontological and political commitments to the body and materiality, postmodernist practitioners may come off as ignorant, arrogant, and privileged.

Hortense Spillers (1997) suggests that the doubleness needs to be worked with—by making a pivotal point of inquiry at the stresses and fractures that create a crisis or a gap. She adds that we must be on guard against the seductive [white] homogeneity and naturalness that prevailing theories of mental disorder hold. As Judith Butler argues, the psychoanalytic framework of Lacan and his feminist followers tends toward a totalizing account of subject formation that fails to explain difference in its complexity.[3] A richer understanding of the symbolic order is needed—one that offers a more nuanced account of how subjectivity is raced, classed, sexualized, and gendered and that will make sense of shifts and changes as subject positions are rearticulated (Rubin and Butler 1994).

Because my version of feminism is one where liberation from *all* dominating structures is desirable and good (to the extent that is possible),

I opt for a feminist account of the subjugation of madness that doesn't position gender as the primary form of subjectivity. I think a Derridean-informed postmodernism is more fruitful than a Lacanian one. It holds more promise for understanding discourse as structuring norms of subjectivity that can be taken up by feminists concerned about the multiple intersections of subject formation and with subsequent readings of those outside the norms as mad.

If, taking these views together, madness is the underside of *logos*, and *logos* is dominating, then it looks like those bodies marked as different are particularly vulnerable to playing out this double bind in the fields of the mad. What happens to those who refuse the subjectivity that the symbolic order offers them? A fascinating psychopathology to examine, from a postmodernist perspective, is the borderline personality disorder.

Borderline Personality Disorder

BPD is one of several mental illnesses that come under the heading of personality disorders.[4] The commitment to the equation of a unified self that has a coherent sense of past and future with a healthy, white or fully raced, heterosexualized personality leads to the assessment of those who fail to exhibit or experience such a self as unhealthy. This modern view of personality permeates the mental health fields as well as popular culture.

The borderline personality is characterized by identity disturbance, feelings of chronic emptiness, impulsive or self-destructive behavior, and unstable intense interpersonal relationships. Loss of ego boundaries, an identity based on multiple contradictory unintegrated self-images that are experienced as an inner void, and aggression that "breaks through" defenses are key characteristics, according to Goldstein (1995). Distrust, all-or-nothing thinking, extreme sensitivity to unfair treatment, and an appearance of normality that quickly unravels under stress are additional features he discusses.

This diagnosis is ripe for feminist postmodernist analysis. Women are far more likely to be diagnosed with BPD than are men (Jimenez 1997); in fact, the DSM-IV-TR (American Psychiatric Association 2000) reports that 75 percent of those diagnosed with BPD are women. Mary Ann Jimenez, who has analyzed psychiatric literature for its evolving thoughts on women, finds that new diagnostic categories nevertheless continue to reflect a psychiatric orthodoxy in which dominant values subjugate women to gender-role conformity (Jimenez 1997). Furthermore, psychiatrists claim to identify BPD in many parts of the world, presumably demonstrating its cross-cultural nature. The vast majority of research into biases in the case of BPD, however, has taken gender to be the salient concept for analysis and bias of concern, thus highlighting Walton's point.

Historically, the term "borderline" marked a boundary between psychotic and neurotic personality types, but it has increasingly come into usage as a noun, carrying a pejorative meaning. This can be seen in language used to describe the treatment of such patients. They are considered difficult to treat because of "the intensity of their engagement with caregivers, the sometimes overwhelming nature of their demands for care, and the strong emotions and conflicts that they provoke in others" (Herman et al. 1989: 1). Put less delicately, one researcher claims to distinguish BPD patients from depressed or schizophrenic ones by "their angry, demanding, and entitled presentation," (Solof 1981; quoted in Mitton and Huxley 1988: 341) and another warns that "any interviewer, whether with a clinical or research purpose, will be exposed to devaluation, manipulation, angry outbursts, clinging or appeal" (Mitton and Huxley 1988: 341). Most bluntly, "borderliners are the patients you think of as PIAs—pains in the ass," as a past chairman of the psychiatry department at New York University put it (*Medical World News* 1983: 51).

The picture of the borderline patient as a demanding, aggressive, and angry woman is a recurring theme over the past 20 years (Jimenez 1997). Perry and Klerman, for example, pathologize the behavior of their borderline patients for what seems like a failure to comply with the social role assigned to women patients:

> Their behavior was judged as unadaptive to the interview. They did things to hinder the interview, such as asking questions irrelevant to its purpose, getting up and changing chairs, or refusing to answer questions. They behaved in predominantly angry ways, expressing anger toward a variety of targets, including the interviewer. They were argumentative, irritable, and sarcastic. Without tact or consideration, they were demanding and attempted to manipulate the interviewer to acquiesce to their wishes. (Perry and Klerman 1980: 168)

Angry, assertive women, and women who resist expectations that they be especially attentive to social nuance, are defying norms for femininity and are vulnerable to being considered mentally ill; such behavior, coupled with their own expressions of emptiness, aloneness, or lack of identity are taken as confirming evidence of BPD.[5]

Modernist Therapy for the BPD Patient? Lacanian Therapy?

Glen Gabbard (2001) suggests that practitioners aim for a flexible and spontaneous attitude rather than allow warnings from literature on borderlines to lead to excessive rigidity. On the other hand, he says that "the inherent instability of the borderline patient demands that structure must be imposed from external sources" (2001: 5). He warns against a tendency of practitioners to resist being turned into the object of the patient's rage and hatred, as such resistance tends to provoke efforts by the patient to transform the therapist into the bad object. The goal is for the patient ultimately to own her own projected hostility, but the practitioner should not rush this task. As "the experience of being incomplete or fragmented is at the core of borderline psychopathology," the goal of therapy is to help the patient achieve integration of her good and bad object-selves (2001: 10).

A psychotherapy that is organized around semiotics and voice, where the aim is to disrupt the force of the symbolic order, would seem to be quite different from typical therapy. Can a postmodernist approach such as that suggested by Irigaray or Kristeva play a role in healing the subjugated?

Although I do not argue for my view, I will say that I am wary of substituting a Lacanian psychotherapy for the prevailing approaches. In brief, I take seriously the criticisms of those who worry that the dualisms inherent in such theories aren't as postmodernist, transgressive, or liberatory as they might appear (Butler 1989; Moi 1992). Derridean thinking tells me that the force of any taxonomical or discursive system cannot be overcome by embracing its opposite. This is the case for feminism, whether the issue is abstract metaphysics or the everyday politics of oppression. Consideration about voice, authorship, and symbolic discourses lead me to the next section, where I explore what *is* possible (and what would be necessary) in order for any therapy to be liberatory.

Psychiatry and Playfulness

The topic of ethics is positioned more comfortably in modern than in postmodernist discourse,[6] but because postmodernity is not a location or historical time that is fully present—because a metaphysics and epistemology of modernity still presses us at every turn—I think a less tidy discussion is in order than an alternative full-blown postmodernist ethics. I offer a sketch of ethics that locates us as actors shifting in-between modernity and postmodernity.

What would it be like for psychiatrists and patients to glimpse the spaces in-between? As Derrida suggests, the thought that there is no center, no origin, no transcendental signified extends the domain and the play of signification infinitely, but how can psychiatrists be playful?

Because discursive practices are simultaneously confining and leaky, allowing the possibility of play at the frontiers, resistances emerge that are beyond the capacity of therapeutic (or political) practices to contain. These sites of struggle suggest a kind of spontaneism[7] which, together with necessity, gives us the range and possibility of play. Spontaneism (and thus play), although never completely banished, is more strictly under wraps in the mental health industry. Much of therapy still exhibits the urge toward unity; theories press toward closure and resolution of contradictions by banishing the troublesome contrary.

Given that in postmodernist thought, subject positions are constituted by and through difference, the discursive formation of subjectivity is inevitably the site of struggles. Subjects, in order to *be* subjects, must assert their existence through *logos,* which simultaneously subjugates through discourse that is normalizing. However, the relation of the subject to the other is neither necessary nor purely relational because the discursive formation of subjectivity is never total and there is always an overflow or an excess (Mouffe and Laclau 1985).

The in-between practitioner works with this excess. She or he works at the edges and in the margins. She or he doesn't try to capture the overflow and contain it, but rather to play with it. Play involves pushing on the boundaries, identifying the madman within, being a fugitive. Play is open-ended; the meanings are not given; the signs are surprising, they catch us off balance and delight us and confuse us in their unexpectedness. This concept of play is related to a kind of dialogical openness that would be helpful for feminist psychiatrists to cultivate with their patients. It is not the openness of looking for signs of the unconscious or for gaps in a patient's story (although there may be that too), but the openness of playing at the margins of meaning and pushing at the borders of thought. Articulating exactly what that looks like, of course, cannot be done without *logos* and so would undermine its own liberatory potential, but let me indicate a possible application.

Within the therapeutic context, a postmodernist ethic calls for the readmission of the Other into the "hard core of the moral self," as Bauman puts it (1993: 84). This state of intersubjectivity is not a Winnicott-derived ebb and flow of subjects, nor a Levinasian ethical encounter with the absolute other, nor a straightforward transference–countertransference relationship between practitioner and patient. Rather, a space is made for madness within that is not ultimately resolved. Rejecting closure of transference as an ultimate goal of therapy, transference is given instead a positive spin (with all the discomfort that that entails.)

An example from the BPD literature illustrates the issues. A female practitioner takes in the projections of a patient who sees herself as "bad and dirty" but finds them extremely uncomfortable to endure. Even though the practitioner understands that the patient's self-image comes from terms the patient's father used about her when he sexually abused her and are not "real" reflections on the practitioner's own diligence and effectiveness, criticisms about her incompetence run her down. Eventually she wonders whether she ought to refer the patient to someone else (Alarcon and Leetz 1998).

While this example, looked at from a modernist perspective, is clearly a case of transference and countertransference, it also indicates the kind of in-betweenness of subjects, where a difference between a modern model of therapy and a postmodernist one is the willingness to remain in the uncomfortable in-between state without pathologizing it. A practitioner who is moving in the in-between would not identify her feelings as projections from the patient but as a grasping of the constitutive outside that conventionally is not resolved without an act of domination and illusory closure.

A further contribution of postmodernism to psychotherapy is found in the reformulation of resistance. With a postmodernist approach, resistance is not pathologized but understood as an integral part of negotiations of power. As Foucault argues, power is not totalizing. There are always resistances, and part of the formation of subjects involves resistance to subjugation and the dominating force of structural power relations.

Allan Young (1993) gives a fascinating account of the difficulties the resistant person encounters in the context of post-traumatic stress disorder (PTSD). Most patients who undergo treatment for combat-related PTSD eventually offer narratives and interpretations of their behavior that are acceptable to the practitioners (1993: 113). Why is that? Young argues that the goal of treatment is not psychiatric transformation, but the production of knowledge in the form of a compliant subject. This subjugated product is molded through talk therapy where he tries out various narratives and disclosures, getting praised for the ones that fit the explanatory model for PTSD—namely, that the patient's pathology originates in an external trauma from which he makes choices. Resistance, for a patient diagnosed with PTSD, typically is cast as a refusal to recall the traumatic memories.

Resistance, however, as Young argues, has two meaning. One refers to a sequence where someone refuses to collaborate, the meaning of his or her behavior is appropriated, and the reinterpreted action is incorporated into knowledge production. The second meaning refers to behavior that impedes that process and that cannot be assimilated (Young 1993). When the practitioner assigns to the realm of repressed memory the patient's refusal to recollect trauma, we see an example of the first kind of resistance. "The patient's claim is meant to take him out of the production process; the therapist's claim inserts him back into it" (Young 1993: 115) A feminist postmodernist psychiatrist must be on the lookout for a liability toward deploying resistance in this way; it is not liberatory but coopting.

The second kind of resistance, in contrast, is potentially liberatory but much harder to work with. As we have seen, the person marked as borderline is characterized as fundamentally manipulative, furious, needy, and resistant. We might begin to imagine a postmodernist-informed approach to BPD that links a postmodernist sense of resistance with the patient's attempts to assert a subjectivity that is not erased by the symbolic order. Because the subject is only given meaning *qua* subject in relation to other elements in structural orders, and that meaning is in relation to what is marked off as different, she or he is both subjugated and resistant to that subjugation. The practitioner could work with this interpretation. The borderline person might be taken to be explicitly performing a postmodernist subjectivity that is on the border between subjectivity and subjugation, but that attempt at articulating the contradictions in subject formation is viewed as celebratory rather than as symptomatic of psychopathology.

Some of those attempts to resist subjugation can be frightening and difficult to understand, especially if the practitioner adopts a modernist view of mental disorders. For example, a person diagnosed with BPD may cut her body, drawing blood and sometimes leaving scars. Psychiatry characterizes such behavior as self-mutilation and decries it for its dysfunction. Postmodernist interrogations of the meaning given to the body—not to mention functional health, mature adulthood, and responsible living—reposition such actions (although their alternative meanings should not be a priori assumed by any practitioner.)

This is not to say that a discourse on metaphysics has no place in psychiatry. As it stands, language constitutes subjects who are sometimes taken to be disordered. Nosological categories, like other conceptual categories, are necessary to thought and to work, if only to understand the force of this kind of subjugation and its effects. However, a psychiatry that breaks with modernity retains the necessity of categorizing while being playful. It does not take those categories to be natural kinds. It recognizes the contingency of its objects and remains open to contestation of power/knowledge infrastructures. The psychiatrist–patient relation itself is contestable. Thus questions must be asked: "From what institutional sites does the doctor and the discourse derive its legitimation?" and "What subject-positions does psychiatry as it is currently being practiced make it possible for the individual to occupy?" (Foucault 1972: 50–55).

Still, concerns about power relations and criticisms about the social function of the construction of madness, although revolutionary, are not particularly new. Much theorizing has been done by practitioners who grasp the postmodernist turn in therapy as it pertains to narrative. Although narrative therapy typically draws upon postmodernist ideas such as deconstruction and narrative coauthorship, most remains committed to a suspect metaphysics of reality (now multiple realities), body, and linear time; and most is unlikely to be liberatory in that it maintains a picture of problems in living, mental health, agency, and experts. Postmodernist critiques of truth and reality are nodded to, yet the argument that *logos* not only dominates but subjugates—and in patterned ways—is almost completely overlooked. While narrative therapy is an advance from more mainstream medical responses to mental disorders, it is distinct from the feminist stance I suggest. My argument is that a stance that teeters around and within the in-betweenness and ambivalences that come with a radically uncertain and shifting metaphysics and epistemology stands a better chance of being liberatory.

An Ethics of the In-Between

It is not that I think modernist concepts and values have no place in feminist postmodernist psychiatry. Deliberate playing in the spaces would be useful, but it is not only a matter of being in-between the subject and the Other; the practitioner drawing on such an ethic occupies a discursive position that is more radical than most narrative therapies.

Teetering between modernity and postmodernity, the practitioner moves between ambiguity and the certainties that discourse continually erects and threatens. Yet uncertainty and ambiguity are uncomfortable, and we necessarily evoke a metaphysics of reality and truth as language-users. It must be openly acknowledged that cultural norms of unity function as gatekeepers of elite clubs to which many find themselves desperate to belong and miserable to be excluded from. It is crucial not to present a nonjudgmental or open therapeutic stance as if epistemological neutrality is a simple and possible thing. Categories, distinctions, and boundaries are unavoidable, but practitioners can deploy them openly, admitting their nongivenness and taking responsibility for the positioning of those concepts and categories. In all this, the goal is less comfort and acceptance of postmodernity than it is a deliberate stance of being and thinking in contradictions and ambiguities.

I would retain some concepts from modernist ethics: responsibility, trustworthiness, solidarity, and attention, but these concepts, like concepts of reality, truth, and unity, would be informed by postmodernist thinking. To what, or whom, might a feminist postmodernist psychiatrist bear responsibility? I would answer: to the patient as subjugated resistor whose resistances are always already threatened with being inscribed within the symbolic order; to the patient's loved ones insofar as they aren't only contributing to the patient's subjugation; perhaps to other feminists, and perhaps to a more general discursive community from which she cannot afford to be entirely cut off.[8] Finally, following Bauman, I suggest that she has a responsibility to "permanent attention, come what may" (Bauman 1993: 88). This kind of attention marks a departure from modernist ethics that tends to conceive duties as contractual and time-bound. A postmodernist kind of attention is never exhausted, never discharged.

Consider, for example, the claims about responsibility and attentiveness with regard to the discussion of racialized subjectivity. What a practitioner attends to is crucial to being an ethically oriented feminist therapist but is also (partially) shaped by the dominant discourse. Interpretations of behavior, diagnoses, and responses tend to reiterate the medical model of mental disorder. Because, as Abel argues, people tend to interpret racialized experiences along racial lines, practitioners have a responsibility to disrupt the master discourse of race. This task requires self-reflection but, more important, it requires that practitioners position themselves so that their assumptions and biases are challenged. This in turn requires that the practitioner (through listening, talking, reading, and reflecting) be actively involved with others whose positionalities differ from his or her own.

Fostering and sustaining trust is recognized as vital to the therapeutic relationship, and sustaining trust requires one to straddle an awkward midlevel position between being trustworthy to one's patient and being trustworthy to one's clinic, one's colleagues, and the psychiatric industry (Potter 1999). Still, this in-betweenness of positionalities of power calls for maintaining trustworthiness toward one's patient and openly acknowledging the compromised position one occupies.[9] In this way, the practitioner's alliance is tipped toward the subaltern, while not pretending that the symbolic is inescapable, or easily eroded with resistance.

Among the myriad ways that trust between practitioner and patient is inflected, trust in the practitioner's understanding of racialized subjugation (and its intersection with other Others) is crucial. Patients whose world-view is materialist or Marxist are likely to distrust a practitioner who presents her or himself as liberation-oriented yet calls into question the reality of embodied and material subjugation. It is unwise to push at the margins of modernity/postmodernity if it gives a patient the impression that the practitioner isn't taking seriously the material effects of discursive structures. In developing a trusting relation, the practitioner must give signs and assurances of his or her trustworthiness, which may involve indicating one's political commitments.

Another tension in trusting relations comes from the use of discourse on mental disorders to interpret behavior. When is it splitting a pathology, and when is it an accurate, if simplistic, representation of a racist world? Indications of distress such as rage at the powerful bad Other, a sense of a fragmented self, and expressions of internalized oppression in the form of self-destructive behavior (all of which behavior might be taken as symptoms of BPD) should be neither pathologized, patronized, nor privatized. As Spillers says,

> To speak is to occupy a place in social economy, and in the case of the racialized subject, history has dictated that this linguistic right to use is never easily granted . . . what must be emphasized here is the symbolic value of the subject's exchanges with others, and it is within the intersubjective nexus that the inequalities of linguistic use and value are made manifest—what one can do with signs in the presence and perspective of others—and it is only within those circuits that a solution can be worked out. (Spillers 1997: 145)

Let me interject into theory another example from the literature on BPD, one that points to the messiness of working in-between the fractures and doubleness of modernity/postmodernity, and self/Other.

> Ms. B, a 29-year-old chronically suicidal borderline patient who started psychotherapy with me, revealed a core feeling of hopelessness about the treatment. She was a survivor of incest, and while sitting in therapy, she had the posttraumatic sensation of her father's hands being all over her. She told me that when she cut her wrist, it was her father's blood that she saw. When she looked at her skin, she said she saw her father's skin. She said that she was rotten inside because of what he'd done to her. She carried him with her. (Gabbard 2001: 7)

As the practitioner has described it, this example illustrates the seriousness of the distress of someone marked as borderline. If I assume the reports of the doctor to be objective, I come face-to-face with the complexity (if not the inappropriateness) of recommending play as a mode of interaction between practitioner and patient. While there are some good reasons not to make that assumption, I am still somewhat hesitant to endorse play within psychiatric practice. There is legitimate concern that the ability to play with meanings, categories, and sense-making requires that one's social, economic, and material positionality be relatively secure.[10] Performing gender in a playful way, for example, is something that the powerful can more safely engage in than the subjugated. Playing with the boundaries of reality is safer for a practitioner who is certifiably mentally healthy than for the person marked borderline, who is likely to be diagnosed as having a psychotic break. Playfulness needs to be tempered with a consideration for the very real consequences that it might bring to the patient whose conceptual and material framework one is playing with. As I noted earlier, the patient diagnosed with BPD is reported to respond well to reality-orienting comments; where a postmodernist stance seems to call for eschewing such an approach, to do so might leave the patient vulnerable to enacting an epistemological uncertainty that further pathologizes her.

Finally, I suggest that any feminist ethics of psychiatry, whether postmodernist or any other kind, needs to be informed by practice. I do not see an ethics of therapy that is theory-driven to be as reliable as one that is responsive to the situated yet fluid interactions between this practitioner and that patient. This is not an ethics of individualism but rather a recognition that the discursively formed and patterned subjectivity that each brings to the therapeutic setting must also be particularized.

Conclusion

Postmodernist ideas and theories may not be useful tools for all diagnoses and clinical interactions. Furthermore, as the *logos maker*, the doctor subjugates the patient even as she or he liberates him or her. For those who are uncomfortable in the role of subjugator, the idea that power is circulating, not totalizing, and the claim that resistances proliferate despite containments and disciplines, may ease the mind. Nonetheless, we cannot escape the logic of discourse, the power of *logos* to constitute subjectivity in ways we might protest; but then, we *can* protest (and that is something.)

Notes

1. *Différance* is (1) the difference between any graphic or phonic entities separated by spaces and (2) the deferral of any transcendental signified associated with signs. Deferment is the continual postponement of origins.

2. For Lacan, the "symbolic order" contrasts with "the imaginary" (trajectories of the ego and its identifications) and "the real," which is the moment of impossibility where the two are grafted (Rose and Mitchell 1982).

3. Spillers (1997) comments that Lacanian theory can inflect race through its three dimensions of subjectivity (see note 2), but the dimension of the "Real" highlights the perversity of assuming race to be given, pure, and simple (1997: 150).

4. Personality disorders are "deeply ingrained maladaptive patterns that have been present since adolescence and which have given rise to personal distress or social impairment" (Rutter 1987: 451). Maladaptive behavior is determined by the degree of deviance from the expectations of the individual's culture (American Psychiatric Association 2000: 685)

5. This phenomenon should vary from one racial group to another: black and Latina women, for example, are often assumed to be exhibiting a "natural" intensity of emotions. This does not mean they are not pathologized, but it means that their "madness" is seen as an essential—and essentially flawed—condition.

6. While there are exceptions to this characterization, especially in feminist work, ethical theory typically rests on modernist concepts such as agency, guiding principles of action, duty and often rights, with a modernist metaphysics to prop it up.

7. This is Rosa Luxemburg's term for the emergence of resistances and movements that are beyond the capacity of regulation and organization of political leadership (Mouffe and Laclau 1985).

8. A rearticulation writing of subjugated voices involves taking on a responsibility to disrupt the symbolic order, not just to create "alternative storying", but to carve out what is not yet: the subaltern. However the feminist practitioner cannot (both in the modern and the postmodern sense of logical possibility) abandon *logos* altogether.

9. Indicating ways one cannot be trusted is not likely to help with so-called paranoid patients, though. Again, suggestions to be this-or-that sort of practitioner cannot be taken as decisive and must be informed by both modernist and postmodernist lenses.

10. I am grateful to Jay Kraus for pressing this point with me.

References

Abel, Elizabeth (1997) "Black Writing, White Reading: Race and the Politics of Feminist Interpretation," in *Female Subjects in Black and White: Race, Psychoanalysis, Feminism,* E. Abel, B. Christian, and H. Moglen (eds.) Berkeley: University of California Press, pp. 102–131.

Alarcon, Renato, and Leetz, Kenneth (1998) "Cultural Intersections in the Psychotherapy of Borderline Personality Disorder," *American Journal of Psychotherapy* 52, no. 2: 176–190.

American Psychiatric Association (2000) *Diagnostic and Statistical Manual of Mental Disorders* (4th ed., revised), Washington, D.C.: American Psychiatric Association.

Atwood, George, and Stolorow, Robert (1984) *Structures of Subjectivity: Explorations in Psychoanalytic Phenomenology.* Hillsdale, N.J.: Analytic Press.

Bauman, Zygmunt (1993) *Postmodern Ethics.* Oxford: Blackwell.

Butler, Judith (1989) "The Body Politics of Julia Kristeva," *Hypatia* 3, no. 3: 104–118.

Derrida, Jacques (1978) *Writing and Difference,* trans. Alan Bass. Chicago: University of Chicago Press.

Fanon, Franz (1967) *Black Skin, White Mask,* trans. Charles Lam Markmann. New York: Grove Weidenfeld.

Foucault, Michel (1972) *The Archeology of Knowledge and the Discourse on Language,* trans. A. M. Sheridan Smith. New York: Pantheon Books.

Gabbard, Glen (2001) "Psychodynamic Psychotherapy of Borderline Personality Disorder: A Contemporary Approach," *Bulletin of the Menninger Clinic* 65:1: 41–57.

Gilman, Sander (1985) *Difference and Pathology: Stereotypes of Sexuality, Race, and Madness.* Ithaca, N.Y.: Cornell University Press.

Goldstein, William (1995) "The Borderline Patient: Update on the Diagnosis, Theory, and Treatment From a Psychodynamic Perspective," *American Journal of Psychotherapy* 49, no. 3: 317–337.

Herman, Judith, Perry, J. Christopher and van der Kolk, Bessel (1989) "Childhood Trauma in Borderline Personality Disorder," *American Journal of Psychiatry* 146, no. 4:1: 490–495.

Homans, Margaret (1997) "'Racial Composition': Metaphor and the Body in the Writing of Race," in *Female Subjects in Black and White: Race, Psychoanalysis, Feminism,* E. Abel, B. Christian, and H. Moglen (eds.) Berkeley: University of California Press, pp. 77–101.

Irigaray, Luce (1985) *Speculum of the Other Woman,* trans. Gillian Gill. Ithaca, N.Y.: Cornell University Press.

Jimenez, Mary Ann (1997) "Gender and Psychiatry: Psychiatric Conceptions of Mental Disorders in Women, 1960–1994," *Affilia: Journal of Women and Social Work* 12, no. 2: 154–176.

Medical World News, New York, April 25, 1983, 51.

Mitton, Jan, and Huxley, Gail (1988) "Responses and Behavior of Patients with Borderline Personality Disorder During Semi-Structured Interviews," *Canadian Journal of Psychiatry* 33: 341–343.

Moi, Toril (1992) "Femininity Revisited," *Journal of Gender Studies* 1:3 324–334.

Mouffe, Chantal, and Laclau, Ernesto (1985) *Hegemony and Socialist Strategy: Towards a Radical Democratic Politics*. London: Verso.

Pellegrini, Ann (1997) *Performance Anxieties: Staging Psychoanalysis, Staging Race*. New York: Routledge.

Perry, J. C. and Klerman, G. L. (1980) "Clinical Features of the Borderline Personality Disorder," *American Journal of Psychiatry,* 137(2): 165–173.

Potter, Nancy (1999) "Terrorists, Hostages, Victims, and 'The Crisis Team': A 'Who's Who' Puzzle," *Hypatia* 14, no. 3: 126–156.

Rose, Jacqueline (1982) 'Introduction II' in *Feminine Sexuality: Jacques Lacan and the ecole freudienne,* eds. J. Mitchell and J. Rose, trans. J. Rose. New York: W. W. Norton, pp. 27–57.

Rubin, Gayle, and Butler, Judith (1994) "Sexual Traffic" (interview), *differences: A Journal of Feminist Cultural Studies* 6: nos. 2–3: 62–99.

Rutter, Michael (1987) "Temperament, Personality and Personality Disorder," *British Journal of Psychiatry* 150: 443–458.

Spillers, Hortense (1997) "'All the Things You Could Be by Now, If Sigmund Freud's Wife Was Your Mother': Psychoanalysis and Race," in *Female Subjects in Black and White: Race, Psychoanalysis, Feminism,* E. Abel, B. Christian, and H. Moglen (eds.) Berkeley: University of California Press, pp. 135–158.

Swartz, Sally (1996) "Shrinking: A Postmodern Perspective on Psychiatric Case Histories," *South African Journal of Psychology* 26, no. 3: 150–157.

Walton, Jean (1997) "Re-Placing Race in (White) Psychoanalytic Discourse: Founding Narratives of Feminism," in *Female Subjects in Black and White: Race, Psychoanalysis, Feminism,* E. Abel, B. Christian, and H. Moglen (eds.) Berkeley: University of California Press, pp. 223–251.

Whitford, Margaret (1991) *Luce Irigaray: Philosophy in the Feminine*. New York: Routledge.

Young, Allan (1993) "A Description of How Ideology Shapes Knowledge of a Mental Disorder (Posttraumatic Stress Disorder)," in *Knowledge, Power, and Practice: the Anthropology of Medicine and Everyday Life,* Shirley Lindenbaum and Margaret Lock (eds.) Berkeley: University of California Press, pp. 108–128.

Zulick, Margaret (1991) "Pursuing Controversy: Kristeva's Split Subject, Bakhtin's Many-Tongued World," *Argumentation and Advocacy* 28:2, 91–103.

7

A Bioethics of Failure: Antiheroic Cancer Narratives

Lisa Diedrich

In this chapter I problematize a particular mode of being ill and writing about being ill that attempts to reverse or revise the crisis of illness by describing a sort of heroism in the face of such a crisis. This *heroic art of existence*[1] is, perhaps not surprisingly, quite common in illness narratives, as individuals who are ill attempt to exert a measure of control over their illness as well as the corresponding stories. In order to challenge and/or supplement the heroic mode of being ill, I discuss two recent narratives about the experience of ovarian cancer: Jackie Stacey's *Teratologies: A Cultural Study of Cancer* (1997) and Gillian Rose's *Love's Work: A Reckoning with Life* (1995). Both authors are British academics, and their accounts of illness represent journeys into uncharted narrative territories, although both writers also draw heavily from the theory and methods of their particular fields of study: Stacey from feminist theory and British cultural studies, and Rose from continental philosophy and critical theory. This chapter demonstrates the ways in which both Rose and Stacey posit what I call an ethics of failure; that is, an ethics that emerges out of the experience of failure and in these cases the failure of the body, of conventional and alternative medicine, and of language. Such an ethics, which draws on both feminist and postmodern formulations of bioethics,[2] challenges autonomy as the primary aim of bioethics, as well as the heroic narratives that limit other ethical formulations that might emerge out of the experience of illness. I take the term "ethics of failure" from the work of feminist literary theorist Jacqueline Rose, who is also, as *Love's Work* reveals, Gillian Rose's sister. Her work informs my readings here. I will also make use of Elaine Scarry's phenomenological discussion of pain, which she takes to be an experience that unmakes the world of the person in pain, and Lyotard's exposition in *The Postmodern Condition* (1984) of two modes of presenting the unpresentable. Lyotard describes one as a modern, melancholic narrative concerned with the consistency of form, while the other he describes as a postmodern, innovative narrative that is not concerned with consistency of form or with achieving unity and wholeness.[3] Both Scarry and Lyotard pay attention to forms of affect that exceed the capacity of representation. Therefore I utilize their particular domains of investigation into new "idioms which do not yet exist" (Lyotard 1988: 13) as frameworks to structure my discussion of these two narratives of ovarian cancer, as well as my attempts to articulate an ethics of failure.

In his work, Lyotard delineates what he calls "phrase regimens," which are various "mode[s] of presenting a universe" that are "incommensurate" and not translatable from one mode to the next (1988: 128). And yet, Lyotard wonders, how can one link phrase regimens? I see Jackie Stacey's work as an attempt to link incommensurable phrase regimens. In *Teratologies,* she juxtaposes personal, political, and theoretical phrase regimens to tell her story of illness. As her work reveals, it is paradoxically the failure to bring the experience of embodiment into language that provides a precarious link between these phrase regimens. Stacey opens *Teratologies* with a chapter entitled "Heroes," in which she critiques the western cultural narratives available to her for describing the experience of cancer, or, for that matter, for describing any crisis of the self. According to Stacey, "In contemporary Western culture, we are encouraged to think of our lives as coherent stories of success, progress and movement. Loss and failure have their place but only as part of a broader picture of ascendance. The steady upward curve is the favoured contour" (1997: 9). With regard to illness in particular, this need to move quickly beyond loss and failure, to show, indeed, that it has been left behind, means that the socially sanctioned illness narratives dwell not on loss and failure, but on the heroic overcoming of loss and failure. According to Stacey, the "fantasies of heroic recoveries and guaranteed survival" so common in narratives of cancer, reveal one of the meanings of the word "teratologies"; that is, "the tales of monsters and marvels that pervade the popular imaginary of cancer subcultures" (1997: 10). Stacey wonders, however, what is missing from this "crisis-rescue-recovery formulation." And, she asks, furthermore, "What remains untold in these heroic narratives? What does linearity exclude? What cannot be restored with closure? Where is the continued chaos and disorder in such accounts? Where is the forgotten pain?" (1997: 14–15). In other words, where are the stories of failure? Where are the stories, not of consolation or of a compensatory imaginary that screens the real, but of dissolution and even the desire for dissolution? And, why are such stories of dissolution and the desire for dissolution necessary?

At the center of her "Heroes" chapter, Stacey begins the personal narrative of her own illness and its treatment that will continue throughout *Teratologies*. Printed in a subtly different typeface, the story of her illness and treatment begins, paradoxically, with the end of treatment and a planned journey to a foreign place. As Stacey discovers, however, "the story of the treatment kept changing," which makes the holiday as an "end-of-chemotherapy treat" something of an impossibility. This is not a simple, linear story; rather, the story she tells is one marked by uncertainty over its ending. The question of an ending matters because this is not only a story *of* treatment, but also a story *as* treatment. My method for reading illness narratives like Stacey's and Rose's keeps in mind the multiple meanings, according to the *Oxford English Dictionary*, of the word "treatment," including "the process or manner of behaving towards or dealing with a person or thing"; "the application of medical care or attention to a patient, ailment, etc."; "a manner or instance of dealing with a subject or work of literature, art, etc."; and, perhaps most important, "a discussion or arrangement of terms, negotiation." In its broadest sense, therefore, a treatment might be understood as an ethical negotiation that is concerned with, in Lyotard's formulation, modes of presenting the unpresentable.

In the midst of the uncertainty surrounding the question of whether her treatment will end sooner or later or ever, Stacey and her partner take a chance on a date and book their holiday. Such decisiveness in the face of uncertainty gives her something to focus on, "an incentive to get [her] through it" (1997: 18). And, arbitrarily selecting a particular time and place leads to a remarkable encounter. In a village on Crete, Stacey discovers something—or someone—unexpected: a woman who looks just like her, a woman who, like Stacey, "had that rather uncannily naked look of someone with no eyebrows or eyelashes" (1997: 18). This woman, "who looked completely familiar and yet totally unfamiliar at the same time," is Stacey's double, and the doubling is not just based on bodily appearance but on shared history.[4] When they eventually speak to each other, Stacey discovers that her double has recently had chemotherapy for cancer, a fact that doesn't surprise Stacey. However, what is surprising—completely coincidental, in fact—is her double's answer to her question, "What kind of cancer have you had?" In a parenthetical remark, Stacey admits (to her double, to her reader, to herself) that she never knows what tense to use to talk about cancer, a comment that reveals again the uncertainty over whether there will be an ending to her cancer, or what that ending will be. Stacey's double agrees that she too doesn't know which tense to use. Thus, in speaking to each other, they confirm the difficulty of finding the proper grammar, or even if there is a proper grammar, with which to speak a narrative of cancer. Nonetheless, in this moment in which the difficulty of speaking of cancer is acknowledged, at the same time speaking of cancer, no matter how inadequately, opens up the possibility of communication and recognition across the gaps of what cannot be said, or what cannot be said well:

> What kind of cancer have you had? (I never know which tense to use. Nor do I.) Well, it's very rare. So is mine. It's called a teratoma. A teratoma? So was mine. You had it removed, and an ovary too? So did I. And chemotherapy? Bleomycin, etoposide and cisplatinum. Me too. I've got these strange scratch marks on my skin as a side-effect. So have I. I'm having AFP tests every week. So am I. My tests are clear so far. So are mine. I've been taking high dose vitamins. So have I. I've tried all the alternative medicines. So have I. I've been seeing a healer. So have I. They offered me a wig, but I refused. So did I. I've read all the cancer books. So have I. But I've never met anyone else. . . . Nor have I. (Stacey 1997: 19)

I quote at length from Stacey's description of this "stranger than fiction" encounter, which she admits is both "[t]oo fictional to even hope for, yet too coincidental to belong in good fiction" (1997: 19), to demonstrate the mirroring between the two women reflected in the narrative form itself. Who is the "I" who is speaking at any one time, and who is the "I" who is listening and then replies? The narrative is punctuated by a repetitive rhetoric of recognition: So is mine. So was mine. So did I. Me too. So have I. So am I. So are mine. So have I. So have I. So have I.

So did I. So have I. Until the last two sentences, which are not separated by a period, but by an ellipses. This "magical meeting" fills Stacey with relief and a "childlike excitement," but the uncanny convergence will not last, and those last lines—"But I've never met anyone else. . . . Nor have I."—take on a different meaning later, in another time and place, as Stacey's and her double's narratives of cancer diverge. The "So have I" becomes "Nor have I," and the moment of recognition becomes the possibility—indeed, the inevitability—of a future misrecognition. Thus, after their uncanny interlude, Stacey and her double return to Britain where their shared history fails to become a shared future, revealing the precariousness of the notion of a shared history. As Stacey notes, "We had rehearsed another story, but it escaped our control" (1997: 20). And so as Stacey continues her return to health, her double experiences the return of cancer. Stacey understands that the splitting of their narratives reveals the "dangers of narrative trajectories which promise closures of certainty" (1997: 21). The gap that opens up between their stories reveals the impossibility of shared histories, and it reminds Stacey that uncertainty and contingency are all that she and her double really share.

Like Stacey, Gillian Rose is interested in telling a story of uncertainty and contingency, and, in *Love's Work*, she attempts to describe the experience of illness—her own illness and the illnesses of others—without resorting to the compensatory imaginary of a heroic cultural narrative. Rose's work is both memoir and philosophical essay; in fact, it might be called a philosophical memoir. As such, her work allows us to consider what Foucault called the "fundamental structures of experience" that link medical thought, philosophical thought, and literature (1973: 198). *Love's Work* opens with a return visit to New York City to see her friend and former lover, Jim. New York is where Rose discovered her life work, continental philosophy and critical theory, and Jim was integral to that discovery. Her first visit to New York in August 1970 was just after she had graduated from Oxford. Oxford, for Rose, had been an educational experience that was not very educational and couldn't have ended too soon.

According to Rose, her real education didn't begin until New York, a trip that was supposed to be for a mere three weeks, but became a year-long sojourn. Yet, her return to New York in 1991 affords her a new view of the city and a different sort of education. And in fact this return begins with misrecognition and the realization that her and Jim's lives have diverged. At the airport, Rose explains, she initially goes up "to someone who looked like a caricature of Jim as I remembered him in good health" (1995: 4). She literally doesn't see, or perhaps doesn't want to see, the Jim who has come to meet her, transformed as he is by HIV/AIDS. Rose writes:

> My formerly laconic and witty friend had become loquacious, needy, addressing with urgent familiarity everyone we chanced to have dealings with over the next few days—taxi-drivers, bell-boys, waiters. And when he wasn't holding forth to those nearest to him, he issued a continuous, low, moaning sound, a piteous cradling for the inner, wounded being that, strangely, had surrendered to the publicity of the city streets (Rose 1995: 4).

Rose is disconcerted by the ways in which Jim's private moaning moves into the public; it's as if his most private pain leaks out into the world, and this leakage between the private and public is something he can no longer control, nor is he even aware of it.

It seems everyone Rose meets in New York this time is "extraordinarily afflicted" (1995: 7); in fact, the city itself is extraordinarily afflicted, and she calls it a "city of death."[5] What Rose doesn't say, because she doesn't know at the time, is that she will be—indeed, perhaps already is—one of the extraordinarily afflicted; and her affliction—ovarian cancer, the "silent" cancer —will only be discovered, like 80 percent of such cases, in an advanced state, having already metastasized to her colon (1995: 83). Her own inner, wounded being remains cradled within, and does not, yet, surrender to the publicity of the city streets. The reader doesn't learn about Rose's illness until halfway through her work, and only after she has wondered how her reader would respond if she were to say she has AIDS—"full-blown AIDS"—and that she has been "ill during most of the course of what [she has] related" (1995: 76). What, Rose wonders, does the revelation of illness (and, presumably, imminent death) do to the reader, who she interpellates here as "you"? Answering her own query, Rose insists:

> I would lose you. I would lose you to knowledge, to fear and to metaphor. Such a revelation would result in the sacrifice of the alchemy of my art, of artistic "control" over the setting as well as the content of your imagination. A double

sacrifice of my elocution: to the unspeakable (death) and to the overspoken (AIDS) (Rose 1995: 76–77).

And yet Rose recognizes the uses of losing us, and of losing control over the setting as well as the content of our imagination. The possibility of losing her reader and of losing control over her story are not reasons for not writing; rather, the possibility of such loss—the inevitability of such loss—is reason itself for writing. No, she doesn't have AIDS; rather, she has something else that is "full-blown," and that is not overspoken,[6] but barely spoken, or, perhaps, like the disease itself until it is too late, silent. Not to write, for Rose, then, is to "die deadly" (1995: 77). Yet, as she explains to her reader and in many ways to herself as well, "by this work, I may die forward into the intensified agon of living" (1995: 77). Writing is not a means for overcoming the difficulty of dying, but rather a means of engaging with the agon of living. Dying forward is not simply leaving a record of one's heroism in the face of one's death, it is grappling with one's inevitable failures in one's reckoning with life.

In *The Body in Pain* (1985), Elaine Scarry offers a phenomenological description of pain and elucidates the ways in which torture and war are structured as that they are capable of "unmaking the world" of an individual. How might Scarry's unmaking be understood in terms of Rose's agon of living? According to Scarry, "Pain is a pure physical experience of negation, an immediate sensory rendering of 'against,' of something being against one, and of something one must be against. Even though it occurs within oneself, it is at once identified as 'not oneself,' 'not me,' as something so alien that it must right now be gotten rid of" (1985: 52). As Scarry sees it, this uncanny sense that one's embodied self has become alien is similar in illness and in torture, but only in torture is this "internal physical experience . . . accompanied by its external political equivalent, the presence in the space outside the body of a self-proclaimed 'enemy,' someone who in becoming the enemy becomes the human embodiment of aversiveness" (1985: 52).

Although I think Scarry is absolutely right to establish the specificity of the experience of pain in torture and to distinguish it from the experience of pain in illness, nonetheless, it can hardly be said that in illness the subjective characteristics of pain are *never* objectified. This is precisely what medicine attempts to do, if usually in a benign, not an averse manner, and it often does so in such a way that it contributes to the patient's distress and to the unmaking of the patient's world. Many critiques of modern medicine, especially feminist ones, have noted the ways in which the patient is objectified and silenced within the isolating spaces and hierarchical relationships of modern medicine. The doctor–patient relationship is often characterized, not by the modernist ethics of beneficence or nonmaleficence, but by paternalism at best and punitiveness at worst.

Rose, for example, experiences conventional medicine as a "carnival of communication" when two consulting surgeons—Mr. Wong, the gynecologist, and Mr. Bates, the bowel specialist—report vastly different prognoses after a second operation on her bowel. Mr. Wong, on the one hand, reports that Rose's cancer has spread considerably, and thus her prognosis is "guarded" (1995: 99). Mr. Bates, on the other hand, reports that she is "living in symbiosis with the disease," and that she should "[g]o away and continue to do so" (1995: 100). Their "utterly discrepant opinions," while perhaps not averse in themselves, are made so by the fact that what Rose's consultants are most concerned with is not her well-being, but whose position is taken as authoritative in relation to her disease. Mr. Wong refuses to talk to his colleague, because, as he tells Rose, "I will not change my position. This is my cancer" (1995: 101). Rose, in a panic, must plead, cajole, beg, flatter, and inveigle Mr. Wong to talk to Mr. Bates (1995: 101). In this absurd scenario, Rose's body becomes the ground upon which disputes over power are fought. There is no person with cancer in this scenario, only a cancer and the surgeons who have the power to either cure or condemn it (1995: 103).

Rose eventually realizes that she is "already in a realm beyond medicine," and that she and medicine "do not have enough command of each other's language for the exchange to be fruitful" (1995: 102). Rose discovers that she and medicine are mute to each other, and such a muteness is what Lyotard describes as a case of a differend between two parties, which "takes place when the 'regulation' of the conflict that opposes them is done in the idiom of one of the parties while the wrong suffered by the other is not signified in that idiom" (1988: 9). Medicine does not speak of the wrong suffered by Rose; it only speaks of the capacity of one or the other consultant to properly diagnose her disease. Yet, through the practice of writing (and reading) her memoir, this incompatibility between idioms becomes an opportunity, in Lyotard's words, for a "philosophical politics" to "bear witness to differends by finding idioms for them" (1988: *xiii* and 13). This philosophical politics emerges, not from the success of heroic medicine in curing Rose's cancer, but from her realization that her illness is in a realm beyond medicine, and that to speak of it requires a new idiom.

Like Lyotard, who is concerned with the state signaled by the feeling "[o]ne cannot find the words" (1988: 13), Scarry is concerned throughout *The Body in Pain* with the failure of language in the face of pain. Her work is often read pessimistically; according to this reading, pain is incommunicable because, as Scarry notes, "[t]o have pain is to have *certainty;* to hear about pain is to have *doubt*" (1985: 13; emphasis in original). Thus, she writes, "To witness the moment when pain causes a reversion to the pre-language of cries and groans is to witness the destruction of language" (1985: 6). However, she does not stop at the destruction of language. Rather, she insists as well that "conversely, to be present when a person moves up out of that pre-language and projects the facts of sentience into speech is almost to have been permitted to be present at the birth of language itself" (1985: 6). Scarry, like Lyotard and Rose, then, is concerned not only with the "difficulty of expressing physical pain," but also with the "nature of human creation," with the ways in which, through "acts of making, human beings become implicated in each other's sentience" (1985: 176).

Two acts of making in *Love's Work,* in which the process cannot be separated from the product, are love and work, or, juxtaposing them as does Rose, love's work. "Love's work" is a form of treatment that is, according to Rose, in opposition to the "iatrogenic materiality of medicine and to the screwtape overdose of spirituality of alternative healing" (1995: 77–78). "Love's work" is both a theory and a method for negotiating loss; it is a theory/method that conveys "the impasses, the limitations and cruelties, equally, of alternative healing and conventional medicine" and "insinuate[s] *démarches* [steps, proceedings, treatments] of healing that have not been imagined in either canon" (1995: 77). These not-yet-imagined *démarches* of healing are an opening to an ethical moment.

In *The Body in Pain*, Scarry is interested in both the making and unmaking of the world, and the ways in which analyzing the processes and structures of unmaking might give us insight into the processes and structures of making. Similarly, in *Love's Work*, Rose moves from a chapter on love to a chapter on illness. In her text, then, love and illness are juxtaposed, not as opposites, but as two scenes of loss (of self, of certainty, of control) in which the embodied self is always already vulnerable. The work doesn't heroically disregard this vulnerability but rather acknowledges it and negotiates with it. She opens herself up to her readers, but this opening reveals not just life in its medical sense as incommensurate with death, but life in its "meaningful sense . . . as inclusive of death" (1995: 79). The literal and figurative opening that Rose reveals is the opening of a colostomy, a procedure she must undergo because her cancer has spread to her colon. Of this decidedly uncanny treatment, Rose notes:

> Nowhere in the endless romance of world literature (my experience is, needless to say, limited) have I come across an account of living with a colostomy. Since the first colostomy was performed in this country in 1797, the first paper on the subject published in 1805, and colostomies have been routine medical practice since the second half of the nineteenth century, this is more than enough time for lyric and lament. (1995: 93)

In fact, it is antilyric and antilament that Rose practices: "Let me make myself clear," she writes, "the colostomy—*stoma* meaning "opening"—is a surrogate rectum and anus" (1995: 93). Linking what she calls "colostomy ethnography" with Holocaust ethnography,[7] Rose intends to speak of shit, to re-site bodily function, to exchange "discretion for an anterior cloaca and incontinence" (1995: 95).

Stacey also speaks of shit, as well as vomit, urine, blood, saliva, sweat, and tears, because these "abject bodily wastes . . . become the currency of everyday life" for the person with cancer (1997: 82). Thus, in her chapter entitled "Monsters," she utilizes Julia Kristeva's theories of abjection to help her describe the "crossing of the border between I/other and between inside and outside that truly disgusts" (1997: 82); such crossings are a crucial aspect not only of the experience of cancer but also of the experience of its conventional treatments. For Stacey and other people with cancer, chemotherapy turns the body inside out, and "the body's flows are set in reverse: where food should enter, vomit exits; where waste should exit, suppositories enter" (1997: 84). Moreover, it is not only the inside of the body that becomes strange and is unable to perform the functions that the healthy body takes for granted, such as eating and eliminating, the outside of the body becomes strange as well. The skin that forms the boundary between the body and world is hairless, "overburdened" with rashes that cause "wild scratching," and flushed with the heat of "hormonal disturbance for all to see" (1997: 85). This body that Stacey describes in detail—her body and yet not her body—"becomes the only reality" (1997: 85). She explains that "[t]his matter is all I am" (1997: 85), which provides an answer of sorts to the question often asked of the ill, "What's the matter with you?" What's the matter is that she *is* matter, and the matter that she is keeps changing its form.

Both Stacey and Rose, therefore, attempt to show the ways that illness disrupts the stability of binary oppositions, including inside/outside and public/private. Illness might be said to transform the slash that separates these binaries, to make it vulnerable and porous. Thus, by speaking and writing indiscreetly of her body and its failures, Rose creates an opening that leads both ways: inside out and outside in.[8] Because she is "already in a realm beyond medicine," (Rose 1995: 102) and because the language of medicine is irreconcilable with her own language, who she is exceeds what medicine might say about her. But it is not only conventional medicine that fails to provide Rose with a grammar and syntax with which to describe "a new bodily function" and the difference it does and does not make (1995). Rose sees alternative healing practices as offering little more than compensation for friends and family who "field the crisis of their own mortality brought on by my illness by serving hard and fast at me the literature and liquids of alternative healing" (1995: 104). As Rose sees it, alternative healing practices provide a discourse for others to take up in the face of the uncertainties that illness reveals. They may provide consolation, but rarely to those who are ill and already beyond consolation. According to Rose, moreover, "The injunction, which pervades the literature of alternative healing, to become 'exceptional' (Bernie Siegal), or 'edgeless' (Stephen Levine), to assume unconditional love, is poor psychology, worse theology and no notion of justice at all" (1995: 104). In contrast to the alternative healing discourses, therefore, the love, psychology, theology, and justice that Rose practices is conditional, meaning, for Rose, not absolute but speculative.

Alternative healing instantiates what Stacey calls in *Teratologies* a "discourse of responsibility" (1997: 204). In order to delineate this discourse of responsibility, she opens her penultimate chapter entitled "Responsibilities" with her own dilemma over whether or not to have a fifth chemotherapy treatment. Her doctor has recommended it, but the previous treatments have been accompanied by devastating and debilitating side effects: unending vomiting and diarrhea, loss of feeling in her fingers and toes, and a maddening ringing in her ears. She—her body, her self, her embodied self—simply can't take anymore. Her decision not to have a fifth dose, she realizes, will be accompanied by, if she falls ill again, a (self and social) judgment that she did not do everything she could have done to defeat her disease; that is, that she was lacking in resolve, the correct attitude, a sense of personal responsibility for her own health. According to this discourse of responsibility, Stacey may be held responsible not only for the failure of her treatment, but also for having the disease to begin with. She relates a visit to a therapist who asks her if she knows why she has cancer. The therapist wants Stacey to find an emotional cause (most likely somewhere in the distant past) with present physical effects. When she refuses to engage in his teleological game of emotional cause and physical effect, he wonders if she is "afraid of self-exploration" (1997: 202). In order to interpret the lessons in responsibility that this therapist is trying to instill in her, Stacey ventriloquizes the doctor's ethical teachings as she understands them:

> Sometimes you have to go right into the depths of despair before you can surface anew (be reborn?). I could do things differently now and stay healthy. It is my choice. Do I really have no idea why I had cancer? Am I willing to take the risk, to seize the opportunity, to receive the gift? It's not a question of blame, but a question of cause and effect, of responsibility. (1997: 202)

Not a question of blame, but a question of responsibility. Stacey recognizes that the distance from responsibility to blame, where illness and health is concerned, is very short indeed.

Thus, for Stacey as well as for Rose, alternative healing provides a "counsel of despair which would keep the mind out of hell" (Rose 1995:

105). In other words, it attempts to speak only in terms of heroic successes in overcoming difficulty and of the possibility of unconditional health and unconditional love. Failure and conditionality are radically excluded from this heroic mode. Alternatively, Rose proposes an ethics based on her book's epigraph: "Keep your mind in hell, and despair not."[9] She is concerned, that is to say, with an ethics that acknowledges that we are all "vulnerable, woundable, around the bounds" and that "conditionality is the only unconditionality of human love" (1995: 106). We must risk relation; we must seek the agon as well as the repose of living. Throughout *Love's Work,* therefore, Rose attempts to articulate what might be called an *ethics of failure,* the term I take from Jacqueline Rose. In a lecture entitled "Why War?" Jacqueline Rose discusses the problem of war in general, and a dispute within the British Psycho-Analytical Society in 1943–44 between Melanie Klein, her supporters, and her critics in particular. Rose asserts, following D. W. Winnicott, that "[k]nowledge will be possible only if we are willing to suspend the final purpose and ends of knowledge in advance" (J. Rose 1993: 36–37). If we are to avoid going to war, according to Rose, we must "[h]ang on to failure" (1993: 37).

Knowledge itself requires a certain suspension of belief in the possibility of total knowledge. It requires a certain willingness to trust in that which cannot be known, or that which can be known only conditionally. Gillian Rose, similarly, understands ethics as the *diaporia,* or, "being at a loss yet exploring various routes, different ways towards the good-enough justice, which recognises the intrinsic and contingent limitations in its exercise" (1995: 124). An ethics, for Gillian Rose, will never come from dissolving "the difficulty of living, of love, of self and other, of the other in the self," it will come from being at a loss yet exploring various routes (1995: 105). Illness does not interrupt love's work, but rather requires that we discover and explore new routes for loving and working, and for living and dying. These routes cannot be mapped in advance, nor will they necessarily be mapped in any conclusive, totalizing way, even as we travel along them.

As I have described it, Gillian Rose's ethics of failure, with its recognition of the contingent manner in which a good-enough justice might operate, articulates certain ideals that I associate with a postmodern feminist bioethics. It is interesting (though perhaps not surprising considering her training) that Rose explicitly opposes both postmodernism and feminism[10] in *Love's Work*. For Rose, both postmodern philosophers and feminists are "in deadly, unironic earnest" (1995: 125), and they fail to recognize "the way that play (fairy stories, terrifying films) teaches the difference between fantasy and actuality" (1995: 126). Making use of Winnicott's psychoanalytic theories of creativity,[11] Rose explains that

> [t]he child who is able to explore that border [between fantasy and reality] will feel safe in experiencing violent, inner, emotional conflict, and will acquire compassion for other people. The child who is locked away from aggressive experiment and play will be left terrified and paralysed by its emotions, unable to release or face them, for they may destroy the world and himself or herself. The censor aggravates the syndrome she seeks to alleviate; she seeks to rub out in others the border which has been effaced inside herself (1995: 126).

The person who censors play in Rose's formulation is a "she," and, as we come to realize a bit further in the text, clearly an earnest feminist. Rose's characterization of feminism appears to be straight out of Camille Paglia, who is Rose's friend and who is described in *Love's Work* as both "a literary wordsmith" and "the *alazon,* The Imposter, who boasts of more than she knows" (1995: 114). Rose admits that "feminism never offered me any help," and this isn't surprising considering her claim that feminism "fails to address the power of women as well as their powerlessness" (1995: 140). Clearly, Rose has a rather limited view of feminism; her view is a caricature of even radical second-wave feminist efforts to expose everyday sexism and violence against women. Her portrait of feminism might have been more generous had she read feminists like her sister, who sees "radical self-questioning . . . not as a block or a ban to political life, but as a necessary part of its procedures" (J. Rose 1993: 232). Jacqueline Rose, moreover, understands such a feminist project as "not exactly utopian but more a bid for the future" (1993: 232).

Gillian Rose views feminism, not as an ethical practice of radical self-questioning invested in a bid for the future, but as a practice that is unable to discern either "the beauty or the limitation" of the sort of love that has most fulfilled her: between an older woman and a younger man, "in which each is equally teacher and taught, Lover and Beloved" (1995: 140). Why Rose assumes that such a love is incompatible with a feminist ethical practice is not entirely clear to me, but I mention it because it is an example of her insistence that feminism be viewed as that which suppresses fulfilling love and work. Rose, ultimately, maintains a "skeptical faith, shaky but persistent, in critical reason" (1995: 139), and she believes such a skeptical faith in critical reason is not to be found in either feminism or postmodernism, nor, for that matter, in a postmodern feminism. In this respect, Rose might seem to come down on the modern side of the differend that Lyotard describes in *The Postmodern Condition*. The two modes Lyotard describes "testify to a difference (*un différend*) on which the fate of thought depends and will depend for a long time, between regret and assay" (1984: 80). The difference, for Lyotard, is both an aesthetic one [between an aesthetics that regrets what has been lost and an aesthetics that assays, that is, "searches for new presentations" (1984: 81)] and an ethical one (between a model of legitimation that emphasizes consensus and the maximization of performance and one that emphasizes pragmatic paradoxes and the production of the unknown).

Although Rose voices a persistent faith in critical reason, nonetheless, her faith is not a nostalgic, sentimental one, meant to offer solace and simple pleasure, but a faith that, paradoxically, requires risk and speculation as she explores the boundaries between fantasy and actuality: "I will stay in the fray, in the revel of ideas and risk; learning, failing, wooing, grieving, trusting, working, reposing—in this sin of language and lips" (1995: 144). Rose's (mis)readings of the theories and practices of feminism and postmodernism are illustrative of the difficulties of articulating a feminist and postmodernist bioethics. Nonetheless, we must heed her advice even as we critique her readings: to stay in the fray and revel in ideas and risk, and ideas that take risks rather than offer comfort.

Unlike Rose, Stacey relies on both feminist and postmodernist theories to present her cultural study of cancer and to generate an art of being ill. Her final chapter, "Endings," comes to no conclusions, but rather speculates on writing itself and the reason in particular that one might write (and/or read) a personal narrative of cancer. Stacey explains that in such personal narratives, the "person who has had cancer is presented as a sagacious messenger whose purpose is to remind everyone of the preciousness and the precariousness of life" (1997: 244). And, she continues,

The so-called "survivors" of cancer are seen to possess knowledge of the secrets of life, as well as the secrets of death. They are heroised for their confrontation with death, which is presumed to have enlightened them about how to live life. They are the bearers of knowledge. They have lived to tell the tale. (Stacey 1997: 244–245).

Stacey herself seems not to identify as one of the "so-called 'survivors' of cancer." She does not offer her readers enlightenment or special knowledge of life and death. What she does do, however, like Rose, is stay in the fray so that she might continue the search for new presentations, new arts of being ill. What we find in *Teratologies* and *Love's Work*, then, is not absolute knowledge, but learning; not heroism, but failing, wooing, grieving, trusting, working, reposing; not someone who has lived to tell the heroic tale, but someone who is in the fray of reckoning with life.

Notes

1. This term is an adaptation of Foucault's term "art of existence." It is Foucault's methodology that interests me most here; he approaches the history of sexuality not, or not only, through an analysis of institutional codes or juridical authority, but through forms of subjectification, or practices of the self, that included in classical Greece, for example, an ethics based on moderation, or, as Foucault explains, the "domination of oneself by oneself" (1985: 65). My work is concerned with forms of subjectification that emerge out of the experience of illness.

2. Some important works that combine feminist and postmodernist (and, of course, postmodern feminist) approaches to the practices and techniques of health include Diprose (1994), Grosz (1994), Shildrick (1997), Shildrick and Price (1998), and Singer (1993).

3. For the most part, within Lyotard's schema, both *Love's Work* and *Teratologies* offer postmodern narratives, but as Lyotard makes clear and these works show, the "nuances which distinguish these two modes may be infinitesimal," and, moreover, "they often coexist in the same piece" (1984: 80).

4. Someone "who looked completely familiar and yet totally unfamiliar at the same time" is almost exactly one of the definitions that Freud gives for the term "uncanny." Thus, according to Freud, "the 'uncanny' is that class of the terrifying which leads back to something long known to us, once very familiar" (1953[1919]: 369–370). Later in his paper, Freud also discusses the "theme of the 'double'" in the work of Otto Rank. The "double," for Freud and Rank, is both a guarantee against the destruction of the ego, as well as, paradoxically, "the ghastly harbinger of death" (1953: 387). Stacey's double is both of these things, as we will see. I should point out that while the story of Stacey's double sounds

metaphorical, there is no reason to believe from the text itself that it is not a true—that is, factual—story.

5. Cities, in Rose's work, stand in for aesthetic, philosophical, and ethicopolitical ideas. In *Mourning Becomes the Law* (1996), Athens represents rational politics; what Rose calls the "New" Jerusalem represents the imaginary community of a new ethics; and Auschwitz represents the irrational.

6. The question of whether AIDS is overspoken is certainly debatable. It seems to me that the question of whose experience of AIDS is spoken and whose is not is important to keep in mind. Having said that, I would agree with Rose that the experience of ovarian cancer, especially in 1995 if less so now, is not overspoken.

7. Rose, whose Jewish father and mother emigrated to England from Poland before World War II, and who lost numerous family members in the Holocaust, interweaves the stories of her three 'Cities of Death'—New York, Auschwitz, and Jerusalem—throughout *Love's Work*.

8. I take the terms "inside out" and "outside in" from Elizabeth Grosz. In her book *Volatile Bodies* (1994), in which she outlines the need for a "corporeal feminism," Grosz takes up philosophies that are either directed "inside out" (e.g., Merleau-Pontian phenomenology, Lacanian psychoanalysis, and neurophysiology) or directed "outside in" (e.g., the philosophies of Nietzsche, Foucault, Deleuze, and Lingis). As Grosz makes clear, the focus in both of these philosophical modes is on the body or perhaps the self as embodied.

9. The quotation is from Staretz Silouan (1866–1938).

10. Although similar in Rose's portrayal of them, the two also appear in her portrayal to be mutually exclusive.

11. See, in particular, *Playing and Reality* (1971), in which Winnicott describes the importance of transitional phenomena for the formation of the ego. According to Winnicott, in adolescence and adulthood, transitional phenomena are manifest less so in particular objects, as they had been in childhood, but through play and other creative activities. After childhood, the transitional object is "not forgotten and it is not mourned," but becomes "diffused" and "spread out over the whole intermediate territory between 'inner psychic reality' and 'the external world as perceived by two persons in common,' that is to say, over the whole cultural field" (1971: 5). Where there is play, there is creative living; and where there is creative living, there is cultural experience. Play, therefore, is a potential—and precarious—space "between the subjective and that which is objectively perceived" (1971: 50).

References

Diprose, Rosalyn (1994) *The Bodies of Women: Ethics, Embodiment and Sexual Difference*. London and New York: Routledge.

Foucault, Michel (1973) *The Birth of the Clinic: An Archeology of Medical Perception*. trans. A. M. Sheridan Smith. New York: Vintage.

Foucault, Michel (1985) *The History of Sexuality*. vol. 2. *The Use of Pleasure*. trans. Robert Hurley. New York: Vintage.

Freud, Sigmund (1953[1919]) "'The Uncanny'," *Collected Papers*. vol. IV. ed. Ernest Jones trans. Joan Riviere. London: Hogarth Press, pp. 368–407.

Grosz, Elizabeth (1994) *Volatile Bodies: Toward a Corporeal Feminism*. Bloomington: Indiana University Press.

Lyotard, Jean-Francois (1984) *The Postmodern Condition: A Report on Knowledge*. trans. Geoff Bennington and Brian Massumi. Minneapolis: University of Minnesota Press.

Lyotard, Jean-Francois (1988) *The Differend: Phrases in Dispute*. trans. Georges Van Den Abbeele. Minneapolis: University of Minnesota Press.

Rose, Gillian (1995) *Love's Work: A Reckoning with Life*. New York: Schocken Books.

Rose, Gillian (1996) *Mourning Becomes the Law: Philosophy and Representation*. Cambridge, UK: Cambridge University Press.

Rose, Jacqueline (1993) *Why War?* Oxford: Blackwell.

Scarry, Elaine (1985) *The Body in Pain: The Making and Unmaking of the World*. New York and Oxford: Oxford University Press.

Shildrick, Margrit (1997) *Leaky Bodies and Boundaries: Feminism, Postmodernism and (Bio)ethics*. London and New York: Routledge.

Shildrick, Margrit, and Price Janet (eds.) (1998) *Vital Bodies: Feminist Reconfigurations of the Clinic*. Edinburgh: Edinburgh University Press.

Singer, Linda (1993) *Erotic Welfare: Sexual Theory and Politics in the Age of Epidemic*. New York and London: Routledge.

Stacey, Jackie (1997) *Teratologies: A Cultural Study of Cancer*. London and New York: Routledge.

Winnicott, D. W. (1971) *Playing and Reality*. London and New York: Routledge.

IV

The Challenge of Biotechnology

8

Biomedicine and Moral Agency in a Complex World

Sylvia Nagl

There is something different about this chapter, which is written by a scientist and has its grounding in ongoing research practice and the lived experience of contemporary biomedical science. I am a computational biologist with a doctorate in molecular biology, based at University College London, one of the largest life science faculties in Europe, where my scientific interests lie in the development of new conceptual frameworks for medicine based on complexity theory. However, the origins of this chapter, and the intellectual journey leading up to it, go back a long time, to my early twenties.

From that point, an increasing awareness about the exclusion of women's experiences, achievements, and life histories from academic disciplines led me to engage also with such issues in relation to people of color and nonwestern ways of knowing. Motivated by a strong desire to reach beyond these boundaries of exclusion and marginalization, I broke with my family's (western) medical tradition and studied eastern philosophy and acupuncture, and worked as a practitioner in this field for several years. Out of the realization that any cultural transformation toward a new integrative medicine would ultimately need to arise from within western culture itself, I pursued further studies in philosophy and the history of western science. Since embarking on my career in molecular biology, I have been committed to building bridges between science and other ways of knowing. This chapter was written for some of my colleagues as an invitation to conversation and possibly to a shared questioning and exploration of the issues it raises.

The Genome, e-Medicine, and the Digital Body

With the near completion of the Human Genome Project, biomedicine is currently undergoing a momentous change in its conceptual foundations. Before taking up the bioethical implications of such work—both in its end use and, more important, in this chapter for those involved in research—I outline some of the developments that concern me. Going beyond the work on inherited single-gene disorders that was of central concern in the 1980s and 1990s, the focus has shifted to an overriding concern with the genome and its information-processing properties. The functioning of bodies in health and disease of any sort, regardless of whether or not the disorder possesses an identifiable inherited component, is being reconceptualized in terms of global expression states of the genome. New "microarray" technologies enable large-scale parallel studies of the simultaneous activation states of thousands of genes in cells that, for example, are responding to particular environmental stimuli, or are at a specific developmental stage, or malfunction in one way or another, or have been exposed to certain drugs (Lee and Lee 2000).

This focus on the information-processing properties of the genome, and of the organism as a whole, brings with it issues of representation. A conceptual framework is now emerging from within biomedicine that encourages the abstraction of living bodies to the status of information-processing machines. Concomitantly, genetic information can be conceived to exist as a disembodied entity. Once the genome is conceptualized as an information structure, it becomes plausible that it can exist in various physical media (Haraway 1997: 246). The DNA organized into natural chromosomes in the living cell, then, only constitutes one type of possible media. Various *engineered* molecular structures such as bacterial plasmids or yeast artificial chromosomes, designed to carry and transfer stretches of DNA, provide another medium. The entire genome of an organism may be cloned into a library of such biochemical information structures. Genetic information can be even further removed from any actual biological context, in that the biochemical composition of DNA can be abstracted into sequences written in a four-letter code, encoded in binary strings of 0s and 1s, and entered in computer databases.

Furthermore, the simultaneous activation states of tens of thousands of genes using microarray chips are seen to provide a readout of bodily information processing. This new technology is currently revolutionizing the understanding of human disease with, as yet, uncertain outcomes. One may note, however, that these developments carry with them the potential for a further silencing of the patient's voice in medical discourse because they are capable of dramatically widening the distance between high-tech medicine and the subjective bodily experience of well-being or illness.

Within this new paradigm, biomedicine is redefining itself as an information science, which in turn is leading to a radical redefinition of the body and of the human itself. We need to ask ourselves who, or rather what, is the human represented by the Human Genome Project? Donna Haraway has described the human to be represented in this way:

> Most fundamentally, . . . the human genome projects produce entities of a different ontological kind than flesh-and-blood organisms . . . or any other sort of "normal" organic being. . . . the human genome projects produce ontologically specific things called databases as objects of knowledge and practice. The human to be represented, then, has a particular kind of totality, or species being, as well as a specific kind of individuality. At whatever level of individuality or collectivity, from a single gene region extracted from one sample through the whole species genome, this human is itself an information structure. (Haraway 1997: 247)

This data structure is a construct of abstract human-ness—without a body, without a gender, without a history, and without personal and collective narratives. It does not have a culture, and it does not have a voice. This electronically configured human is an a-cultural program. Yet in this very construction it is deeply culturally determined. We find ourselves confronted with a universal human, constructed by science as practiced in North America and Europe at the beginning of the twenty-first century.

The full impact that such a representation will have on our understanding of who we are, what it means to be human, and what constitutes a person, is still unknown. There are clearly profound implications for the construction of identity, ethnicity, and gender. Genomic science, as medical science has always been, is as much philosophical as practical, a matter of meaning as much as medical intervention (Kemp and

Wallace 2000). From this perspective, it is thought-provoking to reflect on certain parallels between our contemporary search for self-knowledge by means of genomics and the central role that anatomy has played in this quest from the Renaissance to the nineteenth century.

Much of the highly detailed knowledge about anatomy gained by the dissection of corpses was of no use to the physician, or even the surgeon, because contemporary medical practice simply did not have the means to intervene with the levels of refinement that the representations delivered. Rather, the disclosing of the "divine architecture" that stood at the summit of God's creation remained the central goal of anatomical representation across at least three centuries (Kemp and Wallace 2000). Today, theology does not have any part in scientific inquiry, but a (often unacknowledged) psychological urge to "know ourselves" is arguably still a powerful motivation. While many hopes for medical usefulness may remain unrealized, and the deluge of accumulating genomic data may suffer the same fate as the highly refined anatomical representations of earlier centuries, at least for some time to come, we will, and already are, experiencing the "meaning-making" consequences at all levels of culture and society.

These developments raise a vast number of (bio)ethical questions, in relation to human persons, medical research, diagnosis and treatment, and society at large. There are also a host of issues concerning the commodification of genetic information held in cell lines, clone libraries, and databanks. Arguably, biomedical scientists ought to be involved in the ethical discourse arising from these questions. However, despite calls for scientists to become more ethically sensitive than they used to be (Ziman 1998), the contemporary research culture places severe obstacles in the path of such an involvement. This chapter discusses some of these obstacles and explores strategies for expressing moral agency in research and the creation of a social space that can facilitate scientists' participation in bioethical discourse.

An Ethics of Models and Metaphors

In fundamental ways, *any* kind of representation—as postmodernist thought insists—is linguistically constructed; we can only know something about the world and about ourselves through language:

> Since representations are necessarily structured by language (hence, by culture), no representation can ever "correspond" to reality. At the same time, some representations are clearly better (more effective) than others. In the absence of a copy of truth, we need to search for the meaning of "better" in a comparison of the uses to which different representations can be put, that is, in the practices they facilitate. From such a perspective, scientific knowledge is value-laden (and inescapably so) just because it is shaped by our choices—first, of what to seek representations of, and second, of what to seek representations for. Far from being value-free, good science is science that effectively facilitates the material realization of particular goals, that does in fact enable us to change the world in particular ways. (Keller 1992: 5)

Thus we face questions of ethical agency in relation to the consequences of our chosen models and of our language. It is clear that there *are* choices to be made, that our models are not the embodiment of pure deduction, but are in large part cultural constructs. At the most basic level, the representation of primary data, design decisions about genome databases determine what uses can be made of the data—what can be compared with what. Further interpretation of the data and the dissemination of this information also depend crucially on the medium of language. On a societal scale, science and culture continuously create and recreate each other through language. This traffic of ideas, images, metaphors, models, and theories about nature and human nature is bidirectional. It is at this juncture that wider conceptual frameworks, often only implicit in the language tools employed, exert their constraints by enabling certain representations but not others. In this way, cognitive metaphors as culturally inherited and linguistically reinforced concepts (Margulis and Sagan 1995) play a tremendously important role in the ongoing transformation of our views of reality and of ourselves.

To illustrate this, consider how throughout history the construction of nature has drawn heavily on culturally held beliefs about women. Francis Bacon saw nature as a woman whose veil was to be torn away and who was to be tortured—"put on the rack"—to make her reveal her secrets. Today, "Gaia," intended to represent the feminine principle in nature, has become a familiar metaphor in the culture at large and has been adopted by some scientists as the organizing framework for their research (Lovelock 1979). My purpose here is not to judge the cognitive metaphors themselves but to consider how these contrasting metaphorical constructions of nature facilitate widely divergent science practices.

To name some further examples, science has appropriated metaphors from culture to describe evolution as a Malthusian struggle for existence (Depew and Weber 1996), the cell as a factory (Spanier 1995), and the fertilization of the egg by a sperm cell as a drama of romantic courtship (Martin 1991). In turn, the wider culture has adopted metaphors from science that describe a person as a readout of the genome. Furthermore, the mind is often metaphorically seen as a computer program, although unimaginably more complicated. Following the logic of such metaphors, the mind, and a culture-dependent construct such as intelligence, can then ultimately be reduced to genes as well. These essentialist metaphors circulate widely among academic disciplines and have come to exert a strong influence on the humanities. In bioethics, this type of genetic essentialism often remains unquestioned in itself, and bioethical issues arising from human genetics and the Human Genome Project are discussed as if what such metaphors imply were true. In the media and popular science books, these assumptions have become commonplace.

Scientists occupy a critical position in this flow of ideas and metaphors from the wider culture to science and vice versa. Their agency is constituted by participation in both scientific and cultural discourses; they are transmitters of meaning-making representations in both directions. Therefore, scientists as moral agents carry some responsibility for the language they use and the representations of the world and human nature that they create. From this arise issues about an ethics of representation in science.

Postacademic Science: Obstacles and Dilemmas

The two cultures of science for knowledge and science for profit have begun to merge in recent years by a process that is driven by a complex and as yet poorly understood interplay of social, political, and economic forces that appears irreversible. The following passage (taken from the official press release of the U.S. White House announcing the release of the first draft of the human genome, June 26, 2000) reveals some of the major interests shaping contemporary biomedical science:

> President Clinton, with the British Prime Minister Tony Blair, announced that the international Human Genome Project and Celera Genomics Corporation

have both completed an initial sequencing of the human genome. He congratulated the scientists working in both the public and private sectors on this landmark achievement, which promises to lead to a new era of molecular medicine. . . . He recognized that research and development by biotechnology companies will be key to the translation of human genome sequence data into useful, new health-care products and pledged to strengthen a business environment that will spur research and development in this vital sector. The President also reaffirmed his support for patenting genetic discoveries that have substantial and credible uses. By protecting and rewarding investment in research, consistent with current law, this policy of intellectual property protection will promote rapid conversion of basic knowledge into useful applications. (White House website 2000)

There are no longer any clear demarcation lines between science and business, between academic and industrial science, between basic science and product development, or even between careers in academia and in industry. John Ziman (1998) has called this science enterprise post-academic, since it outwardly preserves many characteristics of academic science but in fact constitutes a hybrid research-business culture where all research stems from problems arising in the context of application. As a consequence, the norms and practices of research in university and industrial settings have converged. Ziman (1998) goes on to argue that postacademic science has features that make nonsense of the traditional barriers between science and ethics. Academic scientists were traditionally expected to follow a code of disinterestedness; in other words, research was to be conducted, presented, and discussed as if it was the product of disembodied minds. Any considerations of the uses to which the knowledge produced might be put, and the possible adverse impact of the research on people, other life forms, or the environment, were not considered appropriate for inclusion in the scientific process. In the professional role assigned to academic scientists, there is no space for values and virtues other than objective, disinterested truth.

This myth of objective truth has of course been thoroughly exploded by several decades of feminist and social critiques of science, and we do not need to consider its fallacy yet again. What is of relevance to the development of the present argument is how this role assignment differs from that of industrial scientists in relation to bioethical considerations. Industrial scientists are much more likely to be directly faced with ethical dilemmas than their academic colleagues. For successful product development, both the interests of their industrial employers and the personal needs and values of customers, patients, and other users have to be taken into account. Yet at the same time, industrial scientists are rarely authorized to address ethical dilemmas arising from their work directly, but are expected to defer this responsibility to their corporate employers. Ziman observes that the two research cultures of academia and industry insulate science from ethics in two distinct ways. On the one hand, academic scientists are supposed to be indifferent to the potential consequences of their work. On the other hand, industrial scientists do work whose consequences are considered too serious to be left in their hands (1998: 1814).

The new phenomenon of the independent scientific entrepreneur who often also maintains an academic appointment creates an additional ethical dilemma. Her or his role combines scientific, ethical, and financial risks. How is the responsibility of the scientist to be defined in this case? How are conflicts between ethical and financial risks to be resolved? Clearly, adherence to an ethos of disinterestedness is not justifiable, but no alternative professional ethos has been developed yet. When these different role prescriptions and dilemmas combine in the new postacademic hybrid culture, an ethical and bioethical void is created.

In the university environment, postacademic culture has created additional new constraints on scientists' agency. Postacademic research is usually carried out in a series of relatively short-term projects funded by external bodies. These funding bodies evaluate research proposals not only on scientific merit but increasingly in terms of their potential for creating wealth. In addition to traditional sources of funding, universities expect researchers to attract industrial funding for contracted research, and seek to exploit any patentable discoveries made by their research staff for maximum financial gain. Knowledge has now become intellectual property, an extremely valuable commodity, and knowledge creation in academia has more overtly than ever been absorbed into the marketplace. It is also significant that projects are increasingly carried out by large networked teams of scientists that collaborate across different disciplines and institutions, and across academia and industry. These collaborations are sometimes of a long-term nature, but often are set up specifically for the attainment of a specific goal and are only short-lived. The particular characteristics of this dispersed and ephemeral organizational structure create their own set of ethical issues. Where does ethical responsibility lie? It is not difficult to see that it can easily result in a fragmented moral space populated by isolated individuals where no one feels a personal obligation to shoulder ethical responsibility.

All of these developments have rapidly and profoundly changed the roles of academic scientists. As science in general, and biomedical science in particular, become increasingly central to society's concerns and its economic aspirations, there is a new social dimension to the practice of science that could support a stronger social and ethical commitment on the part of scientists. However, because the economic stakes are higher now, and there is more to be gained from the knowledge that scientists produce, there is a new constellation of interests that benefit from promoting a hybrid ethos of disinterestedness (from traditional academic research), and deferment of moral agency to the institution (from industrial research). All of these factors combined severely restrict possible roles for scientists in social and ethical discourse.

Rewriting the Script

It is obvious that the meaning society attaches to human genetics already influences personal expectations, institutional practices, and social policies, and will increasingly do so in the future. Therefore, as agents sharing in this redefinition of the human self with other cultural agents, scientists need to be ethically sensitive to the choices they make about the definitions they will support and those they will oppose. However, this kind of discourse is unfamiliar territory for many scientists and is often seen to lie outside their professional role. Given that an orthodox view of scientific agency, centered on a disembodied mind outside of social discourse, does not support such involvement, effective participation may require a reevaluation of the models of agency that are available to scientists.

Such a reevaluation is facilitated by postmodern approaches to moral agency. Drawing on Foucauldian analysis, Susan Hekman reminds us that no one is ever offered only one discourse. We create our self out of the many discourses that are available to us:

On Foucault's account, this self-creation is accomplished through a kind of discursive mix. At any given time we find ourselves confronted with an array of discourses of subjectivity, scripts that we are expected to follow. We can accept the script that is written for us or, alternatively, piece together a different script from other discourses that are extant in our particular circumstances. It is important to note that this concept of subjectivity does not involve an appeal to a core, or essential, self. It is not a matter of "finding" our true, authentic self. Rather, we employ the tools (or scripts) available to us in our situation. Furthermore, our application of these tools is a creative act; it can even be an act of resistance. (Hekman 1995: 82)

Contrary to modernist models, we are not predetermined subjects, with our identity and values fixed prior to our participation in any discourse, but construct our sense of self as we participate in discourses of many kinds. Nonetheless, the individual scientist is not determined by the discourses in which she or he participates. Rather, scientists participate in, and can influence, a number of different discourses through which they (have responsibility to) negotiate what sort of subjectivity they will express. We express moral agency as we decide what sort of subjects we are, how we will position ourselves in history, what social and political projects we commit ourselves to, what practices of power we will participate in and on what terms, and where we will offer resistance to the discourses that would construct our subjectivity.

Moral Agency as Contextualization: Helen Longino's Theoretical Virtues

A scientist wanting to piece together a different script for her or himself has to make choices. These choices become more transparent when taking into account that scientists are both knowledge-producing *and* social agents. If the scientist's role as a producer of knowledge is taken to be one of the focal points of her or his agency, one can ask which kinds of cognitive values support which kind of agency in science practice. Every scientist is familiar with the traditional cognitive values of accuracy, simplicity, internal and external consistency, explanatory power, and fruitfulness. As Helen Longino states, these theoretical values are customarily invoked in theory choice, retrospective appraisal, rationalization of commitments, plausibility assessments, etc., not to mention hallway gossip (1996). This set of values supports traditional scientific agency but excludes moral agency because the values function within the code of disinterestedness.

The moral agency of scientists as knowledge producers is strongly linked to contextualization, i.e., addressing likely consequences of scientific research arising in social, political, ecological, and other contexts. Longino's critique of the assumption that a cognitive value can serve independently of context as a universally applicable criterion of epistemic worth, and her discussion of six "feminist theoretical virtues" (1996: 44–50), offer an alternative approach in support of contextualization. The six theoretical virtues are:

- empirical adequacy
- novelty
- ontological heterogeneity
- mutuality of interaction
- applicability to human needs
- diffusion or decentralization of power

These values are seen as virtues in the sense that they function as qualities of a theory, hypothesis, or model that are regarded as desirable (Longino, 1996). It is worthwhile for our argument to consider the first four as primarily related to the content of theories and models and the last two as related to the effects of adopting a particular theory or model. My central argument is that all six together provide a useful framework for moral agency in science. Space does not permit an extended discussion of Longino's theoretical virtues, but I will briefly highlight their usefulness to first, contextualization in theory or model choice, and second, to social contextualization of research.

Empirical adequacy is a virtue common to both a traditional and alternative set of values. It concerns standards of appropriate research design and statistical methodology, and its relevance to contextualization can be seen in its power to reveal gender, race, and class in the phenomena under study and to make visible gender, race, class, and cultural bias in the interpretation of research.

Novelty is defined by Longino as a quality of models or theories that differ in significant ways from currently accepted ones by attempting to elucidate phenomena that have not been previously studied, by postulating different processes, by adopting different principles of explanation, and, by incorporating alternative models and metaphors. As Longino states,"treating novelty as a virtue reflects a deep skepticism that mainstream theoretical frameworks could be adequate to the problems confronting us, as well as a suspicion of any framework developed in the exclusionary context of modern European and American science" (1996: 46). Novelty as a virtue of theory and model choice encourages scientific creativity in the broadest sense. Regarding contextualization, it supports integration of different knowledge systems across deeply entrenched boundaries, such as research subject–scientist, patient–doctor, community–scientific experts, western–nonwestern, and thus plays a crucial role in addressing social and ethical issues in research. Novelty functions in close conjunction with the virtue of diffusion of power (see later discussion).

Ontological heterogeneity emphasizes respect for specificity and individual differences by insisting on the priority of particulars over abstractions. Barbara McClintock's attention to the individual kernels of a corncob in her studies of genetic mobile elements is a paradigmatic example of this virtue; it enabled her to detect subtle patterns of change that would have remained hidden otherwise. It is important to note that this virtue rejects theories of inferiority. Theories of inferiority grant ontological priority to a particular type chosen as the standard (for example, the average white male, the "normal" gene for a trait.), and all others are seen as failed or incomplete versions. It is easy to see that this virtue has far-reaching implications for the choice of theory and model in human genetics. Its adoption would lead one to pay attention to genetic differences among individuals without imposing a framework of normal versus abnormal or deficient. It supports contextualization through the study of individual entities, be they genes or persons, under specific circumstances.

Mutuality of interaction values theories and models that treat relationships between entities and processes as mutual, avoid causal explanations based on single factors, and take complex interaction as a fundamental principle of explanation. The virtue avoids simple asymmetric models such as the postulation of control genes, or active–passive interaction modes, such as traditional models of fertilization of the "passive" female egg by the "active" male sperm. Instead, it supports models based on networks of dynamic mutual interactions, context sensitivity, and cooperativity rather than control. It too is closely related to the virtue of diffusion of power.

Arguably, these four virtues can be seen to support the moral agency of scientists in their role of knowledge producers by supporting contextualization in theories and models. I now consider the social contexualization of knowledge production as another indispensable requirement. Longino's virtues of *applicability to current human needs* and *diffusion of power*—which are familiar in humanism, if often absent from modernist science—provide just such a framework. The first supports research that meets human and social needs; alleviates pain, suffering, and deprivation; and leads to the improvement of the material conditions of human life. In turn, diffusion of power supports conceptual change by, for example, redefining theories and models employed in midwifery as scientific, developing medical procedures that empower patients to make decisions about their health and treatment options, or by making scientific knowledge accessible to nonscientists.

In order to develop a strategy for ethical and social engagement by scientists, it is vital to extend the virtue of *diffusion of power* beyond its application to theories and models and to place it in the context of social agency on the part of scientists. Moral and social agency go hand in hand. In order to function as a moral agent in society, one needs to make choices about the kinds of relationships one engages in. In the strategy explored here, moral and social agency are understood as intrinsically relational. Social space is seen as embodied in actual human relationships rather than as an abstract vehicle for negotiating interactions and potentially adversarial interests. In order for scientists to fully express ethical engagement, they need to go beyond the traditional boundaries of science practice and reflect on which kinds of social relationships they want to build. Among the many possible options, interdisciplinary alliances, alliances with philosophers and social scientists, and a greater number of partnerships with marginalized groups, groups of diverse cultural backgrounds, and nongovernmental organizations than exist today could create a new kind of deterritorialised social space. Since they are familiar with the processes and dynamics of self-organizing research communities, scientists already have at their disposal collective knowledge about how to create partnerships and networks. Over time, a richly textured, socially inclusive space for ethical discourse could emerge.

Scientists and Art: Going beyond the Boundaries

Another way to create a space for the social contextualization of science would be through alliances with artists who could be very powerful allies for ethically and socially sensitive scientists. With regard to the questions raised earlier about the radical redefinition of the body and the profound change in our self-understanding arising from biomedicine's current preoccupation with genomics, art offers a unique medium for exploration and challenge. Collaborative relationships between artists and scientists might create a social space for critical and ethical engagement with the representations of bodies, diseases, and selves created by genetic medicine, and the medical and cultural practices that result from these representations. The artist John Isaacs maintains that "the fundamental difference between science and art is that the methodology of science describes and institutionalizes the 'other,' while art naturally leans more towards an articulation of 'self'" (Kemp and Wallace 2000: 158). How do positions of objectivity and subjectivity intersect? Where are the tensions, and where are the points of convergence, between disease, as objectified by genomic science, and illness, a person's subjective experience? Is there a clear-cut distinction or is illness at the crossroads of biology, science, and culture?

References to the human body, illness, and medicine have emerged in contemporary art from the 1960s onward, notably in feminist art, and several recent exhibitions have crossed the boundaries between art and science (Kemp and Wallace 2000). Some artists have taken a personal and intimate approach. Jo Spence, whose breast cancer forced her to reevaluate her health and "normal" body, used photography to document the changes that ensued with her illness. Maud Salter filmed her hysterectomy, and John Bellany recorded events around his liver transplant from his hospital bed, using painting and drawing. Other medical themes, such as pregnancy, abortion, brain science, mental illness, AIDS, sickle-cell anemia, muscular dystrophy, the invasion of the body by high-tech medical interventions, and the differences between the physical and emotional impact of disease have also been addressed in recent works (Kemp and Wallace 2000; Brodie 2000). In going beyond the traditional boundaries between art and science, many artists have spent extended periods in residence at scientific institutions. It is now up to scientists to reach out on their part.

Is Biomedicine Ready?

Biomedicine is in a phase of rapid conceptual transformation, driven by the data flooding in from the Human Genome Project and rapid technological change. New questions, new ways of thinking, and new models are being explored, but we are surer about what we have left behind than what we are moving toward. A new global biology is emerging that aims at understanding the systems properties of genomes, cells, and bodies. As concepts of interaction, network, and complexity have taken center stage, the need for context-sensitive, integrative approaches is becoming increasingly apparent. While this appears to signal a significant change, it is important to realize that the deep-rooted stance of control over nature, so pervasive in all of biomedicine, has not been seriously questioned. Integrative approaches are encouraged on the ground that they promise new possibilities for intervention and control. Systems thinking has so far not led to an exploration of biomolecular therapies that seek to cooperate with, rather than control, biological processes. Nevertheless, in the present climate, there is a new openness to conceptual change based on contextualization in theory and model development. Consequently, one can expect Longino's virtues of novelty, ontological heterogeneity, and mutuality of interaction to become more acceptable to mainstream science, although how far the boundaries can be pushed is by no means clear. If such virtues are applied in ways that leave existing power relationships unchallenged, in other words by splitting them from Longino's virtue of diffusion of power, acceptance is probably gained relatively easily. Models of cooperatively acting genes or gene–environment interactions, for example, may find ready support, whereas a disease model that seeks to place genetics, social factors, and patients' experience of the disease on equal terms would most likely face opposition.

Once scientists reach out beyond science practice in the strict sense and seek to express their moral and social agency through nontraditional alliances, they risk a range of reactions from their peers. Some initiatives would be seen as desirable and worthy of support and others would incur negative reactions. What is permissable, even to be encouraged, and what is not, vitally depends on the local culture of the scientific field, institution, and research group an individual scientist finds her or himself in. Questions of power play a role, with different scientific subcultures situating themselves differently in relation to existing power relationships. Diffusion of power, such as by empowerment of marginalized groups, will be regarded then as a value by some and a threat by others, and emerges as the potentially most contested of Longino's virtues. In conclusion, each setting creates its own mix of obstacles and opportunities, and there are no easy or universal answers.

In Closing: A New Zealand Perspective

Having spent a long period of my life in New Zealand, I aim to integrate Longino's virtues with bicultural and postcolonial perspectives in rewriting my own script as a scientist. Living in a bicultural society intrinsically undercuts universal knowledge claims and facilitates the recognition that we need to take an active part in choosing which scripts we follow. Sandra Harding comments that multicultural and bicultural feminists

> show how much communities and individuals have had to learn to negotiate between unequally powerful, conflicting cultures. They have not been permitted the dangerous luxury of assuming that one and only one conceptual framework can provide all the answers in order to survive and flourish. Cognitive dissonance is for them an uncomfortable but necessary and valuable resource for negotiating daily life. (Harding 1996: 271)

Politically mandated biculturalism in New Zealand seeks to enhance and support different voices, different but equal agents, and to address unequal power relations. The Treaty of Waitangi, New Zealand's founding document, defines relations between Maori—the indigenous people of New Zealand—and *pakeha*—the British colonists, their descendants, and people of European descent in general—as a partnership. The concept of partnership ought to be the foundation of all aspects of New Zealand society. Partnership should also extend to the relationship between the two distinct knowledge systems of New Zealand, those of the Maori and of the *pakeha*. Although this dialogue has not been entered into by mainstream *pakeha* scientists in the past, some progress is being made now, as in the exchange among Maori, Pacific Islanders, and *pakeha* scientists and philosophers initiated at a national level in 1995 (Baird 1995); and in the Second National Conference on Women and Science (New Zealand Association for Women in the Sciences 1996). In this process of change currently under way, exclusive eurocentric models of knowledge seeking are required to enter into a dialogue with indigenous ways of knowing.

In no area of science is the need more keenly felt than in the field of human genetics. Maori culture understands the gene in ways radically different from these of western science, as Aroha Mead's writing shows clearly:

> A physical gene is imbued with a life spirit handed down from the ancestors, contributed to by each successive generation, and passed on to future generations. Maori have two terms to describe a human gene, both of which are interlaced with a broader reality than western scientific definitions. The first is *ira tangata*, which is the actual word for a gene and translates as "life spirit of mortals." The second term is *whakapapa*, which means to set layer upon layer. It also means genealogy and is the word most commonly used by Maori to conceptualize genes and DNA. (Mead 1996: 47)

Whakapapa is an immensely rich concept; it encompasses the physical heritage of the ancestors as well as the the cultural values and beliefs, languages, histories, spirituality, and relationship to the land of the Maori (Mead 1996). It is a relational, nonessentialist concept. *Whakapapa*—setting layer upon layer—in all its dimensions reminds us of what we are in danger of losing by genetic reconstructions of our humanity; we are in danger of losing our agency in genetic reconfigurations. We become a-cultural programs with no place to stand, no place to act from. Genetic essentialism reduces us to a disembodied, uprooted abstraction that is utterly dispossessed of agency and human creativity. Agency and creativity depend on the particular and the embodied, the lived experience and the lived history; they depend on *whakapapa*.

I have argued that the choice of the scripts we follow as scientists, the metaphors and models we adopt, are ethical choices. Choosing to engage with the concept of *whakapapa*, a rich and multidimensional sense of being human, invites reflection on which kind of bioscience would be facilitated in the course of such a dialogue. Which direction would the study of human genomes take? How would it differ from a science influenced by metaphors that describe humans as genetic programs? How would our vision of our future societies, of ourselves, and of medicine be shaped by an epistemology that sees all cultures and all people as equal partners in our search for a reflexive self-knowledge?

What do we, as western scientists, have to offer as a basis for such a dialogue for change? At the beginning of the chapter, I claimed that a new integrative medicine depended on cultural transformation from within the West as much as on openness to other ways of knowing. In working toward such a transformation in medicine, postmodernism continues to provide both support and creative challenge for me. For example, I see many connections between relational, contextual concepts in postmodernism and those embodied in *whakapapa*, which could facilitate a dialogue across cultural boundaries. Furthermore, where technology has been instrumental in creating modernist text metaphors and metanarratives of the human genome, and representations of bodies as machines, these issues can be critiqued from a postmodern standpoint. However, in order to transform representations of the patient currently being created by postgenomic medicine, by integrating cross-cultural insights (as well as patients' narratives of disease and recovery), engagement with postmodernism needs to occur at a much deeper level. My interest here centers on postmodern ideas regarding embodiment, the collection of signs that make up human bodies, and the possible roles of information technologies. Within the next decade, we will witness the synthesis of large amounts of medical data, such as in simulations of whole body systems or even "virtual patients" over global grids linking supercomputers around the world. It is possible to envisage the use of these technologies as a medium for integration far beyond the boundaries of current biomedicine, and this is still largely unexplored by postmodernism.

References

Baird, Deborah et al. (1995) "Whose Genes Are They Anyway?" in *Report from the Health Research Council on Human Genetic Information*. Wellington, New Zealand: Health Research Council of New Zealand. Available at: www.hrc.gov.nz/assets/pdfs/publications/whosegenes.pdf

Brodie, David (2000) *It's In Your Head*. London: Spacetime Publications.

Depew, David J., and Weber, Bruce H. (1996) *Darwinism Evolving: System Dynamics and the Genealogy of Natural Selection*. Cambridge, Mass.: MIT Press.

Haraway, Donna J. (1997) *Modest_Witness@Second_Millennium.FemaleMan@_Meets_OncoMouse@@*. New York: Routledge.

Harding, Sandra (1996) "Multicultural and Global Feminist Philosophies of Science: Resources and Challenges," in *Feminism, Science, and the Philosophy of Science*, Lynn Hankinson Nelson and Jack Nelson (eds.). London: Kluwer Academic, pp. 263–287.

Hekman, Susan J. (1995) *Moral Voices, Moral Selves: Carol Gilligan and Feminist Moral Theory*. University Park, Pa.: Pennsylvania State University Press.

Keller, Evelyn (1992) *Secrets of Life, Secrets of Death*. New York and London: Routledge.

Kemp, Martin, and Wallace Marina (2000) *Spectacular Bodies: The Art and Science of the Human Body from Leonardo to Now*. London: Hayward Gallery.

Lee, Pat S., and Lee, Kelvin H. (2000) "Genomic analysis," *Current Opinions in Biotechnology* 11: 171–175.

Longino, Helen E. (1996) "Cognitive and non-cognitive values in science: Rethinking the dichotomy," in *Feminism, Science, and the Philosophy of* Science, Lynn Hankinson Nelson and Jack Nelson (eds.) London: Kluwer Academic, pp. 39–58.

Lovelock, James E. (1979) *Gaia: A New Look at Life on Earth*. Oxford: Oxford University Press.

Margulis, Lynn, and Sagan, Dorion (1995) *What Is Life?* London: Weidenfeld & Nicolson.

Martin, Emily (1991) "The egg and the sperm: How science has constructed a romance based on stereotypical male-female roles," *Signs* 16: 485–501.

Mead, Aroha Te Pareake (1996) "Genealogy, sacredness, and the commodities market," *Cultural Survival Quarterly* Summer 1996: 46–51.

New Zealand Association for Women in the Sciences (1996) *Proceedings of Women, Science and Our Future*. Wellington, New Zealand: NZ Association for Women in the Sciences.

Spanier, Bonnie B. (1995) *Im/partial Science: Gender Ideology in Molecular Biology*. Bloomington and Indianapolis: Indiana University Press.

White House website (2000) President Clinton announces the completion of the first survey of the entire human genome. Available at http://www.whitehouse.gov/WH/New/html/20000626.html.

Ziman, John (1998) "Why must scientists become more ethically sensitive than they used to be?" *Science* 282: 1813–1815.

9

Reproductive Technology and the Political Limits of Care

Carol Bacchi and Chris Beasley

The ethics of care is a prominent theme in feminist ethics. References to "care" and relatedly to "connectedness" can also be found increasingly in mainstream ethical debates,[1] in bioethical theorizing (Martin 1999; Koski 2000), and in policy documents that deal with aspects of biotechnology affecting reproductive technology (Royal Commission, 1993a,b). Such references suggest that care ethics represents a site of feminist influence and intervention in the growing arena of biotechnological innovation. On the one hand, these developments may appear to signal a kind of triumph for feminism, a degree of success in challenging rationalist and objectivist approaches to thinking in these areas. On the other hand, an examination of some of these contributions indicates that there are good reasons to be wary of the turn to care.

First, we suggest that the focus on interpersonal morality and individual moral development in most proponents of an ethics of care (hereafter referred to as care ethicists) indicates a limitation to its political usefulness. Care ethicists tend in the main to describe care as a moral virtue possessed by some individuals. They typically assume that people who learn to care in one-to-one relationships will bring a humane concern to the design of social arrangements locally, nationally, and even internationally. At the same time they disavow rule setting as narrow, bureaucratic, and instrumental (Sevenhuijsen 1998).

We find the distinction between individual and interpersonal moral character and the creation of rules unhelpful in that moral rules continue to be made, in law and in legislation. Developments in biotechnology have produced a proliferation of rules, emanating from institutional ethics committees, select committees, and royal commissions, for example, and doubtless these will increase as new questions arise about permissible uses of these technologies. Establishing a barrier between moral vision on the one hand and procedures or rules on the other, leaves little space to reflect upon the conditions that could produce more ethical policy decisions in these and other areas.

Second, there are difficulties with the leap in faith from caring for intimate others to humane social visions. A move from care for particular others to a concern for distant others suggests that all forms of interconnection are in some sense alike and are transferable, which may be difficult to sustain. A further problem arises in relation to the emphasis on feelings such as empathy and compassion. Although it is prompted by a concern with interdependence, such an emphasis paradoxically is inclined to produce another variant of individualistic ethics—that is, a moral actor motivated by concern for others replaces the rational actor operating out of self-interest.

Third, the reliance on appeals to feelings like sympathy and compassion gives care an overly and narrowly prescriptive normative character. This is ironic, given that care ethicists reject rule- or principle-based ethical theories precisely on the grounds of their universal claims. Furthermore, the prescriptive orientation of care ethics is advanced despite the rather woolly meaning of its core term, "care." The consequence of this conjunction of a prescriptive moral agenda and an uncertain meaning for care is sometimes dubious political outcomes. We offer examples from reproductive policy in Canada and Australia to show that care can be used to justify political programs that many care ethicists would find problematic and even disturbing.

More specifically, we argue that the normative content within the care paradigm is in conflict with claims that an ethics of care emphasizes the importance of context in ethical decision making. Here, we draw upon research into the experiences of users of reproductive technologies to place in doubt some central tenets associated with the ethics of care; that is, connectedness, relationships, and particular others. These voices lead us to conclude that contrary to the claims of care ethicists, the ethics of care evokes quite limited notions of specificity and difference. While the insistence on the importance of context sounds postmodern, care ethicists deal only with quite specific contexts—those to do with their interpretations of the concerns of dependent and vulnerable others.

Finally, we examine themes associated with the ethics of care—the challenge to the possibility of impartiality, the sensitivity to human interconnectedness, the place of emotion in human decision making—to make preliminary recommendations for reshaping bioethical decision-making practices. Instead of trying to shape individual moral actors, we suggest putting in place strategies that allow differences to emerge.

Caring for Others: Starting from Interpersonal and Individual Morality

It is important to note at the outset that the main contributors to the development of an ethics of care, at least initially, were social psychologists and moral philosophers. In a sense this background explains their focus on interpersonal morality and individual moral character (Young 1995). However, each of the authors considered here explicitly reflects upon the implications of her approach for collective social organization. Hence, it is relevant to consider the kinds of claims they make regarding this area of political action.

Carol Gilligan (1982), a social psychologist, launched a major challenge to Lawrence Kohlberg's "levels of moral development." In Kohlberg's model, women tended to cluster at level three, which tied moral decision making to relationships with particular (meaning intimate) others, while men tended to dominate level six, where general principles for moral decision making were generated. In Gilligan's view, this implied that justice-based principled decision making was a higher level of moral development than the kind of responsiveness to relationships supposedly evinced by women. Gilligan wanted to show, not simply that there are other ways of evaluating moral development, but that by excluding a consideration of gender, Kohlberg had narrowed his understanding of possible legitimate moral responses. "Care" became a shorthand for both a sensitivity to context and a willingness to consider the preservation of relationships as a moral priority.

Susan Hekman argues that there are two ways to read Gilligan. In one reading Gilligan is challenging the possibility of truth in the area of moral psychology since "implicit in Gilligan's articulation of the different voice is the assumption that what we, as listeners, hear is a function of the interpretive framework we use" (Hekman 1995: 7). In a second reading, according to Hekman, Gilligan wants to defend the "truth" and validity of care as a moral virtue. This tension between an epistemological claim about the impossibility of impartiality and hence of universal abstract norms, and the desire to direct attention to particular aspects of people's lives—their need for care and their position in relationships—runs throughout debates about the validity of an ethics of care. The first position can be associated with a postmodern insistence on the situatedness of all knowledge; the second fits uncomfortably with this claim since it posits a prescriptive normative value for a particular moral behavior called care.

Kohlberg meanwhile claimed that his level six was meant to indicate, not superior moral development, but that "the universal principles he defines are more likely to resolve moral problems" (in Hekman 1995: 28). In effect this argument reinforces the judgment of classical and modern philosophers alike. It reiterates the judgment that women are incapable of principled decision making, which is detached and hence rational, because of their emotional commitments to particular others (Lloyd 1983).

While the dispute between Gilligan and Kohlberg is revealing in terms of gender bias, a conflation of debates is evident. Are these interlocutors talking about personal moral character as evinced in our immediate relationships, or are they talking about the possibility (or impossibility) of ethical collective decision making? In Brian Barry's (1995: 191–194) view, summarized by Held (2001: 69), care ethicists and procedural theorists, like Rawls, are talking about different problems. This is because second-order impartiality theories, like Rawls' theory of justice, are "designed for judging institutions, not the actions of persons in personal situations." Recognizing a conflation of issues here does not, however, mean coming down on the side of Barry and Kohlberg. It does not mean accepting that abstract principles are preferable because they facilitate the kinds of decisions around law and policy that are necessary to run a society. Rather, identifying the tension between a focus on interpersonal (one-to-one) morality and a search for ethical means of institutional design suggests that we need to consider the possibility that the analyses offered by care ethicists have limited relevance for making law and policy.

Indeed, for the most part, care ethicists themselves appear ambivalent about the applicability of their insights to realms beyond the interpersonal. Gilligan's examples are all at a "close-up" scale—children playing games, adolescents forming relationships, and women making abortion decisions—and are described in interpersonal terms. Nevertheless, she wants to imply that the kinds of decision making that go on in these settings could offer an alternative model for decision making in law and the public domain. She criticizes adversarial models in law, and notes that the male model of decision making associated with "the legal elaboration of rules and the development of fair procedures for adjudicating disputes" is considered better "since it fits the requirements for modern corporate success" (Gilligan 1982: 10). By contrast, her analysis is based upon the dynamics generated in affiliative relationships and on the production of a singular caring individual. It is at best unclear why or how this would be transferable, let alone produce a "premise of nonviolence—that no one should be hurt" beyond that realm (Gilligan 1982: 174).

Sara Ruddick attempts to elaborate the nature of the connection between attention to particular others in one's own life and an attitude of concern for those more distant, for strangers. Her hope is that the practices of attending to children generate "conditions of respect for unpredictable and as yet unimagined difference and variety among and within people" (Ruddick 1990: 134). In this interpretation, maternal practice becomes a natural resource for peace politics. Her example is the *Madres* of Argentina.

> They (the *Madres*) did not "transcend" their particular loss and love; particularity was the emotional root and source of their protest. It is through acting on that particularity that they extended mothering to include sustaining and protecting any people whose lives are blighted by violence. (Ruddick 1990: 232).

There is still a good deal here that remains assumed rather than explained. The mechanisms by which or the channels through which this transference from particular others to a general concern for nonviolence takes place continue to be taken for granted and are not spelled out. This is especially open to question, given Ruddick's willingness to acknowledge the parochialism and indeed violence often associated with protecting one's children (Ruddick 1990). More important, the emphasis on individual moral character suggests that connectedness is much the same in any social sphere and, in particular, that politics is simply a matter of individual conviction and commitment whatever the setting.

Virginia Held has a similar preoccupation with the ways in which a person's social practices produce a particular kind of moral character. She agrees with Ruddick that "the content of mothering can be a fruitful source of insight concerning how peace should be sought in other domains" (Held 1993: 39). To her credit, she confronts head-on the question of how and whether concern for flesh and blood others can become a broader consideration for those more distant from us. On this point she concludes that it is transferable, but is rather more circumspect than Ruddick about the extent of its transferability:

> [W]e have limited resources for caring. We cannot care for everyone or do everything that a caring approach suggests. We need moral guidelines for ordering our priorities. Though the hunger of our own children comes before the hunger of children we do not know, the hunger of children in Africa ought to come before some of the expensive amusements we may feel like providing for our own children. Her suggestion is that making links between intimate relationships and relationships with those more distant is about limited alteration of individual priorities, such as diverting money from luxuries for our children to sending money to Oxfam. (Held 1993: 74).

Such recommendations are hardly limited to the care paradigm. More to the point, it is very difficult to see how this example can generate a revised vision of sociopolitical life.[2]

Here we take issue, not necessarily with Held's conclusion, but with what follows from it. She elaborates that in her view this moral commitment to particular others means that care ethics has its own domain, a domain separate from law and legalistic approaches (Held 2001). Her concern then is not to challenge the rule of law, but to assert that "the perspective of universal rules should be limited to the domain of law, rather than expected to serve for the whole of morality" (2001: 77). Lawrence Kohlberg said something very similar in his reply to Gilligan—that the focus on care and responsibility was indeed appropriate in familial domestic settings, but not outside these (in Gilligan 1982: 18). In this interpretation care ethics has a limited domain, the private, set by its own proponents (Tronto 1993).

Others who endorse versions of care ethics also set at odds "the male fixation on the special skill of drafting legislation" and attention to relations of care and trust (Baier in Held, 1993: 86). Rosemary Tong draws a similar conclusion regarding bioethics. She does not want bioethics to become "just a subfield of law—another rule, regulation, and policy generating enterprise" (Tong 1996: 89). Rather she wants it "to help vulnerable people work through complex issues of choice, control and caring." In the same vein, she argues "we do not need more policies dealing with any 'agent x' but more hands-on approaches for communicating and connecting with each particular patient" (1996: 89). Here it seems that Tong wants to remain specifically within the domain of conventional clinical bioethics, doctor–patient relationships. The question we are asking is whether care ethics has any relevance for those *policies* that will be created to handle biotechnological developments.

Will Kymlicka (1993) specifies new reproductive technologies (NRTs) as one area where the ethics for policy is somewhat distinct from doctor–patient ethical issues. Following Kymlicka, issues requiring judgment and decision that involve a social rather than a primarily clinical or professional ethical dimension would also include all the recent debates about surrogacy, access of lesbians and/or single women to assisted insemination (AI) and in vitro fertilization (IVF), cloning, research on stem cells, and so on. The list is long and expanding. And of course there is a long history of policies with an ethical component that goes beyond professional protocols. Abortion and euthanasia immediately spring to mind. In fact, it is difficult to think of a policy issue that does not have this kind of broad ethical dimension. It follows, to our mind, that it is impossible and indeed unethical not to examine the bases of decision making in this area. However, it seems that care ethicists in the main (exceptions follow later) have little to say about policy. Indeed their focus on individual moral character and/or on one-to-one interactions indicates a limited engagement with or interest in political processes, not just in the strict traditional sense of governance, but in the sense most feminists employ; that is, they display an oddly restricted concern with power relations in society.

Recognizing the Other: From One-to-One to Distant Others

It is important to recognize that care ethicists deal with questions that are dominating a good deal of ethical debate today—the nature of moral responsibility and ethical techniques of the self. Indeed, influential postmodern philosophers are finding versions of care attractive as a grounding for ethical relationships. Emmanuel Levinas (in Bernasconi and Critchley 1991) and Zygmunt Bauman (2001a,b), for example, have attempted to take a concern with interdependence from the realm of the particular to that of distant and different others. These approaches have received careful and at times highly critical scrutiny among feminists studying ethics (see Irigaray 1991; Russell 2000; Bell 2001).

For Levinas, human interdependence indicates an ethical responsibility that precedes politics. This is because the existence of others makes "being" possible. Theorizing ethical responsibility in this way has meant that Levinas is seen as "on the side of the other." Sarah Ahmed questions the possibility of taking the other's side "through philosophical language" (Ahmed 2000: 142). In her view, the way in which the other, the stranger, is abstracted from particular others produces the stranger as a fetish.[3] This reification is also evident in Levinas' use of the mother–child dyad as a means to configure our responsibility to others. Moreover, his use of the mother–child dyad neglects the many feminist concerns regarding the characterization of the nature of the mother–child relationship as prepolitical, and in particular the tendency to glorify maternal self-sacrifice (Borgerson 2001).

Bauman bases his hope for a postmodern ethics in the ambiguity surrounding individuals today, which leads, he suggests, to a greater willingness to consider the stranger within and hence the stranger without.[4] Once critical of care talk as paternalistic (Bauman 2001a), the language of care is finding its way into his more recent writings:

> [I]f there is to be a community in the world of individuals, it can only be (and it needs to be) a community woven together from sharing and mutual care, a community of concern and responsibility for the equal right to be human and the equal ability to act on that right. (Bauman 2001b: 149–150).

While these sentiments are laudable, it is at best unclear what is to generate such a community.

It can be argued, moreover, that in quite different ways Levinas and care ethicists produce a version of the personal versus political in the sense that politics is placed outside the realm of (personal) ethics.[5] This distinction is paradoxical since it is at odds with their claim to offer a new vision for a social life, not just a way of dealing with intimates.

In contrast to Levinas, we would concur with Held that intimate relationships are not necessarily straightforwardly replicable with strangers. However, we do not think that this in any way supports the view, promulgated in different ways by both Levinas and Held, that personal ethics are distinct from and opposed to politics in the sense of systematized social or public policy or rules. Rather, we suggest the issue is one of maintaining a critical agenda regarding interpersonal morality and interpersonal connectedness, including a cautious view of its transferability as a guide to decision making at a community, national, or international level.

Political Caring: Broadening Interconnection, Enhancing the Possibilities of Care

Political theorists Joan Tronto (1993, 2001) and Selma Sevenhuijsen (1997, 1998) have attempted to deal directly with the limitations of a moral philosophy version of the ethics of care. They insist that feminists need to stop thinking about care as a moral disposition. Rather, care ought to be seen as an important social practice that should be considered in political deliberations about institutional responses to need. This move shifts the discussion from one-to-one caring relationships to institutional caring arrangements, in this way challenging the kind of public and private boundary reinforced by the "domain relativism" of Held and others (Hekman 1995). Tronto (2001) states explicitly that care is a collective, not an individual, responsibility.

We would certainly agree that it is important to get the effort expended in physical and emotional nurturance recognized by public institutions (see Beasley and Bacchi 2000). Nonetheless, how this should be accomplished remains very much a matter of debate. Sevenhuijsen (1998) recommends that governments create the space for men to be caring by ensuring that they have the resources, including the time, to care, instead of coming down on one side or the other in child custody disputes. By the same token, however, some versions of fathers' rights could be and are often defended in the language of children's needs, a possible interpretation of care (Shanley, 1997). The Dutch health document that Sevenhuijsen so effectively deconstructs could also be defended on the grounds that a caring society is one that dispenses health resources wisely. In fact, the document builds its argument on a vision of collective need versus selfish individual preferences (Sevenhuijsen 1997). With care as our yardstick of ethical practice, we remain very much in the realm of interpretation. Sevenhuijsen is well aware of this, as reflected in her careful phrasing of the possibilities of care: "[T]he feminist ethics of care *might* be able to provide new perspectives on the politics of custody, provided that it is carefully *interpreted*" (Sevenhuijsen 1998: 107; emphasis added). This, of course, implies that you accept her interpretation.

Sevenhuijsen elaborates a slightly different position in her defense of care as a viewpoint, a pair of spectacles with which to approach social issues, which requires the cultivation of epistemological virtues—attentiveness, responsibility, responsiveness, and the commitment to see issues from differing perspectives (1997). While there is something useful in this shift in attention from the presumed nurturing activities of caring to a scrutiny of one's way of approaching political issues, the focus of attention remains the individual actor. In this version, a moral actor is one who judges with care.

Sevenhuijsen's larger goal is to try and create "rhetorical and discursive space for moral narratives of care, which are marginalized in dominant discourses" (1998: 60). In effect she wishes to put on the agenda a "politics of care interpretation" (1998: 60) to match Nancy Fraser's (1989) "politics of needs interpretation." The question then becomes, does adding care to the range of rhetorics expand the debate in useful ways? We suggest not. In fact, we will argue that the common alignment between care and family and indeed between care and women makes the rhetoric more dangerous than useful.

What Has Care Got to Do with It?: Its Prescriptive, Normative Associations

Sevenhuijsen admits that "all definitions of care contain normative dimensions" (1998: 22). This normative component takes a particular shape. It evokes a sense of compassion or sympathy. As we noted previously, when care ethicists venture beyond one-to-one relationships, it is with the hope that people can learn to care about distant others (see Tong 1993; Tronto 1993). This is their singular policy guideline. We have already discussed the limited usefulness of this message for policy making. Here we consider some of the dangers associated with endorsing care as a political norm. Our examples come from contemporary policy proposals in the area of reproductive technology.

The 1993 Canadian Royal Commission on the New Reproductive Technologies adopted the title *Proceed with Care* for its report as an indicator of a commitment to the ethics of care. In a separate volume on the ethical aspects of new reproductive technologies, Will Kymlicka (1993) included the ethics of care as an important ethical theory. The commission's report and accompanying volumes thus offer a litmus test for the political uses and limits of care.

In the first instance, it is clear that those associated with the commission did not agree on what an ethics of care meant or on its usefulness. In an introductory section to the final report, the commissioners declared their adoption of an ethics of care *over* "overarching ethical frameworks like utilitarianism or social contract theory" (Royal Commission 1993a: 50). In direct contrast, Kymlicka asserts that the ethics of care is a theory *akin to* utilitarianism, and he is scathing in detailing its problems. Chief among these, he argues, is its lack of specificity, so that care can be associated with any number of positions on key bioethical issues.

> For example, some proponents of the ethic of care say that once we focus on the importance of relationships, rather than competing rights, public policy should treat the pregnant woman and her fetus as a single unit and not restrict the woman's rights in the name of the fetus. Others, however, argue that a concern for relationships and responsibilities suggests that the law should impose a "duty of care" on pregnant women to protect the fetus. (Kymlicka 1993: 10).

He argues that since concepts such as care are so hard to interpret, theorists who work in the area of applied ethics need to devise a set of more concrete, middle-level rules that focus "on more specific and tangible human interests, such as people's desire for autonomy and the need to prevent harm" (Kymlicka 1993: 10). Kymlicka's comment on the possible varied interpretations of care is useful, although we fail to see anything more tangible or middle-level in the principles he proposes.

Despite Kymlicka's critique, the final report recognizes the shaping influence of a "version" of the ethics of care that "fosters care and community" and that "seeks to prevent adversarial situations whenever possible" (Royal Commission 1993a: 50). On these grounds the report condemns commercial surrogacy and accepts regulated altruistic surrogacy. In each case the woman "gestating and giving birth" is declared "the legal mother of the resulting child" (Royal Commission 1993a: 50). While some readers might be in sympathy with these recommendations, the terms of the argument need to be considered. Are commercial surrogacy arrangements any more likely to generate conflictual relationships than so-called altruistic ones? This is at least debatable (see Lessor 1993). More important, should bioethical determinations be based on avoiding conflict and preserving relationships? We want to ask, are there not times when conflict is appropriate and necessary, especially if exploitation or coercion is occurring?; and which relationships deserve to be preserved? The executive summary of the report declared,

> [h]aving children and healthy families are important goals to most Canadians: but some people cannot reach those goals without help. If there are technologies that can be used to help, a caring society should provide these. (Royal Commission 1993a: xxxi)

We draw attention to the presumptions lodged within this statement about the value of children and families, and the government's role in encouraging the production of more of these. Along similar lines, a paper setting out the brief of the Law Reform Commission of Canada to the Royal Commission stated that the role of government is "to nurture procreative and family health" (Jones 1992: 121). To its credit, the Royal Commission comes down in favor of lesbian and/or single women's access to AI and IVF, but it stops short of endorsing access for postmenopausal women. In other words, the ethics of care is being used to bolster a particular normative societal vision.

Furthermore, it is clear that endorsement of relationships and of care often lines up with traditional conceptions of family and sexuality. For example, the submission of the Canadian Medical Association to the Royal Commission criticized the growing emphasis in our society on individual autonomy, which they call "a granular view of people." An alternative is offered: "no biological organism . . . exists in isolation" (Royal Commission). On these grounds it is argued that "a healthy organism is one that is capable" of reproducing itself (1993a: 74). In these terms infertility is declared to be a biological problem and the "social infertility" of lesbian and/or single women is denied (Kluge and Lucock 1991).

Feminists should be particularly sensitive to the ways in which appeals to care, relationships, and even to human interconnectedness have been and can be used to control women and sexuality. In our research on AI in New South Wales, the need for a husband's consent to the procedure is justified on an understanding that "promotion and support of the heterosexual and married family is a justifiable policy for the legislature to adopt" (NSW Law Reform 1984: 34). This conclusion is reached despite the recognition that such a requirement "would be a diminution of the wife's personal autonomy and human rights" (NSW Law Reform 1984: 34).

We noted at the outset increasing references in bioethical theorizing to care and connectedness. Our concern is the way in which these terms tend to line up with references to family and community without any discussion of the normative assumptions these necessarily imply. In a recent issue of the *Journal of Law, Medicine & Ethics*, Greg Koski counters "principlism" with "connectedness," a notion he traces to "so-called 'feminist principles'."

> While making decisions in a detached manner may foster great objectivity and impartiality—the hallmarks of principle-based decision making—it can ignore the broader impact of those actions and decisions on loved ones, family, community and even society at large. (Koski 2000: 330–331)

No care ethicist could wish for more! Our point is that the level of generalization leaves as a real concern which kinds of families and which community concerns will be considered legitimate (see Burkitt 1999).

If care is a vague precept open to interpretation and use (Bacchi, 1996), we have to consider just what is risked by wedding our ethical proposals to it. A more useful exercise, following the advice of Nicola Lacey (1995), would be to map the ways in which care is interpreted and applied in particular contexts. Of course, the risk of misuse might be outweighed by the greater sensitivity to alterity that some care ethicists claim will follow from cultivating a caring perspective (Ruddick 1990; Sevenhuijsen 1998). We now intend to challenge this proposition, using surrogacy to illustrate the limits to recognizing difference in care approaches.

The Problematic Particularities of Care: What is Context?

Early critics of care ethics drew attention to the way in which the focus on the mother–child dyad reinforced traditional assumptions about mothers' responsibities for caring for their young (Tong 1993). A new dimension is added to these criticisms by developments in reproductive technology around surrogacy, which make it increasingly difficult to identify "the" mother in a relationship. Indeed, key bioethical debates are generated by exactly this question. Should the gestational mother or the genetic mother or the social mother be recognized as primary, and/or are these categories relevant to the users of the technology (Goslinga-Roy 2000)? The suggestion that the social mother should be favored since she actually does the caring does not seem to help, given the number of feminists who insist that gestation itself generates a caring relationship (see Held 1987). This is certainly the presumption that informed the recommendation of the Canadian Royal Commission:

> [C]ommercial preconception arrangements commodify women's reproductive functions and place women in the situation of alienating aspects of themselves that should be inherently inalienable. A preconception contract obliges the gestational mother to sell an intimate aspect of her human functioning. (Royal Commission 1993a: 683–684)

Is this always so? This position appears to be based on assumptions about biological connection that are at least open to debate. If we listen to the voices of some of the users of biotechnologies, this certainly seems to be the case.

In this context, Helena Ragoné relates the stories of gestational surrogates who state that they prefer gestational surrogacy because "they are uncomfortable with the prospect of contributing their own ovum" (1998: 120). Black gestational surrogates feel even less connectedness if they produce a child of a race different from themselves (Ragoné 1998). Meredith Michaels (1996) relates stories of surrogates that suggest that surrogacy can open up the possibility of special relationships between women, bypassing men. Instead of adjudicating which form of family or mother should win, Warnke (1994) suggests that the law should facilitate and help us deal with the multiple relationships within which we find ourselves. These examples reinforce the proposition that biotechnology produces a cultural revolution that creates new cultural forms, while at the same time demonstrating "how vexed the meaning of 'flesh of my flesh' has always been" (Brodwin 2000: 13).

By contrast, care ethics in theory (Held 1987) and in application (Royal Commission, 1993a) tends to be associated with conventional understandings of family and biological connection. This indicates a limit to the claim that the approach fosters sensitivity to difference and context. Instead of challenging the impossibility of impartiality, we find that care ethicists in the main pay heed only to particular particularities, those to do with their interpretations of dependence and vulnerability. Iris Young identifies the project of care ethicists more precisely: "[t]he ethic of care emphasizes *contextualized issues of harm and suffering* rather than a morality of abstract principle" (Young 1995: 115; emphasis added). Delineating a kind of context that demands attention conflicts with the postmodern insistence that all knowledge is situated and every contextual factor is relevant. Indeed, the postmodern view of the importance of context means that "the search for systematic norms of epistemic evaluation, in morals or elsewhere, may seem seriously misguided" (Campbell and Hunter 2000: 24).

While it is important that care ethicists have put particular lived bodies on the agenda and challenged the dominant bioethical representation of bodies as "gross material" (Shildrick 1997), they retain assumptions about natural biological connections that are deeply problematic. Moreover, even in their broadest and most useful form (Sevenhuijsen 1998; Tronto 2001), care ethicists deal only with quite specific aspects of embodiment—those to do with bodily maintenance and nurturance. Bioethical debates require a broader conception of embodied (inter)subjectivity.

Social Flesh in an Ethical Third Space[6]: An Alternative Maneuver

This leads us to put forward a different ethical project, one that picks up the challenge to the possibility of impartiality and the attention to lived bodies, but one that is less prescriptively normative. Our focus is precisely the realm abandoned by care ethicists, the space within which rules governing biotechnologies get discussed and decided. Our goal is to address the conditions that would be most likely to produce guidelines responsive to the varied contexts of experience.

Currently this decision-making space is dominated by particular voices, primarily those of professionals (Shildrick 1997). We believe that it is important to challenge the privileged status granted these voices. To this end we endorse the need to make visible "the subjectivity of the socially powerful participants" (Nicholas 2001: 59). In addition, we support a broadening of the decision-making constituency to include lay participants in biomedicine, including the direct users of biotechnologies (see Saetnan 2000).

However, we would want to caution against a version of subjects as "talking heads" making choices. It is crucial to recognize all participants as embodied and to take into account the ways in which embodiment affects the views expressed. We offer the notion of "social flesh" as a way to talk about the complex nature of the interaction among embodiment, social processes, and subjectivity (Beasley and Bacchi 2000). The notion of social flesh offers a challenge to the dominant language of consumer participation, which produces debates about the uses of biotechnologies as matters of individual choice. It also pays heed to significant differences in position along a number of axes, including both those more commonly identified, such as gender, race, class, disability, and sexual orientation, and those less commonly noted, such as distinctions between users and nonusers, and between the articulate and relatively silent ill (see Broom, 2001).

We do not claim that this approach to bioethical decision making is easy or straightforward. Hunter (2001) indicates as much in her warnings about ease of cooption and manipulation. This should not, in our view, be used as a rationale for adopting principle-based approaches that pretend that impartiality is possible and the ultimate aim. The chief defense of principle-based approaches is that they facilitate decision making. A more democratic response would acknowledge that decision making in the contested areas around biotechnology should *not* be easy, and that encouraging dissent may be more important than finding a simple solution. An ethic of "care" to our mind also tries to find a simple solution, and this indicates its most notable failing. As long as care is associated with attempts to install a particular value framed by a conception of interpersonal relations as a guide to political action, it is open to abuse and its applicability is necessarily limited.

Notes

1. In the fourth edition of their *Principles of Biomedical Ethics* (1994: 85–92) Tom Beauchamp and James Childress note that, "the care ethic provides a needed corrective" (Beauchamp and Childress in Wolf 1995: 15).

2. In a more recent contribution, Held again opts for the favoring of one-to-one flesh-and-blood relationships over consideration for strangers (Held 2001).

3. By particular others, Ahmed means living people as opposed to abstractions. By contrast, most care ethicists use the term "particular others" in the sense of intimates.

4. Ahmed's point concerning the abstracted and hence fetishized character of the conception of a stranger applies here as well.

5. Levinas' "hiatus" between ethics and politics accomplishes exactly this; the assumption is that politics is always manipulation (Bell 2001).

6. We borrow this term from Homi Bhabha (1995) to set the stage for thinking about the conditions that would produce a genuine possibility of exchange of views.

References

Ahmed, S. (2000) *Strange Encounters*. London: Routledge.

Bacchi, C. (1996) *The Politics of Affirmative Action*. London: Sage.

Bacchi, C., and Beasley, C. (2002) "Citizen Bodies: Is embodied citizenship a contradiction in terms?" *Critical Social Policy* 22(2): 324–352.

Barry, B. (1989) *Justice as Impartiality*. Berkeley: University of California Press.

Bauman, Z. (2001a) *The Individualized Society*. Cambridge, UK: Polity.

Bauman, Z. (2001b) *Community: Seeking Safety in an Insecure World*. Cambridge, UK: Polity.

Beasley, C., and Bacchi, C. (2000) "Citizen bodies: Embodying citizens—A feminist analysis," *International Feminist Journal of Politics* 2(3): 337–358.

Beauchamp, T., and Childress, J. (1994) *Principles of Biomedical Ethics.* New York: Oxford University Press.

Bell, V. (2001) "On ethics and feminism: Reflecting on Levinas' ethics of non-(in)difference," *Feminist Theory* 2(2): 159–171.

Bernasconi, R., and Critchley, S. (eds.) (1991) *Re-Reading Levinas.* Bloomington: Indiana University Press.

Bhabha, H. (1995) "Cultural diversity and cultural differences," in B. Ashcroft, G. Griffiths, and H. Tiffin (eds.), *The Post-Colonial Studies Reader.* London: Routledge. pp. 206–209.

Borgerson, J. (2001) "Feminist ethical ontology: Contesting 'the bare givenness of intersubjectivity'," *Feminist Theory* 2(2): 173–89.

Brodwin, P. (2000) "Introduction," in P. Brodwin (ed.), *Biotechnology and Culture*: Bodies, Anxieties, Ethics. Bloomington: Indiana University Press. pp. 1–23.

Broom, D. (2001) "Public health, private body," *Australia and New Zealand Journal of Public Health* 25(1): 5–8.

Burkitt, I. (1999) *Bodies of Thought.* London: Sage.

Campbell, R., and Hunter, B. (eds.) (2000) *Moral Epistemology Naturalized.* Calgary: University of Calgary Press.

Fraser, N. (1989) *Unruly Practices.* Minneapolis: University of Minnesota Press.

Gilligan, C. (1982) *In a Different Voice.* Cambridge, Mass.: Harvard University Press.

Goslinga-Roy, G. (2000) "Body boundaries, fiction of the female self," in P. Brodwin (ed.), *Biotechnology and Culture: Bodies, Anxieties, Ethics.* Bloomington: Indiana University Press, pp. 121–146.

Hekman, S. (1995) *Moral Voices, Moral Selves: Carol Gilligan and Feminist Moral Theory.* Cambridge, UK: Polity.

Held, V. (1987) "Feminism and moral theory," in E. F. Kittay and D. Meyers (eds.), *Women and Moral Theory.* Totowa, N.J.: Rowman and Littlefield, pp. 111–128.

Held, V. (1993) *Feminist Morality.* Chicago: University of Chicago Press.

Held, V. (2001) "Caring relations and principles of justice," in J. Sterba (ed.), *Controversies in Feminism.* Lanham, Md.: Rowman & Littlefield, pp. 67–81.

Hunter, L. (2001) "Listening to situated textuality: working on differentiated public voices," *Feminist Theory* 2(2): 205–217.

Irigaray, Luce (1991) "Questions to Emmanuel Levinas: on the divinity of love" (trans. Margaret Whitford), in R. Bernasconi and S. Critchley (eds.), *Re-Reading Levinas.* Bloomington: Indiana University Press, pp. 109–118.

Jones, D. (1992) "Brief of the Law Reform Commission of Canada to the Royal Commission on New Reproductive Technologies," *Health Law in Canada* 13(1): 119–124.

Kluge, E.-H., and Lucock, C. (1991) *New Human Reproductive Technologies*. Ottawa: Canadian Medical Association.

Koski, G. (2000) "Risks, benefits, and conflicts of interest in human research: Ethical evolution in the changing world of science." *Journal of Law, Medicine & Ethics* 28(4): 330–33.

Kymlicka, W. (1993) "Approaches to the ethical issues raised by the Royal Commission's mandate," in Royal Commission on New Reproductive Technologies, *New Reproductive Technologies: Ethical Aspects*. Volume 1 of the Research Studies. Ottawa: Minister of Supply and Services Canada, pp. 1–46.

Lacey, N. (1995) "Feminist legal theory beyond neutrality," *Current Legal Problems* 48(2): 1–38.

Lessor, R. (1993) "All in the family; social processes in ovarian egg donation between sisters," *Sociology of Health & Illness* 15(3): 393–413.

Lloyd, G. (1983) "Reason, gender and morality in the history of philosophy," *Social Research* 50(3): 490–513.

Martin, P. (1999) "Bioethics and the whole: Pluralism, consensus, and the transmutation of bioethical methods into gold." *Journal of Law, Medicine & Ethics* 27(4): 316–27.

Michaels, M. (1996) "Other mothers: Toward an ethic of postmaternal practice," *Hypatia* 11(2): 49–70.

Nicholas, B. (2001) "Exploring a moral landscape: Genetic science and ethics," *Hypatia* 16(1): 45–63.

NSW (New South Wales) Law Reform Commission (1984) *Artificial Conception: Discussion Paper 1: Human Artificial Insemination*. Sydney: New South Wales Law Reform Commission.

Ragoné, H. (1998) "Incontestable motivations," in S. Franklin and H. Ragoné (eds.), *Reproducing Reproduction*. Philadelphia, Pa.: University of Pennsylvania Press, pp. 118–131.

Royal Commission on New Reproductive Technologies (1993a) *Proceed with Care*. Final Report, vol. I. Ottawa: Minister of Supply and Services Canada.

Royal Commission on New Reproductive Technologies (1993b) *Proceed with Care*. Final Report, vol. II. Ottawa: Minister of Supply and Services Canada.

Ruddick, S. (1990) *Maternal Thinking*. London: Women's Press.

Russell, R. (2000) "Ethical bodies," in P. Hancock, B. Hughes, E. Jagger, K. Paterson, R. Russell, E. Tulle-Winton, and M. Tyler (eds.), *The Body, Culture and Society*. Buckingham, UK: Open University Press, pp. 101–116.

Saetnan, A. (2000) "Women's involvement with reproductive medicine: Introducing shared concepts," in A. Saetnan, N. Oudshoorn, and M. Kirejczyk (eds.), *Bodies of Technology: Women's Involvement with Reproductive Medicine*. Columbus: Ohio State University Press, pp. 1–30.

Sevenhuijsen, S. (1997) "Feminist ethics and public health care policies: A case study on the Netherlands," in P. DiQuinzio and I. Young (eds.), *Feminist Ethics and Social Policy*. Bloomington: Indiana University Press, pp. 49–76.

Sevenhuijsen, S. (1998) *Citizenship and the Ethics of Care*. London: Routledge.

Shanley, M. (1997) "Fathers' rights, mothers' wrongs? Reflections on unwed fathers' rights and sex equality," in P. DiQuinzio and I. Young (eds.), *Feminist Ethics and Social Policy*. Bloomington: Indiana University Press.

Shildrick, M. (1997) *Leaky Bodies and Boundaries: Feminism, Postmodernism and (Bio)ethics*. New York: Routledge.

Tong, R. (1993) *Feminine and Feminist Ethics*. Belmont, Calif.: Wadsworth.

Tong, R. (1996) "Feminist approaches to bioethics," in S. Wolf (ed.), *Feminism and Bioethics: Beyond Reproduction*. New York: Oxford University Press, pp. 67–94.

Tronto, J. (1993) *Moral Boundaries: A Political Argument for an Ethic of Care*. New York: Routledge.

Tronto, J. (2001) "Who cares? Public and private caring and the rethinking of citizenship," in N. Hirschmann and U. Liebert (eds.), *Women and Welfare*. New Brunswick, N.J.: Rutgers University Press. pp. 65–83.

Warnke, G. (1994) "Surrogate mothering and the meaning of Family," *Dissent*, 41(4): 466–73.

Young, I. (1995) "Punishment, treatment, empowerment: Three approaches to policy for pregnant addicts," in P. Bowling (ed.), *Expecting Trouble*. Boulder, Col.: Westview Press.

10

Genetics and the Legal Conception of Self

Isabel Karpin

Much feminist legal scholarship has attempted to critique the legal concept of selfhood for its reliance upon an artifice of physical boundedness and unity. Feminists who reject the law's embrace of a self produced in response to what Lacan called the "lure of spatial identification"[1] (Lacan 1977: 5; Meek 1998) do so because the political, social, and legal consequences that follow from this ascription of selfhood work against the bodies of women. Women's bodies, it is argued, are least able to conform to an optics of the skin, particularly in the context of pregnancy. Unbounded corporeality is not however, confined to women's bodies. Haraway, for instance, points out that in these days of biotechnological seeing, "even the most reliable Western individuated bodies . . . neither stop nor start at the skin, which is itself something of a teeming jungle threatening illicit fusions" (Haraway 1991: 215). The self is a construct that extends beyond the limits of the physical by simply being in the world. Its extension in time and space undermines the alleged autocracy of the individual. Susan Ballard argues, "every act of viewing becomes an event in which the boundaries of our bodies are imbricated in relations with other bodies" (Ballard 2001: 1). Similarly, Avital Ronell argues that once the telephone enabled the distant projection of the voice in space, the boundaries that demarcated our bodies were fundamentally questioned (Ronell 1989; see also Ronell 1994). In this chapter I want to show how genetic discourses, indifferent to the surface of the body as a marker of identity, demand a more complex understanding of the self in law. What happens, for instance, when genetic discourses reveal that we are all "leaky,"[2] boundaryless, and transgressive?

In her discussion of conjoined twins, Margrit Shildrick describes the leakiness of self as corporeal ambiguity. She says: "[a]bove all it is the corporeal ambiguity and fluidity, the troublesome lack of fixed definition, the refusal to be either one thing or the other, that marks the monstrous as a site of disruption" (Shildrick 1999: 78). I will argue in a related approach that biogenetic discourses, which emphasize shared identity and participation in the common genetic pool, reveal the monstrousness in all of us. This is challenging to law because such discourses expose the impossibility of the autonomous, self-sufficient individual of liberal legalism. The individual in the age of the gene is fundamentally connected and vulnerable. The individual in the age of the gene always contains a trace of the other; not-one but not-two (Karpin 1992).

I turn to the normative individual of liberal jurisprudence and show how even he (and I use the gendered pronoun deliberately) can no longer sustain the essential distance and difference between one and another (Callois 1987). Allen Meek writes of how Lacan extrapolated from Callois's writing to explain that "the autonomous self is produced as an optical effect as a body attempts to conform to an encoded visual surface and to inhabit a landscape constituted as a field of the other's gaze" (Meek 1998: 3) It is this differentiated self, certain of its limits, that we are taught to prize. The failure to articulate and determine fixed and impenetrable boundaries is a failure of selfhood. The discourse of genetics requires us to lose ourselves (or more correctly to find ourselves) in a genetic code that imbricates us with the other. In this case we recognize a selfhood that is based on interconnection and intermingled identity.

In this chapter I examine both legislative and quasi-legislative attempts to restore the visual surface of the body as the marker of individual identity. In the case of genetic discourses, the primary means by which this has occurred is through privacy legislation. Such legislation aims to secure one's right to keep one's genetic identity to oneself. The problem is how to identify the rights-bearing individual in the first place. Each person's genetic code reveals not only who we are but also who else we might become. If we are always implicated in the genetic profiles of our relatives, can we hope to keep ourselves private and can it offer us any solace to do so? We share our genes with others by decreasing degrees of exactitude reaching out from the familial and ending in the common genetic pool of the species. Individuality then is the recognition of ourselves in others. "He has my eyes."

Genetic discourses reveal the individual in biomedical moments of self-recognition in the other. They do not do away with individuality but complicate it. They suggest that what makes us individual also joins us to others. In law, however, the liberal subject is still the preeminent mode of selfhood. This rights-bearing subject finds its greatest recognition in those moments when it fends off incursion by others. These are boundary-defining moments that carry with them the promise of invulnerability and autonomy—but the kind of autonomy that is characterized by self-interest. It is no surprise then that in this frame those most successful at asserting themselves are those who have garnered sufficient social, economic, cultural, and political resources to minimize the impact of their indistinction, dependencies, and interconnections. Bodily transgressions do reside within these individuals, but they are accommodated to a point where they appear value-neutral, enabling the façade of independence to be reified in their favor. Those who demand an autonomy of self that incorporates care, responsibility, connection, dependence, and even immersion with the other are seen as a definitional paradox—transgressive, messy, mixed-up failures. However, it is this conception of self around which law, social, and biomedical discourses must circulate in order to ensure equality and justice.

My aim here then, is to use genetic discourses to generate anxiety about the stability of liberal identity so that its current beneficiaries find themselves at the margins with the rest of us. To do this, I posit a legal norm of transgressivity. Law, in this new frame, must take as its base unit a subject that is inevitably connected, vulnerable, and dependent. Because the transgressive is by definition that which goes beyond the limits, normative transgressivity is both an oxymoron and a standard state of being. (In being you I am me. In needing you I am self-sufficient. In having you I am free.)

Genetic discourses, then, are creating new tensions within the traditional conceptualization of the autonomous individual constructed around or out of a biogenetically connected family. Anthropologist Kara Finkler and legal theorist Janet Dolgin raise concerns about the relation of the individual to a family that is constructed or mapped over a genetic pedigree.[3] This form of individuality, which immediately connects one to genetically related others, disables the liberal individual premised on a distinct and separate selfhood. Instead, it enables or renders able-bodied a transgressive individual whose very selfhood is already connected and vulnerable to the embodiment of someone else. I argue that this is not the end of individuality or indeed autonomy, but that transgressive selfhood demands of us a new understanding of each of these two terms. Before I make this argument, however, it is useful to use both Finkler and Dolgin's concerns as a stepping-off point.

Finkler argues that the hegemony of the gene is undermining what she describes as the "mark of a modern individual" namely, "autonomy, independence and detachment from kinship ties" (Finkler 2001: 237). Her focus is on the way that the gene reestablishes kinship as a biogenetic connection rather than a relationship established on the basis of choice. She states:

> Beyond issues associated with gender, family and kinship ties have been given a new dimension that stresses faulty genes rather than social status, position or even poverty. Cultural significance is given to genetic transmission for better or for worse. (Finkler 2001: 239)

Finkler bases her argument on research she conducted involving several adoptees who sought out the identity of their birth parents. Many of them were motivated by a need to ascertain their medical histories. Others found themselves seeking out genetic relatives because they suffered from a genetically inherited form of disease (Finkler 2001).[4] In examining these cases Finkler argues that the geneticization of kinship[5] has given rise to the possibility of a connection between individuals who may otherwise be nonintimate relations or strangers.

Although Finkler never expressly identifies what is wrong or right with these new directions, the language that she uses suggests that there are significant benefits in the biogenetic model of kinship. She says:

> It recasts our dispersed and loose kinship ties as inexorable genetic ones and reestablishes our continuity with family and kin. Once uprooted we have been reunited by the medicalization of family and kinship. Willingly or not, we must recognize our connectedness, albeit by our dysfunction and disorders. DNA joins the compartmentalized, fragmented postmodern individual to his or her ancestors. (Finkler 2001: 249)

However, while Finkler reads the move back to connectedness as a cure for our postmodern fragmentation, there is more at stake than she appears to be aware of. The compartmentalized individual of contemporary America and other western nations is for law the liberal individual, a modernist construction determined to fend off intrusions and interconnections and enable a self-sufficiency that promises selfhood. The threat of incursion by others or unwilling connection to others is the threat of postmodern indistinction. This is what I have been describing as the transgressive, and it is what Janet Dolgin finds so troubling.

Dolgin laments the primacy of the biogenetic family over the new modern "family of choice," suggesting that it results in the demise of both individuality and autonomy. According to Dolgin, the family-by-choice is being surpassed and in its place a new family entity is created without recourse to the intimacies of social relationships. She terms this entity the "genetic family." Its coalitions are made across gene lines and shared genealogies, which offer the knowledge of an inheritance in the form of disease. As Dolgin describes it:

> Genetic information alone becomes relevant. Genes suggest nothing about social relationships. They are simply data. As such, they neither represent nor demand particular moral links among the people they describe. The notion of the gene as the arbiter of personhood could replace culture, morality, religion, and history—indeed time itself—with mapped sequences of DNA. (Dolgin 2002: 544)

Dolgin goes on to describe the genetic family as giving rise to a new conception of personhood that has neither the traditional hierarchically arranged relationships nor the modern autonomy-based relations of "families-of-choice." In this context she argues there is a confusion between the individual and the group. It becomes almost impossible to tell them apart, to distinguish one from the other. Dolgin however, appears stuck in an old dyad between top-down oppressive power on the one hand (hierarchically based families) and individual power (autonomy-based families) on the other. There is no room in her imaginary for an empowered but vulnerable and connected self.

While I do not agree with Finkler that the biogenetic family represents a recuperative antipostmodern turn, Dolgin's alternative analysis, with its failure to offer an account of our humanity outside either the hierarchy or the autonomy model, raises an even greater concern. Her discomfort with the way in which the individual cannot sustain its distinction from the group in the face of genetic immersion fails to recognize that group membership or identification is not self-evidently negative. It only becomes so when one is aligned with a disadvantaged group in society. Just as the gene can replace culture, morality, religion, and history as the arbiter of personhood, so can skin color, disability, sexuality, gender, and so on. It is for this reason that the gene is so interesting—it may draw into the web of potential social disadvantage those who have so far managed to keep themselves out of it. In response to Finkler, Dolgin remarks:

> [T]his construction of family . . . replaces the notion of autonomous individuality with a notion of a larger group, defined through the metaphor of the individual but within which each person is indistinguishable from each other and from the genetic group. (cited in Finkler 2001: 250)

Dolgin here reiterates a point she has made elsewhere that the move from individual to group implicates "individuals assumed on other grounds to belong to that group" (Dolgin 2002: 544).

For Dolgin this kind of indistinction results in the subordination of the individual's interests to the larger group. This is an affront to the primacy of the liberal individual that has been the project of liberal legalism.

Both Dolgin and Finkler, along with many scholars examining familial claims to genetic information, fall prey, however, to the same inexplicable assumption that it is my aim here to challenge. Namely, that by giving effect to our connectedness we must subordinate our individuality to the claims of the community. This assumption has led many scholars to describe the debate as an argument between individualist and communitarian accounts of identity. For instance, this has been the limited response to innovative scholars such as Loane Skene, who have sought to challenge the rigidity of individualist accounts of the self by, at a minimum, creating a communal familial genetic identity.

In her article "Patient rights or family responsibilities?: Two approaches to genetic testing" Loane Skene (1998) describes two possible models for dealing with genetic information. The first closely reflects the rationale behind both the Australian genetic privacy and nondiscrimination bill and its U.S. counterpart—a legal, rights, privacy model—and is based on autonomy and self-determination (discussed later). The second model was developed by the Cancer Genetic Ethics Committee of the Anti Cancer Council of Victoria and is a medical and family-centered model (Skene 1998: 1–41). In this second model, it is envisaged that genetic information (and the tissue that is tested) would be shared among blood relatives. Furthermore, individuals would not have the ultimate right to "control . . . their information and the use of the tissue taken for genetic testing" (Skene 1998: 24). Instead, ownership would reside in the doctor or hospital that prepared the tissue or genetic information. This is an approach that accords with the treatment of medical records in Australia (Skene 1998: 27).

Bennett and Bell, among others, have called this family-centered model communitarian and have responded by arguing that it is unnecessary because the current common and statute law allows encroachment on the rights of the autonomous individual in the extreme circumstances in which it is warranted. Instead, they prefer to rely on a notion of autonomy that encompasses one's relationship to others. Bennet and Bell suggest that the assumptions behind moves to communalize genetic information "rest on highly individualised and atomised notions of autonomy, which fail to take account of the relational aspects of the exercise of autonomy" (Bennet and Bell 2001: 158). They rely on Nedelsky's view that "autonomy is a capacity that exists only in the context of social relations that support it and only in conjunction with the internal sense of being autonomous" (Nedelsky 1989: 7). This conceptualization of relational autonomy offers a useful strategy for empowering the interconnected individual of transgressive normativity. However, Bennett and Bell do not consider such a radical revision of autonomy as requiring amendment to existing legal structures. Instead we are asked to accept the existence of this form of autonomy and to find its accommodation within the legal structures currently in place. I argue, however, that this kind of accommodation is simply not possible because it challenges the very framework that the legal structure seeks to enforce.

In contrast to Bennett and Bell, Ann Sommerville and Veronica English take communitarian theory as a way to modify liberal individualism in order to take into account the interconnectedness that genetics exposes. According to them:

> Interconnectedness and responsibility to others are brought to the fore in the genetic sphere in a manner which seems to run counter to current ethical and legal orthodoxy. Extreme notions of individual rights and autonomy are insufficient to deal with these complex and interwoven interests. A more useful framework is gained by combining notions of autonomy with a modified version of communitarianism which recognises decisions made by one person inevitably affect others and that an individual cannot have rights without also accepting that he or she has certain duties. (Sommerville and English 1999: 150)

While Bennett and Bell's relational autonomy and Somerville and English's modified communitarianism are significant attempts to grapple with the problem of the transgressiveness of selfhood, neither is, in my view, adequate. In both versions the subversive potential of transgressivity is not realized. In Bennett and Bell's account, the moments when an autonomous individual must accede to his or her relation with others are anomalous moments for which law can always make an exception. In the normal course, however, laws must be written to protect individual rights to control information about the "individuated" self. In Somerville and English's choice of communitarianism, a certain kind of coherence is sought in the formation of tight bonds of responsibility and connection. Just as with Finkler, the move toward interconnection, when read through a communitarian lens, is a desire to create "ties that bind."

However, Michael Walzer describes the transgressive as antithetical to communitarianism because no community can be a stable entity where there is always the possibility of rupture and interposition. In other words, the kind of transgressions, if we even call them that, that will be sustainable in the context of communitarianism are those that enable interconnection among self-sustaining individuals rather than interpenetration among individuals. It is because of this that Walzer argues that a communitarian critique must be continuously applied as a corrective to the excesses of liberal individualism. He says:

> If the ties that bind us together do not bind us, there can be no such thing as a community. If it is anything at all communitarianism is antithetical to transgression. The transgressive self is antithetical even to the liberal community which is its creator and sponsor. (Walzer 1990: 14–15)

Here we see the limits of even the kind of communitarianism about which Sommerville and English write. Those who are most marginalized in the community are generally those who find themselves least accommodated by the social, political, and economic structures in place. They are seen as transgressive because they cannot meet the standards of selfhood in place. It is unlikely, therefore, that bonds of responsibility and duty can operate fairly to bind individuals who are struggling for a legitimate position within the community in the first place (discussed in the next section). Indeed, their insistence on membership in that community will itself be seen as disruptive.

Unruly transgressive bodies threaten the stability of the community because those bodies do not abide by its limits. Nevertheless, finding ourselves necessarily connected with, dependent upon, and vulnerable to others is in fact the state in which we all exist. The only question is where power resides in these interconnected selves. It is the operation of power moving within these inevitable interconnections that needs to be regulated.

In the next section I expose the transgressive body of the apparently autonomous individual through the use of legal discourses surrounding genetics. In particular, through some examples of failed attempts to regulate the use and disclosure of genetic information it becomes clear that an individuated and separate subject around which a cohort of legal rights and responsibilities are built is unsustainable. Rather than suppress that transgressivity, I argue we should embrace it as a starting point for dealing justly with people. We should give significant value to those identities that are not self-contained and independent but instead rely on a transgressive interconnectedness to sustain selfhood.

The Genetic Privacy and Non-discrimination Bill of 1998 (Cth) was the first major attempt in Australia to pass national legislation specifically dealing with issues arising out of the genetic biotechnologies. Its primary aim was to protect the individual's privacy rights over their genetic information and to prevent discrimination that might arise when information about genetic status is revealed. The bill failed to get the necessary support in Parliament, and the Australian Law Reform Commission, in conjunction with the Australian Human Ethics Committee, has now been charged with the role of reporting on the issues raised by the bill.[6]

This bill attempted to create a regulatory regime that dealt with not only the collection, storage, and analysis of human DNA samples and the genetic information characterized from them, but also discrimination that might arise generally and in employment and insurance as a consequence of disclosure of that information. The bill was based heavily on its U.S. counterpart and, as such, the emphasis was primarily on genetic privacy. However, it quickly became evident that it is very difficult to reconcile the individualist premise of privacy legislation with the nonindividual nature of genes. The nature of personal genetic information is that it is never just personal. Knowing an individual's genetic makeup means that you also know something about his or her genetic relatives. Who or what an individual is cannot be taken for granted, and in fact there is recognition of this in the bill itself, where an individual was defined as:

> the source of a human tissue sample from which DNA is extracted or genetic information is characterised. The term includes a subject of genetic research and, where appropriate, includes the parent, guardian or legal representative of the individual. (*Genetic Privacy and Non-discrimination Bill 1998*: Clause 4)

The individual who is protected by the legislation is the individual who physically gave up the tissue for analysis. Yet as we have just seen, an individual's consent to disclosure of DNA information about him or herself may also reveal information about that person's genetic relatives. If an individual were defined in the bill in terms that recognized this interconnected status, a very different kind of legislative regime would result. A genetic relative might be able to deny access to the DNA information of an individual who had freely given his or her consent to its release. The bill would have to protect both its source and those who can be charactersized as connected to that source. Indeed, the second part of the existing definition, which includes the parent or guardian (of the source) within the terms of the individual, accepts that legally and socially the individual may not correspond to a spatially identified physically bounded subject. In this way the normative status of the transgressively embodied (inevitably connected, vulnerable, and dependent) subject takes a central position. This is a reasonably simple accommodation where the example involves intimate relatives, although many would see it as a clear violation of the rights of the autonomous individual to do with their bodily bits and pieces as they see fit. However, when the connections are more tenuous or less human, transgressivity as a norm is significantly more radical.

The submission by the University of Sydney's Faculty of Medicine to the Senate Constitutional and Legal Issues Committee inquiry into the bill, pointed out, for instance, that an ambiguity arises when an individual's DNA is incorporated with a viral DNA. The point made in the submission is that the viral DNA actually becomes part of the individual's DNA, and the question that necessarily follows is whether the viral DNA is part of the individual (Leeder 1998) This is obviously of concern to research scientists who may want to conduct research and analysis of viral DNA intermingled with human DNA and to exploit that research for commercial gain. From a legal perspective, a determination of where the human begins and ends appears to be impossible. In this sense rather than, as Dolgin would have it, undermining individual autonomy, a radically transgressive understanding of human identity is necessary to ensure the autonomy of the connected individual involved. Obviously a person whose DNA is intermingled with viral DNA is still a person. If we take the geneticization of identity to its extreme, we will find ourselves inexorably defined out of existence unless a level of transgressivity is embraced. However, the law is not in the habit of accommodating infiltration by the other.

How then does this most unreliable of individuated bodies, to refer back to Haraway's question, seek legal protection for its privacy and against discrimination? The law requires its subject to be stable, autonomous, self-sufficient, and independent, but the body as the law knows it is in fact a fabrication that mimics material fixity. Accordingly, legal responses to bodily transgressions are generally boundary policing, and a singular individual is artificially carved out through juridical force. This sometimes occurs literally on living bodies, as in the case of conjoined twins, or through the sterilization of intellectually disabled girls (Shildrick 1999, Karpin, 1992, 1999).

Here we are exploring how it occurs at the microlevel of genes. We see how the law and scientists struggle to find the viable individual. Yet another example of this struggle to identify exactly who or what is the rights-bearing individual occurs, not surprisingly, in the section of the now defunct bill dealing with rights over the DNA of a fetus. Clause 24 reads:

(1) Where genetic information is available from genetic analysis before the birth of a person about that person's genome, the genetic information is the genetic

information of the person's biological mother but becomes the genetic information of that person when he or she is born alive. (Genetic Privacy and Nondiscrimination Bill 1998)

This was perhaps the most disputed clause in the bill because its critics claimed it failed to understand the basic difference that genes make. If, for instance, the biological mother is what is sometimes called a gestational surrogate, that is, she is carrying the fetus in her womb for the genetically related mother, then, some would argue, it is inappropriate for the bill to give ownership of genetic information about the fetus to her. Alternatively, the biological mother could be the recipient of a donor ovum, so that even though she is not genetically related to the fetus, it is the intent of all parties that she, as the guardian of the fetus and subsequent child, ought to have all rights over the genetic information pertaining thereto.

The Australian Medical Association, in their submission, further complicate fetal DNA ownership when they question the bill's choice of the biological mother as the appropriate recipient of these rights. They suggest "it is possible to identify which component of DNA, gene or chromosome is paternal and which is maternal; therefore why should the genetic information belong solely to the 'biological mother'"? (Australian Medical Association 1998: 345).

This medical response is interesting in light of the legal conception of the fetus. Kristin Savell examines the English case of *Attorney-General's Reference* (*No. 3 of 1994* ([1997] 3 WLR 421) where a pregnant woman was stabbed, causing the birth of a premature child who died shortly after (Savell 2002). At each instance the court came up with a different conceptualization of the fetus. At the first instance it had no existence in law; on appeal to the court of appeal, it was held to be part of the mother; and in the House of Lords it was held to be an *organism sui generis*. The basis of the House of Lords decision is most interesting. Both Lord Mustill and Lord Hope rejected the argument that the fetus was a part of its mother on three grounds. The first ground was the fact that the genotype of a fetus consists of shared genetic material from its mother and its father. The second was the fact that an embryo could be created outside the womb, and the third was the characterization of the relationship between a woman and her developing fetus as symbiotic.

What is interesting is how the court used the genetic connection with both the father and the mother as a signifier of individuality and therefore separation, rather than considering these joint contributions as giving rise to an interconnection between the genetic progenitors and the fetus.

It is clear from both the scientific and legal discourses discussed here that geneticization of identity is a kind of underpinning ideology, which means that those issues that would otherwise be determined by normal social arrangements are instead complicated and in some instances overridden by a genetic claim. The interesting twist is that in this intense classificatory activity the autonomous individual is not so much fragmented but revealed as already grafted onto others. In other words, the process of geneticization reveals the very transgressivity of our selves at the same time as genetics is touted as offering the capacity to identify us in our very uniqueness.

Having identified the ways in which genetics forces the recognition of a state of interconnection and interpenetration, I now go on to show how that interconnectivity cannot be neutralized through a legal or social regime that prioritizes a shared heritage, since this significantly underdescribes the complex interplay of power, expertise, and resource distribution in the context of genetic heritage. I show how there is a danger in looking to discourses of genetics as a way of describing interconnection because at the same moment that connection is foregrounded, it is also territorialized and racialized. Without an understanding of the transgressive in the context of the communal there will be no means by which to realign the existing inequities and power claims. In the final part of this chapter I examine the proposal by various indigenous and environmental groups for a "genetic commons" to see if this radical reconceptualization of the rights over and access to genetic information offers a partial solution.

Many have argued that the Human Genome Project (HGP), which had as its goal the mapping and sequencing of "the" entire human genome, relates to everybody while in fact relating to nobody at all. As the HGP confined its sampling to largely white, northern populations and yet premised its usefulness on the creation of a generic genome, the Human Genome Diversity Project (HGDP) was conceived as a necessary corrective aimed at mapping ethnic diversity. The HGDP originally sought to collect samples from a broader range of ethnic populations. However, the project quickly became focused, not on obtaining samples from all the world's populations, but on targeting particular populations that were on the verge of disappearing, and on preserving, not the populations, but the cell lines. In other words, where the HGP created an apparently generic human genome (but where generic means primarily white and northern European), the HGDP identified marginal genetic identity (the exotic other). In these two projects we see a tension between non-territorial "human genome" and a racially specific "community genome." The former can only claim its normative generic status by presenting the specified identities in the HGDP as marginal, small, threatened outposts of the other that cannot endanger the normativity of the generic genome.

This is why the decision by indigenous groups to object to the HGDP is so poignant. Indigenous groups represent the point of view of those whose bodily interconnection has been used as a means to subordinate them. In the context of the HGDP they are offered the opportunity to further negotiate the transgression of their bodies, while there is no recognition of the ways in which the most reliable western individuated bodies are never open to negotiation. The language of altruism, used in the context of discussions about the human genome as the common heritage of humanity, fails to take account of the myriad ways in which marginal bodies are already operating as common property. For instance, when the World Medical Association resolved that "the information [from the HGP] should be general property and should not be used for business purposes" (World Medical Association 1992), or when the guidelines to the HGDP describe its primary aim as "[u]ltimately, to create a resource for the benefit of all humanity and for the scientific community worldwide" (International Planning Workshop 1993: 4), there is a fundamental failure to understand the unequal distribution of common resources worldwide and the way that inequality is mapped along race and gender lines. The harvesting of genes from indigenous people is to be compared, for instance, with the harvesting of the genetic information of the people of Iceland, which has become both a multimillion dollar joint venture between the government and two multinational corporations (deCode Genetics and Roche Pharmaceuticals) and a debate about nationalism and the ideology of racial purity (see later discussion).

Yet scientists involved in the HGDP are, it seems, genuinely perplexed when having offered a rigorous commitment to informed consent (the liberal individual model) in conjunction with a generous sensitivity to group cultural attributes, they are rebuffed by indigenous groups of would-be participants. Victoria Tauli-Corpuz, an indigenous activist, describes the difference in understanding:

> I was on a panel with Andre Langanay a former committee member for the Human Genome Diversity Project (HGDP) at the "Patents, Genes and Butterflies" conference in Berne, Switzerland. He was asked to talk about the HGDP and I presented my critique of this project. During the open forum he said he couldn't understand what indigenous peoples have against the extraction of their blood in order to help others get well, he would have no second thoughts about it, he argued. (Tauli-Corpuz 2001: 252)

Andre Langanay's statement shows the importance of a commitment to a situated account of identity. While Laganany sees the project as benign, Tauli-Corpuz views the project from the perspective of someone who knows all too well the power of colonizing forces to appropriate and control bodies, territories, resources, cultures, and knowledges. In the same way, the submission by the Aboriginal and Torres Strait Islander Social Justice Commissioner, Dr. Bill Jonas, to the Australian Law Reform Commission's inquiry into the protection of genetic information highlights the context in which indigenous Australians think about the extraction of genetic information from their citizenry:

> As the most disadvantaged members of Australian society, Aboriginal and Torres Strait Islander peoples are especially vulnerable to exploitation. Their past encounters with colonisers have been characterised by the stealing of land, knowledge, culture and the arts. Genetic mutations found in discrete populations are providing yet another rich field for exploitation, this time by trans-national pharmaceutical companies acting with the explicit or implicit support of national or state governments. (Jonas 2002: 3).

It is clear then, that one can no more advocate an altruistic model premised on the sharing of what is already shared genetic material, than a model in which individual rights over that shared material are enshrined.

The HGDP Model Ethical Protocol for Collecting DNA Samples, for instance, attempts to overcome these inequities by requiring those collecting samples to obtain appropriate consents from the communities being sampled and to work in partnership with them (Human Genome Diversity Committee 1993: 18). At the same time, long-term storage of the information is contemplated that would enable general access to the scientific community, and the expertise to make use of that information resides squarely in the hands of that scientific community (Human Genome Diversity Committee 1993: 20, 29). The set of ethical issues enumerated in the Model Ethical Protocol indicates how researchers might return some of the benefit to the sampled population. Ethical issue no. 3, for example, states:

> Researchers should actively seek ways in which participation in the HGD Project can bring benefits to the sampled individuals and their communities. Examples of such benefits include health screening, medical treatment or educational resources (Human Genome Diversity Committee 1993: 32).

However, these gestures insist upon using a liberal individualist model of consent and profit. It is taken for granted that the means to achieve justice is through this model.

An alternative model posited by Hilary Cunningham exposes the way in which the liberal individualist model fails. She describes her model as relational and rejects a model in which the scientist and the indigenous group operate as two separate negotiating identities. Instead she posits the following:

> I do not mean a traditional collaboration in which a project is designed and then implemented with the consultation of a research constituency. The collaboration which I mention here makes the scope, design, goals, methods of implementation and access to research results all negotiable items. Empirical researchers in particular, whose objectives and methods are said to be governed by acontextual laws and procedures will find this collaboration particularly difficult since it challenges the very epistemological basis of scientific knowledge. Such collaboration suggests that just as valuable to any project's scientific objectives is the formation of a viable relationship with research subjects. This social hermeneutic indicates that the object of research is not simply "information" (a knowledge commodity that can be acquired and controlled by one party) but "insight," a relational kind of knowledge that can be developed only through negotiation of two engaged parties. (Cunningham 1998: 227–228)

It is clear that what is being suggested here is more along the lines of my transgressive normativity model. The research subject is no longer kept at arms length but instead becomes both researcher and researched.

The boundaries between the two, no longer strictly held, challenge the way in which western research is standardized or apparently made objective. Cunningham recognizes the radicalness of this position when she says:

> Yet how many granting agencies—especially in the sciences—would be willing to fund projects whose goals and methods were so fundamentally contingent upon the negotiation of research methodologies and results? (Cunningham 1998: 227–228)

It is the power plays of interconnection that are operational when, for example, the target of research is not a disenfranchised indigenous group but a group who, in racialized terms, identify themselves with the norm and in so doing posit the purity of their genetic pool as an indicator of superiority. I am referring to the genetic database of the Icelandic population constructed by deCode in collaboration with Roche Pharmaceuticals. In this case, the subjects of the research—the Icelandic population through their government representatives—negotiated the terms under which the research would take place. Arguably the Icelandic statutes, the Health Database Act of 1998 and the Biobanks Act of 2000, represent a substantial governmental intrusion into research methodologies. The opt-out form of consent, although not everyone's idea of a fair and appropriate method of obtaining research subjects, was something that was explicitly legislated in both acts.[7] While controversy continues over whether the results and profits from the research should be in the hands of a private corporation, the fact remains that the license provided to deCode under the legislation is for twelve years only. Icelanders then, are not unconnected research subjects, but have had a say in the manner in which the research will proceed and have set in place provisions to ensure that some of the financial achievements are funneled back into Iceland.

It is worth considering then why Iceland has been able to do this and yet indigenous groups targeted by the HGDP have not. Skuli Sigurdsson has characterized the debate around the advantage of Iceland as a research population for genetics as surrounded by the "invocation of myths, clichés, fantastical tales about Iceland, past and present, pieties and regurgitated half-truths." He identifies the eugenic past of Iceland as having "hardly left a dent in public memory" (Sigurdsson 2001: 108).

That past, however, is quite significant. Finnbogason, one of the most influential Icelandic intellectuals of the first half of the twentieth century, invoked the "science of eugenics" to argue for the "purification of the Icelandic race to preserve its spiritual and physical assets" (Palsson and Harðardóttir 2002: 282). Einar Arnason, professor of evolutionary biology and population genetics at the University of Iceland, has made similar statements about the way that the deCode project has "evoked the myth of the homogen[e]ous Aryan Icelanders" (Arnason, 1999) and has challenged those claims with research suggesting that Iceland is one of the most genetically heterogeneous nations in Europe (Arnason et al. 2000: F3).

What we are left with then is two different kinds of interconnected communities. The Icelandic community has to some degree (although within the bounds of an all too inadequate democratic governance) ensured that the power plays over their interconnectivity do not result in their exploitation. Here their connectivity does not undermine their power but instead gives effect to it. However, in the case of indigenous communities, their connectivity is negated by the requirement for individual consent imposed by researchers coming from western legal traditions that favor the autonomous individual. These groups then find themselves with seemingly no legal recourse for protection of their genetic information as a group.

Conclusion

My aim in this chapter has been to utilize genetic discourses to challenge the stability of the autonomous and individuated liberal self. I have done this in order to open a space for subjects who are connected, vulnerable, and dependent and who cannot shed their dependencies in order to become the liberal subject. These are the people whose very selfhood is then seen as unruly and threatening. Once we have taken as a base unit the interconnected self, regulatory effort will need to be directed to determining where power resides in these interconnected selves. This is in contrast to the call for a "genetic commons" which, while offering the genome and genetic discourses as a resource held in common to be used equally by all people, will not be successful unless some further account is taken of the unequal society onto which such a commons must be mapped. The treaty initiative to share the "genetic commons" that was formally launched in February 2002 at the World Social Forum in Porto Alegre, Brazil, reveals this tension in its text, which states:

> Therefore, the nations of the world declare the Earth's gene pool, in all of its biological forms and manifestations, to be a global commons, to be protected and nurtured by all peoples and further declare that genes and the products they code for, in their natural, purified or synthesized form as well as chromosomes, cells, tissue, organs and organisms, included cloned, transgenic and chimeric organisms, will not be allowed to be claimed as commercially negotiable generic information or intellectual property by governments, commercial enterprises, other institutions or individuals. (*Treaty to Share the Genetic Commons* 2002: 6)

However, in the explanatory material that accompanies the text, the authors say that the "Treaty must support the sovereignty of nations and of communities to exchange or withhold genetic materials they hold in trust. . . . We wish to affirm national sovereignty and community rights as well as the right of individuals whose genetic makeup is subject to discrimination . . . to have their own genetic integrity and rights ensured" (*Treaty to Share the Genetic Commons 2002*).

It is this tension that I have been discussing throughout this chapter. How do we assert our autonomy over our genetic integrity yet recognize our inevitable interconnection with others? I argue that if we have an account of the self that is transgressive, that understands that we are both one and an other at once, we offer a self that is vulnerable to the interests and incursions of others as well as being sensitive to them. The law must accommodate this newly dependent interconnected self. It is this that the authors of the treaty are trying to accomplish when they say:

> The Treaty to Share the Genetic Commons is designed to make every government and Indigenous Peoples a "caretaker" of their geographic part of the global genetic commons and to establish the appropriate statutory mechanisms to ensure both national sovereignty and open access to the flow of genetic information. (*Treaty to Share the Genetic Commons* 2002: 2)

In this statement we have an attempt to bring together the traditionally opposed positions of self-sufficiency and dependence. What I have been arguing is that the concept of the idealized individual of western liberal legalism is challenged by genetic discourses. However, rather than regard this as an assault, we should embrace the transgressivity of all selves.

In so doing, those traditionally disempowered by a vulnerable and uncontained selfhood would find some recourse in the law.

Notes

1. Lacan cites Roger Callois's essay "Mimicry and Legendary Pyschaesthenia" to explain how the formation of the ego has its origins in a process of depersonalization by assimilation to space (Lacan, 1977). See also Meek's discussion of this point (Meek 1998).

2. This term is borrowed from Shildrick (1997).

3. Geneticists distinguish between a pedigree, which is a representation of biological relatedness, and a family, which is the named, identified collection of individuals defined in terms of their kinship relations with one another.

4. In one case, for example, "Eve noted she felt closer to her sister and husband and her father but had also become closer to her cousins" because they shared a genetic susceptibility to cancer.

5. In Finkler's response to her critics she notes, "I prefer to use the concept of hegemony of the gene instead of geneticization because the Gramscian construct of hegemony encompasses the concept of the power of dominant institutions to impose an ideology by their very authority which permeates the social and cultural fabric of daily life, without the use of force" (Finkler 2001: 257).

6. The Australian Law Reform Commission and the Australian Health Ethics Committee released a final report, discussion paper 66, '*Protection of Human Genetic Information,*' in August 2002.

7. Icelanders were given the right to opt out of the database, but until they do so, they are presumed to have opted in. This was further entrenched in the BioBanks Act, which was passed in May 2000 without any public discussion (Sigurdsson, 2001). By the middle of March 2001, 19,697 citizens had opted out of the HSD and as Sigurdsson describes it, "in the process become entities in a second-order HSD, registering those socially deviant whereas the first-order HSD is still empty" (2001: 113).

References

Arnason, Einar (1999) Letter to the editor, *New York Times*, February 15. Available at http://www.mannvernd.is/english/articles/ea.nytimes.html.

Arnason, Einar, Sigurgislason, Hlynur, and Benedikz, Eirikur (2000) "Genetic Homogeneity of Icelanders: Fact or Fiction?" *Nature Genetics* 25: 373–374.

Australian Medical Association (1998) "Submission no. 24" to the Senate Legal and Constitutional Legislation Committee on the Genetic Privacy and Non-Discrimination Bill 1998, vol. 2, p. 345.

Ballard, Susan (2001) "My viewing body does not end at the skin", Available at http://www.voyd.com/ttlg/textual/ballardessay.htm 2001.

Bennet, Belinda, and Bell, Dean (2001) "Genetic Secrets and the Family," *Medical Law Review* 9: 130–161.

Callois, Roger (1987) "Mimcry and Legendary Psychaesthenia," trans. John Shepley, *October* 31 (Winter): 17–33.

Cunningham, Hilary (1998) "Colonial Encounters in Postcolonial Contexts: Patenting Indigenous DNA and the Human Genome Diversity Project," *Critique of Anthropology* 18 (2): 227–228.

Dolgin, Janet (2002) "Choice, Tradition and the New Genetics: The Fragmentation of the Ideology of the Family," *Connecticut Law Review* 32: 523–566.

Finkler, Kara (2001) "The Kin in the Gene," *Current Anthropology* 42(2) (April): 235–263.

Genetic Privacy and Non-discrimination Bill 1998 (C th).

Haraway, Donna (1991) *Simians, Cyborgs and Women.* New York: Routledge.

Human Genome Diversity Committee (1993) *Summary Report of International Planning Workshop,* Sardinia (Italy) 9–12 September 1993. Available at http://www.stanford.edu/group/morrinst/hgdp/summary93.html(accessed 12 October 2004).

International Planning Workshop (1993). "Human Genome Diversity Project: Summary Document" Available at http://www.stanford.edu/group/morrinst/hgdp/summary93.html *@30/8/02.*

Jonas, Bill, (2002) (Aboriginal and Torres Strait Islander Social Justice Commissioner, HREOC) "The Protection of Genetic Information of Indigenous Peoples." Submission to the Australian Law Reform Commission inquiry into the protection of genetic information." Available at http://www.humanrights.gov.au/social_justice/genetic_information.html May 13.

Karpin, Isabel (1992) "Legislating the Female Body: Reproductive Technology and the Reconstructed Woman," *Columbia Journal of Gender and the Law* 3(1):325–349.

Karpin, Isabel (1999) "Peeking through the Eyes of the Body: Regulating the Bodies of Women with Disabilities," in L. A. Marks, (ed.), *Disability, Diversability and Legal Change.* The Hague: Kluwer International Law Publishers.

Lacan, Jacques (1977) *Ecrits: A Selection,* trans. Alan Sheridan. New York: W. W. Norton.

Leeder, Stephen (1998) Faculty of Medicine and the Centre for Values, Ethics and the Law in Medicine, University of Sydney, "Submission no. 3" to Senate Legal and Constitutional Legislation Committee on the *Genetic Privacy and Non-Discrimination Bill 1998,* vol. 1, p. 9.

Meek, Allen (1998) "Benjamin, the televisual and the 'fascistic subject'." Available at http://www.latrobe.edu.au/screeningthepast/ /firstrelease/fir998/AMfr4e.htm.

Nedelsky, Jennifer (1989) "Reconceiving Autonomy: Sources, Thoughts and Possibilities," *Yale Journal of Law and Feminism* 1:7–36.

Palsson, Gisli and Harðardóttir, Kristín (2002) "For Whom the Cells Toll: Debates About Biomedicine," *Current Anthropology* 43(2):271–302.

Ronell, Avital (1989) *The Telephone Book: Technology, Schizophrenia, Electric Speech*. Lincoln: University of Nebraska Press.

Ronell, Avital (1994) "The Walking Switchboard," in *Finitudes Score: Essays for the End of the Millenium*. Lincoln: University of Nebraska Press.

Savell, Kristin (2002) "The Mother of the Legal Person," in S. James and S. Palmer (eds.), *Visible Women: Essays on Feminist Legal Theory and Political Philosophy*. Oxford: Hart, pp. 44–46.

Shildrick, Margrit (1977) *Leaky Bodies and Boundaries: Feminism, Postmodernism and (Bio)ethics*. London: Routledge.

Shildrick, Margrit (1999) "This Body Which Is Not One," *Body and Society* 5(2/3): 77–92.

Sigurdsson, Skuli (2001) "Yin-Yang genetics, or the HSD deCODE Controversy," *New Genetics and Society* 20 (2): 113–117.

Skene, Loane (1998) "Patient's Rights or Family Responsibilities? Two Approaches to Genetic Testing," *Medical Law Review* 6:1–41.

Sommerville, Ann, and English, Veronica (1999) "Genetic Privacy: Orthodoxy or Oxymoron?" *Journal of Medical Ethics* 25:144–150.

Tauli-Corpuz, Victoria (2001) "Biotechnology and Indigenous Peoples," in Brian Tokar (ed.), *Redesigning Life : The Worldwide Challenge to Genetic Engineering*. London: Zed Books.

Treaty to Share the Genetic Commons. (2002) Available at http://www.antivivisezione.it/TreatyRifkin.html.

Walzer, Michael (1990) "The Communitarian Critique of Liberalism," *Political Theory* 18(1):6–23.

World Medical Association Declaration on the Human Genome Project (1992). Adopted by the 44th World Medical Assembly, Marbella, Spain. Available at http://www.wma.net/e/policy/96.htm.

11

The Devouring: Genetics, Abjection, and the Limits of Law

Karen O'Connell

"The Devouring" is the Romany term for the Holocaust, in which up to half a million Romany people died and an unknown number were harmed (Rittner and Roth 1993). "Devouring" is a word that in the context of the Holocaust describes a form of destruction that is also consumption. In the Holocaust, people, ways of life and thought that were fundamental to European life were not simply expelled, but destroyed in a self-annihilating violence. The Nazi regime tried to destroy the roots of its own European culture, steeped as it was in Judaic tradition.

The Holocaust is a cultural reference point for genetics and bioethics because it continues to represent in western consciousness the ethical failure of those things that are supposed to protect and save us from the horrors of bodily suffering and ill-treatment: science and law. In addition, the Nazi regime represents the ultimate historical attempt to create a purified race by using science and law to expel unwanted peoples—Jews, Romanies, homosexuals, and disabled people—from the purity of the *Volk*.

Nevertheless, as the Romany term reminds us, when we reject others we do not expel them. "Devouring" evokes one of the central arguments in this chapter: that rejection through expulsion is an impossible fantasy. Where the Other has been invested with the qualities that are unacceptable in the Self, it is impossible to expel the Other, which is separate only in imagination. Nevertheless, it remains a stubborn human fantasy that the qualities represented by the Other can be cast out and denied.

This chapter is an attempt to apply postmodernist ethical thought about refuse and otherness to genetics and genetic discrimination. I begin with a discussion of abjection by looking in particular at the work of

Julia Kristeva to consider where our horror of refuse originates and why the fantasy of expulsion is such a powerful one. I then turn to feminist writings on identity and abjection in order to "flesh out" the theoretical meaning of abjection. Second, I turn to postmodernist ethics, to consider what it might say about abjection. I argue that postmodernism does suggest an ethical stance to take in relation to abject otherness. Finally, I examine a specific case study of disability as the object of genetic attention. I argue that disability discrimination models, when looked at through the lens of a postmodern ethical stance, offer us a possibility to accept what is rejected by revealing the refuse within our own body boundaries. This opportunity is being ignored, as lawmakers rush to protect us from the knowledge of our own flawed bodies by drawing the cover of privacy over us.

Clean and Proper Bodies

Abjection

In *Powers of Horror* Kristeva outlines a theory of abjection in which she argues that a precondition of being a "speaking subject" is possessing a clean and proper body in the form of a bounded self (Kristeva 1982). Subjectivity and a position in the social order require that what is improper and unclean in the self be rejected and expelled. Kristeva's theory demonstrates at an individual level that any object or process that disrupts a body boundary will evoke horror:

> [R]efuse and corpses show me what I permanently thrust aside in order to live. These body fluids, this defilement, this shit are what life withstands, hardly and with difficulty, on the part of death. There, I am at the border of my condition as a human being. My body extricates itself, as being alive, from that border. (Kristeva 1982: 3)

Abjection is a kind of sickness; a horror at the body's vulnerability to a blurring of self. Kristeva identifies various forms of disgust: oral disgust and disgust surrounding waste, death, and sexual difference. Eating, defecating, disease, death, and reproduction transgress body boundaries directly or indirectly and must be controlled.

This idea is a standard one in psychoanalysis (Freud 1950), but Kristeva's account differs because she argues that the denial, or expulsion, of what is not clean and proper does not mean that the unclean is destroyed.

It exists at the edges of the body, threatening the constitution of the self. Elizabeth Grosz describes abjection as "the subject's reaction to the failure of the subject/object opposition to express adequately the subject's corporeality and tenuous bodily boundaries" (Grosz 1989: 70). The subject feels horror of that which potentially disrupts the clean body, the delimitations of self that define the speaking subject. Despite the urge to control what is abject, it can never be adequately obliterated, expelled, or controlled, because it is an integral part of the body's existence. Following Kristeva's theory, the subject is in an unrelenting and unsuccessful process of attempting to expel the abject in order not to acknowledge the tenuous nature of selfhood.

The ongoing struggle to maintain unreliable body borders, and the anxiety that accompanies it, means that the sites at which the border fails to delimit the clean and proper body require regulation. Regulation includes not only the individual's attempts to control or purify his or her body, but also external regulation. Abjection stimulates a social response in the communal regulation of law and taboo. Kristeva discusses numerous examples of regulation of the abject through law, ritual, and taboo. As one example, she examines the biblical laws laid down in Leviticus, which relate to diet, disease, childbirth, incest, and menstruation. In the Torah, unclean food is associated with indeterminate beings or practices. Fish without gills, birds that do not fly, and animals without cloven hooves are not to be consumed as food. Biblical laws also forbid eating blood and cooking a young goat in its mother's milk. Circumcision as a ritual separates the male child from his mother. There are further prohibitions and rules about the burying of corpses and about menstruation. Laws that regulate the horrors of the indeterminate body strive toward the attainment of purity.

The clean and proper body, then, is one that is managed according to law, science, or other ritual. Bodies that are indeterminate—pregnant, sick, disabled, of uncertain gender—remind us that body boundaries are not closed. Such bodies fascinate and repel us and require further regulation.

Fleshing Out the Abject Body

Women writers have for many years described the way in which their bodies are seen as abject in the sense of being more biological, sexual, excessive, and in need of control than male bodies. Women bleed, lactate, swell with child, and give birth. They produce slimy vaginal secretions when aroused, accompanied by fishy odors.[1] The reproductive capabilities of a woman's body are abject:

> [Women's pregnant and birthing bodies] swell bleed and contract, their "otherwise concealed parts" are broken open. Lactating bodies leak and dribble, irregularly and at times, uncontrollably. The blood of menstruation, which precedes pregnancy, must be contained and hidden. Unlike other bodily secretions: urine, feces, even semen, its secretions are not subject to voluntary control and are therefore subject to social regulation. (Mykitiuk 1994: 86)

The unclean and improper body is the female body. The abject body is the body that does not match the clean and proper body of the representative white male.

Feminist postmodern philosophy has gone some way in revealing the violence that is done to women's bodies when they are defined as abject. In particular, women of color have written about the abjection that attaches to their race and gender. The body of a black woman is seen as excessive to such a degree that it necessitates greater external control and self-regulation for the body to be seen as acceptable. Boundaries are defined with reference to the white male body, so that women of color, or anyone removed from this reference point, will inevitably transgress more boundaries. Toni Morrison writes about the "dreadful funkiness of passion, the funkiness of nature" that African-American women fight to be acceptable:

> Wherever it erupts, this Funk, they wipe it away; where it crusts, they dissolve it; wherever it drips, flowers or clings, they find it and fight it until it dies. . . . They hold their behind in for fear of a sway too free; when they wear lipstick, they never cover the entire mouth for fear of lips too thick, and they worry, worry, worry about the edges of their hair. (Morrison 1981: 77,78)

In the white fantasy of the black woman's body, black women secrete odors and substances. They are oily, they have a muskiness that indicates (to the white man, at least) at once a lack of hygiene, promiscuous sexuality, and the primitive. The abject is also associated with sexuality, since (according to Lacan) erotogenic zones are a rim, a zone between the inside and outside of the body (Grosz 1989). Being black and being female associates the self with excessive corporeality and therefore abjection. In the white imagination, blackness is also associated with savagery, which in turn is associated with all kinds of boundary transgressions, including incest and (perhaps the ultimate border transgression) cannibalism.

Morrison's image of "funk" is a representation of self, or an aspect of self, that is described in terms of fluidity and motion. Feminists, mostly women of color who critique the essentialism of white feminism, describe an alternative selfhood that undermines the assumptions about the individually demarcated, static, and bounded self that impregnate not only white feminism, but the liberal philosophy from which it developed. Representations of this alternative selfhood focus on images that are fluid, shifting, and fragmented. Angela Harris cites Zora Neale Hurston's description of herself as "a brown bag of miscellany propped against a wall" (Harris 1990: 613). Luce Irigaray in *This Sex Which Is Not One* uses the image of water to describe women's sexual identity (Irigaray 1985). Patricia Williams writes about self-control, like Morrison, as a holding back of the excess that repels others: "I edit myself. . . . I hold myself tightly and never spill into the world that hates brown spills" (Williams 1991: 183).

Other writers have identified concepts of selfhood that also differ from the mainstream, and that involve recognition of body boundaries that do not involve the strictly defined and anxiously maintained borders of the liberal male subject. An example is Isabel Karpin's reimagining of maternal selfhood, which examines the way that the mother–fetus relationship is understood in terms of an antagonistic self–other distinction and suggests a more complex "nexus-of-relations" (Karpin 1994).

Such self-descriptions of women demonstrate differing experiences of body boundaries and abjection, and reveal that where body boundaries are regulated, this must be done with greater vigilance according to gender and race. Self-descriptions also suggest a concept of selfhood alternative to that of the abject transitional self. Since descriptions of self from the social perspective tend to be negative, while descriptions from a personal perspective are more positive, it seems that for many women the ideal of a bounded self is imposed rather than spontaneously experienced.

These alternative perspectives on abjection offer two insights into Kristeva's theory. First, they reveal that abjection is not experienced uniformly. Abjection is not only about the individual casting out the aspects of self that are unwanted, as Kristeva suggests. Those properties not only exist at the edges of the body, they are also projected onto abject others who then bear their weight. Second, talking about real bodies rather than the abstract bodies of psychoanalytic theory makes clear the potential pain caused by defining bodies as abject others, and by rejecting the qualities that they display. Each of these points invites us to develop an ethical response to bodies considered abject.

The Rag and Bone Man: A Postmodern Ethical Stance

In feminist and postmodernist writing, abjection emerges both as lived experience and as a trigger for ethical practice. The final part of this chapter considers the ethical significance of abjection in the context of genetics. First, however, I want to address what abjection means as it attaches to Otherness, and to demonstrate the ethical implications of abject Otherness.

Most postmodernists would agree that there is no single system of ethics that can protect against the violence done to people in the name of science and medicine or some other system of power. There can be no single form of bioethics. Nevertheless, postmodernist feminist philosophy offers an ethical orientation that illuminates abjection and can be used to deconstruct cultural readings of genetics. Drucilla Cornell renames deconstruction "the philosophy of the limit" (Cornell 1992) and she offers a reading of postmodernist philosophy, and of Derrida specifically, that reveals its ethical imperative. Cornell's postmodernism focuses on the construction of systems of thought and on the limits of such systems. She argues that postmodernism is an ethical philosophy because, as well as examining and revealing the limits and boundaries of systems, it also asks what has been excluded or rejected by that system.

In other words, postmodernism has a two-pronged approach to questions of ethics and exclusion. The first approach is to consider the point at which a system (of law, philosophy, science) ends. For example, the limit of law is probably its origins in illegality. Every legal system at some point had to establish itself and its authority within a territory. For every legal system, therefore, there was a point at which its authority did not yet exist; what would become an authoritative force was simply an illegal and unrecognized exercise of power. In Australia, for example, the British colonial government established its authority within the colonial territories through an exercise of force over the indigenous population for whom it had no legal legitimacy.

The second postmodernist approach questions what lies beyond the limits of the system. Another way of putting this is to say that postmodernists are concerned with what is excluded or expelled—laid waste—by that particular system. As such, postmodernism has an orientation toward what is abject. Cornell refers to "the ethical significance of the *Chiffonier*." The *Chiffonier* is the rag and bone man who goes about salvaging pieces of what has been discarded and is worthless to others. This is the image of the ethical component of postmodernism.

The ethical stance of postmodernism is not in itself a solution to the creation of abject otherness. As Cornell points out, "[w]e cannot escape representational schemes. Yet, at the same time, we must recognise their inevitable infidelity to radical otherness" (Cornell 1992: 70). Furthermore, we cannot simply include what has been excluded:

> What of the rest that has been pushed out of the system? To ask the question is already a kind of tribute to the forgotten Other, whose remains have been scattered. . . . Indeed, for Derrida, it is only through mourning that we can remember the remains because there has never been, nor can there be, a gathering of the rest that makes fully present what has been shut out: For what has been shut out is literally not there for us. (Cornell 1992: 63)

Nevertheless, this ethical stance does illuminate particular aspects of otherness, even while acknowledging that what has been destroyed by expulsion can never be fully present.

A key point of the philosophy of the limit is that exclusion or expulsion is a form of violence to the Other or to otherness. In the social manifestation of abjection, not only are certain activities and processes thought of as abject, but certain bodies are too. One particular interplay of abjection and otherness reveals the violence of this relation and suggests an ethical response: genetics and the disabled body.

"Welcome To The Club": Law, Ethics, Genetics, and the Disabled Body

Although issues of genetic discrimination [raise] images of Aldous Huxley's *Brave New World* in its most sinister sense, I have to say—at the risk of overworking my metaphor—that the newly discovered, uncharted territories of this harsh new continent, too, are ones where some of us have been living for a considerable time.

So one possible response from people with disabilities to concerns from people who do not have a disability yet but are worried by possible genetic discrimination on the basis of a disability they may develop in the future would be a fairly unsympathetic "welcome to the club." (Innes 2000)

Genetics and the Clean and Proper Body

Kristeva's theory of abjection is an illuminating lens through which to view current assumptions and ideologies surrounding genetic technologies. As Grosz says:

> Understanding abjection involves examining the ways in which the inside and outside of a body are constituted, the space between the self and the other, and the way that a child's body becomes a bounded, unified whole. (Grosz 1989: 71)

Understanding genetics in the period following the decoding of the human genome is a similar and similarly daunting project. There are several overlaps between Kristeva's writing on abjection and the current focus of genetic experimentation. First, the kinds of abjection and boundary transgressions Kristeva identifies correspond closely to areas of genetic technological attention. Food, disease, death, and reproduction all threaten defined body boundaries and invite both anxiety and regulation. Transgenics regulates food, gene therapy aims to overcome disease, cloning attempts to control death, and gene mapping aims to direct reproduction.

Second, genetics presents a vision of the body that appears to overcome abjection because it is manipulable and therefore under control. I am referring here, not to the way that geneticists understand the body, but the way that the genetic rendering of the body resonates through cultural media and images. In the genetic map of the body, there is no uncomfortable excess. A blueprint or map of the body represents the self stripped of fleshiness, of blood and excrement: a body without abjection. Dealing with disease and mortality at the level of genetic representation does not produce the horror of facing the boundary transgressions of death and disease because genetic representation is merely a signifier of corporeality.

> A wound with blood and pus, or the sickly, acrid smell of sweat, of decay, does not *signify* death. In the presence of signified death—a flat encephalograph, for instance—I would understand, react, or accept. (Kristeva 1982: 3)

Genetics, therefore, represents expulsion of the abject and reinforces the boundaries of the clean and proper body without the subject having to face its own corporeality.

However, genetic representation also has disruptive capacities. Genetic science works with identity borders, potentially controlling the food we ingest (the self ingesting the nonself), disease and death (the destruction of self), and reproduction [the self(mother)–nonself(fetus); the reproduction of self]. In doing so, it is playing at the boundaries of identity, which, although it offers a means of producing a clean and proper body, also inspires an anxious social response.

Genetic technologies, even as they seem to promise the perfectly delimited and controlled human body, break down and disrupt other boundaries. In learning how to control body boundaries, geneticists inevitably shift them, producing anxiety, horror, and disgust. Modernist definitions of the body, based on boundaries of self and other, human and animal, organism and machine (and the context of nature and culture), are disrupted by a blueprint that allows unprecedented interaction, swapping over, interference, and convergence of the subject. This is genetics at its most threatening, at least to a self-conception based on stable boundaries. The greatest degree of visceral horror in the social reaction to genetic technologies is reserved for those things that blur the distinctions of self or merge other objects with which the self has contact. The insertion of the DNA of fish into a tomato seems a distortion or disruption of the natural. Inserting human DNA into pigs to provide greater quality or content of consumable pig meat makes us transgress, at least in imagination, the border of self and other that prohibits cannibalism. The cloning of a human being threatens selfhood, as does the potential to create beings that dissolves the human–animal demarcation. Here genetic science is not providing a stable form of identity, but is a disruptive, deconstructive agent.

Genetics and Disability

Genetics therefore plays a role in both creating and disrupting the clean and proper body. As the feminist critical perspective on abjection suggests, genetics offers protection against not only those aspects of the body that are sources of abjection but also those people who represent a greater threat to the bounded concept of self because they do not conform to the male and able-bodied norm. If genetics is a way of achieving—in fantasy—a clean and proper body, then those subordinated in society will be most likely to be viewed as abject and most subject to genetic examination.[2] However, genetics is not only about examining bodies but also about altering characteristics of identity. Paul Rabinow (1996) points out that research on the human genome seems predicated on the idea that any identified gene can be changed. It is also likely, therefore, that abject bodies will not only be those most examined by genetic scientists, but will be those most likely to be regulated or manipulated. Geneticists commenting on the Human Genome Project see its benefits extending not only to the cleansing of the individual's body but also to the cleansing of society through the expulsion of those citizens defined as abject: criminals, alcoholics, the unemployed, drug addicts, and people who are violent (Lewontin 1994: 117).

One major focus of genetic research is disability. Genetics has a particular role to play in defining and disrupting the disabled body. Prenatal testing allows fetuses with genetic flaws to be identified and treated or aborted. In the genetic research aimed at eradicating disease (and so, having some degree of control over death) there is never any question that the clean and proper body is one that is able-bodied. This involves certain assumptions about disease and disability:

> Prenatal diagnosis presupposes that certain fetal conditions are intrinsically not bearable. Increasing diagnostic capability means that such conditions, as well as a host of variations that can be detected in utero, are proliferating, necessarily broadening the range of what is not "bearable" and restricting concepts of what is "normal." (Lippman 1991: 25)

It is never open for discussion, for example, whether Down syndrome children are effective and valuable people exactly as they are. It is assumed that children would have been better in some way if their genes could be altered to free them of the particular characteristics of Down syndrome. This is despite the fact that Down syndrome children are usually affectionate and gentle, with strong attachment to people. There is no distinction between disabilities. No distinction is made, for example, between disabilities that cause the person pain and suffering, and disabilities that produce physical malformation. If we accept that disability is, at least to some degree, a social construct, there is also the potential problem that Lippman alludes to—that the increased potential to examine the biology of an individual will lead to a more rigorous definition of disability. As Lippman has pointed out, the definition of disability is dependent on social constructions, since "malformation, a biomedical phenomenon, requires a social translation to become a 'problem'" (Lippman 1991: 45). When those who write about genetics do not acknowledge this, genetics does not add to the adequacy of our approach to disability, but attempts only to eradicate it.

The disabled body is the subject of genetic attention because of its abjection. As I argued earlier, genetics has a role to play in both controlling and disrupting the clean and proper body. Genetics has a specific role to play in the control and disruption of the disabled body. It has the potential to control the disabled body by removing whatever is "wrong" with it through gene therapy, personalized medicine, or termination of the disabled fetus. Yet it also has a disruptive element in its capacity to disturb conventional understandings of self. Able-bodied people view disabled people as "other" and may view with fear and horror the idea of physical and mental incapacity. Genetics, on the other hand, has the capacity to reveal every individual as disabled, because every person potentially has within his or her genes some flaw, even if it has not manifested itself as an existing ailment or characteristic.

The disabled body is particularly vulnerable to genetics in its controlling aspect but also offers transformative possibilities in its disruptive aspect. This disruptive capacity threatens the capacity to reject or expel disability by interfering with the fantasy that disability can only be located in the bodies of others, the disabled, and making such bodies subordinate. Such disruption invites regulation, particularly legal regulation.

The Secrets in My Genes: Genetic Discrimination and Privacy

When genetics is playing a part in controlling identity, law is not deemed necessary to regulate its effects. On the other hand, genetics in its disruptive aspect invites a flurry of legal regulation. As feminist and postmodern scholars have revealed, defining a body as abject and then regulating it is a form of violence to the Other. Despite this, when conventional understandings of self are disrupted, law is called upon to protect those whose power is threatened rather than support those whose status might be enhanced by the change. Genetic technologies demonstrate, in a most uncomfortable way for those of us who are able-bodied, that our bodies are flawed. Disease, disability, and even death are not miraculously absent from some bodies, inhabiting only the disabled body. Disease, disability, and death exist as possibilities within all bodies. We have enjoyed our ignorance of our genes, which guaranteed that as long as no symptom was manifest we retained full physical and mental ability. Now genetic science and technology promise us that we will know the details of our own present and future disability. Even if we do not have a specific genetic disorder, we may have a tendency to a form of cancer, or a recessive gene that marks us as a "carrier" of disability.

What do we do with this knowledge? In Australia, as in the United States and other western countries, such developments in genetic science have fuelled moves to increase the privacy protection offered to citizens. In Australia, genetic technologies have inspired attempts to legislate specifically on genetic privacy, in the Genetic Privacy and Non-discrimination Bill of 1998 (Cth), and a reference to the Australian Law Reform Commission requiring the commission to report on potential law reform in the areas of genetic privacy and discrimination. In addition, growing fears about genetic technologies have coincided with the passing of the Privacy (Private Sector) Amendment Act of 2001 (Cth), which regulates, among other things, the storage, management, and disclosure of health and genetic information.

The problems with using a privacy model to protect genetic information have been documented elsewhere (Karpin 2000). Genetic information is particularly difficult information to keep private, owing to its unique characteristics. For example, genetic information about individuals also provides information about their biological relatives. It is information that is consistent over the life span, meaning that one wrong disclosure has greater implications than information about, for example, a temporary health complaint. Any biological sample, one as simple as a single strand of hair, holds the entire genetic information available about a person.

The difficulty of protecting the privacy of genetic information has only increased the pressure on legislators to provide more stringent privacy laws. The call for protection of such information is couched in the language of consumer rights and public interest: benign terms that hide any personal fears and have undertones of unfair grievance:

> The potential benefits [of genetic testing] are significant, but there are real risks for consumers. Who owns my DNA and how can I control the way it is used? Will the secrets in my genes stop me getting insurance, or see me out of a job? Could insurers ask us to undergo genetic tests , and exclude those of us who "fail" from cover? (Petschler 2000: 10)

The concerns here are about ownership and control of personal information and identity, protection of existing social status, and the fear of failing a genetic test. Privacy laws are typically modelled to give greater control to individuals over the use, storage, and disclosure of personal information. In relation to genetics, such laws are appealing to those who fear the "secrets in their genes" and do not want them revealed.

The push for further regulation of the privacy aspects of genetic technologies is particularly striking in light of the current system that is in place to regulate disability discrimination. The *Disability Discrimination Act* (Cth) was passed in 1992, with the aim of eliminating discrimination against disabled people in a range of public activities such as work, accommodation, education, access to premises, and the provision of goods and services. The act attempts to secure for all disabled people, as far as possible, equality in Australian public and social life, including equality before the law.

What is most interesting about the act for the purposes of this chapter is its definition of disability. Disability is defined in section 4 as:

(a) total or partial loss of the person's bodily or mental functions; or
(b) total or partial loss of a part of the body; or
(c) the presence in the body of organisms causing disease or illness; or
(d) the presence in the body of organisms capable of causing disease or illness; or

(e) the malfunction, malformation or disfigurement of a part of the person's body; or
(f) a disorder or malfunction that results in the person learning differently from a person without the disorder or malfunction; or
(g) a disorder, illness, or disease that affects a person's thought processes, perception of reality, emotions or judgment or that results in disturbed behavior;
and includes a disability that:
(h) currently exists; or
(i) previously existed but no longer exists; or
(j) may exist in the future; or
(k) is imputed to a person.

The definition of disability in the act is broad, and has been interpreted just as widely. In a recent case, *Marsden* v *HREOC and Coffs Harbour & District Ex-Servicemen and Women's Memorial Club* [2000] FCA LEXIS 992 the federal court of Australia found that this definition of disability extended to drug dependence. In *Marsden*, the complainant alleged that the club had discriminated against him by refusing to serve him alcohol. Mr. Marsden used prescribed methadone to manage his heroin addiction. His use of methadone meant that he sometimes was unsteady on his feet, slurred his words, was uncoordinated, and appeared intoxicated. The club made Mr. Marsden's membership dependent on his not consuming alcohol because they were concerned, without medical evidence, that alcohol should not be consumed on a methadone program. The federal court found that addiction was a form of disability, and that it continued to be a disability even if it were satisfactorily treated and no symptoms were present. The court also said that Mr. Marsden could be discriminated against on the grounds that he "had previously been addicted to heroin, might in the future be addicted to heroin or another opiate, or because [the Club] imputed a disability to him"(56).

That such a broad definition covers genetic disorders, including those that are not manifest, is clear from complaints made under the act. In 2000, Graham Elliot[4] made a complaint of disability discrimination to the Australian Human Rights and Equal Opportunity Commission. At the time, Mr. Elliot was an inmate at a minimum-security, state-based correctional facility. Mr. Elliot was nearing the end of a long-term sentence for multiple serious assaults and had recently applied for parole. The parole board refused it, saying that they would not consider his application unless he underwent genetic testing for Huntington's chorea. Mr. Elliot's father had Huntington's disease, therefore Mr. Elliot had a 50 percent chance of having the disease. The rationale given by the parole board was that Huntington's chorea is often accompanied by loss of mental capacity and antisocial behavior, and they were not prepared to release Mr. Elliot into the community if he were so affected. Mr. Elliot said that he wanted to have the test, but only after release, when he could be appropriately counseled. The complaint was heard under the Disability Discrimination Act, but no conciliation was reached and the complaint was terminated as unconciliable.

The *Elliot* case demonstrates that a remedy already exists to protect people from ill-treatment on the basis of their genetic characteristics, as long as they are prepared to define themselves as disabled, and as long as they are prepared to share knowledge about their genes. In light of calls made to regulate genetic information, the lack of attention given to this already existing mechanism is notable. It seems explicable only if disability laws are seen as irrelevant to ordinary people who simply fail their genetic test.

As I understand it, regulation under antidiscrimination law represents the most practical course in terms of the protection of genetic information. Privacy legislation attempts to control every use of genetic information, which is difficult to manage at all. On the other hand, discrimination models do not attempt to control genetic information, but aim to prevent information about disability from being used to treat genetically disabled people differently. Genetic information is regulated only when it is used to the detriment of an individual.

A discrimination approach to regulating genetics also appears the most ethical course to take. Genetics offers us an opportunity to remove the divide between self and abject other. The limit of our system of thought about disability is the line that distinguishes between able-bodied and disabled. By opening up the possibility that we contain future or nonmanifest disabilities in our genes, genetics reveals that line to be a construction. The definition in the Disability Discrimination Act, along with genetics, tells us that future, potential, or imputed disability *is* disability. At the very least, disability hovers within our bodies or is contingent on the attitudes of those that surround us.

The disruptive potential of genetics offers possibilities to reconsider traditional conceptions of selfhood. In relation to disability, it offers the specific possibility of reconsidering definitions of ourselves as able-bodied or disabled. The postmodern ethical stance requires a striving toward the Other in any form, without incorporation or "devouring." Since we can never genuinely expel what exists in our own bodies, the violence that is done by investing only particular bodies with the qualities of abject Otherness is also done to ourself. The ethical stance in relation to the knowledge offered by genetics is attentiveness to what will be lost or rejected if the strict distinction between disabled and able-bodied is maintained. What will be lost is a way of seeing particular bodies that is not tainted by the fear, anxiety, and cruelty that accompanies perceptions of the abject Other.

Notes

1. According to male writers. For example: "I've been writing to you since seven and it's now nine-thirty, I only stopped half an hour for dinner (pea soup, filet of Brill Bercy that smelled so much of woman I had half an erection)" (Jean-Paul Sartre to Simone de Beauvoir in Beauvoir 1992: 84).

2. One example of this is the genetic examination of the body of the male homosexual. See Waldby, (1995) for an examination of the threat the male homosexual body poses to the male heterosexual body.

3. The broad scope of the definition of disability remains controversial, particularly where it offers protection against discrimination to people who could be characterized as less deserving. Following the Marsden case, the federal government introduced a bill to Parliament to amend the Disability Discrimination Act 1992 (Cth) to remove the protection against discrimination on the grounds of a person's drug addiction. The Disability Discrimination Amendment Bill 2003 was referred to a parliamentary committee for report at the end of 2003. The committee, the Senate Legal and Constitutional Legislation Committee, produced its report in April 2004, recommending further consultation on the bill. Two dissenting reports from nongovernment senators opposed the bill. The bill remains in the Senate, awaiting further action.

4. This is a fictional name because complaints to the Human Rights and Equal Opportunity Commission are confidential. Other identifying details have also been altered.

References

Beauvoir, Simone de (1992) *Witness to My Life: The Letters of Jean-Paul Sartre to Simone de Beauvoir,* trans. Lee Fahnestock and Norman MacAfee. New York: Scribners.

Cornell, Drucilla (1992) *The Philosophy of the Limit.* New York: Routledge.

Disability Discrimination Act 1992 (No. 135, 1992).

Ferenczi, Sandor (1938) *Thalassa: A Theory of Genitality.* trans. H. A. Bunker. New York: *The Psychoanalytic Quarterly.*

Freud, Sigmund (1950) *Totem and Taboo.* New York and London: W. W. Norton.

Grosz, Elizabeth (1989) *Sexual Subversions: Three French Feminists.* Sydney: Allen & Unwin.

Harris, Angela (1990) "Race and Essentialism in Feminist Legal Theory," *Stanford Law Review* 42: 581–616.

Innes, Graeme (2000) "Disability Discrimination and Insurance," Speech to the Australian Life Underwriters Association and Claims Association Conference. Sydney. Available at http://www.hreoc.gov.au/disability_rights/speeches/underwrite.htm.

Irigaray, Luce (1985) *This Sex Which Is Not One,* trans. Catherin Porter. Ithaca: Cornell University Press.

Karpin, Isabel (1994) "Reimagining Maternal Selfhood: Transgressing Body Boundaries and the Law," *Australian Feminist Law Journal* 2: 36–62.

Karpin, Isabel (2000) "The Genetic Connection: Owning our Genetic Heritage," *Journal of Law and Medicine* 7(4): 376–389.

Kristeva, Julia (1982) *Powers of Horror.* New York: Columbia University Press.

Lewontin, Richard C. (1994) "The Dream of the Human Genome," in Gretchen Bender and Timothy Druckery (eds.), *Culture on the Brink: Ideologies of Technology.* Seattle: Bay Press, pp 107–127.

Lippman, Abby (1991) "Prenatal Genetic Testing and Screening: Constructing Needs and Reinforcing Inequities," *American Journal of Law and Medicine* 17: 15–50.

Morrison, Toni (1981) *The Bluest Eye.* London: Triad.

Mykitiuk, Roxanne (1994) "Fragmenting the Body," *Australian Feminist Law Journal* 2: 63–98.

Petschler, Louise (2000) "Access Denied: Genetic Testing and Your Insurance," Consuming Interest 10.

Rabinow, Paul (1996) *Essays on the Anthropology of Reason.* Princeton, N. J.: Princeton University Press.

Rittner, Carol, and Roth, John K. (eds.) (1993) *Different Voices: Women and the Holocaust.* New York: Paragon House.

Senate Legal and Constitutional Legislation Committee (2004) *Report on the Provisions of the Disability Discrimination Amendment Bill 2003*, Parliament of Australia, Canberra.

Waldby, Catherine (1995) "Destruction: Boundary Erotics and Refiguration of the Heterosexual Male Body," in Elizabeth Grosz and Elspeth Probyn (eds.), *Sexy Bodies: The Strange Carnalities of Feminism*. London: Routledge, pp. 266–277.

Williams, Patricia J. (1991) *The Alchemy of Race and Rights*. Cambridge, Mass.: Harvard University Press.

V

Rethinking the Materiality of Embodiment

12

A "Genethics" That Makes Sense: Take Two

Rosalyn Diprose

This DNA, this double helix, this bare substance of our chromosomal being, source of our sameness, root of our difference.
—Fay, Weldon (1989: 20)

The claim that it is in DNA that science could discover the source of our sameness and the root of our difference not only points to the central vision of modern genetics (that it has at its disposal the means for mapping human identity and difference) but also to why genetics is of ethical interest.[1] The issue of human identity and difference and, in particular, concerns about the effacement of and discrimination against different ways of being, also lies behind interest in poststructural revisions of assumptions about human subjectivity, identity, and difference. The potential impact of some of those revisions on genetics is part of my concern here. Primarily however, my concern is to indicate the potential consequences of some of these revisions for ethics itself. The point at which genetics, ethics, and poststructural critiques of models of self-present identity and difference come together is over the issue of the body and sense (meaning). The claim to be elaborated here is that it is as bodies that we make sense. It is as bodies that our finitude and uniqueness are signified to others; hence it is as bodies that we are both social and moral beings. This uniqueness is expressed through, and is inseparable from, being open to others within a social context of discourses (scientific, ethical, sociological). As such, identity, and therefore difference, is never self-present; the body makes sense, but never completely or in and of itself. In this schema, the ethics of genetics, and biomedical science in general, does not reside in deciding whether genetics is right or wrong about the source of identity and difference. Rather, the ethics of genetics lies in recognizing the way that scientific and other discourses make sense of bodies and in ensuring that in this social expression of bodies scientific and other discourses remain open to difference and hence open to the openness by which bodies make sense.

The Meaning of Ethics

Poststructural critiques of models of self-present identity and difference either explicitly or implicitly revise the meaning of ethics to something that is as much premodern as it is postmodern, and this revision involves restoring a moral status to the body. In general terms, ethics is the question of being positioned and taking up a position in relation to others. "Ethics" is derived from the Greek word *ethos*, meaning dwelling, or habitat—the place to which one returns. Habitat encompasses habits that, as the product of the repetition of bodily activities, make up one's character, one's specificity, or what is properly one's own.[2] To belong to, and project out from an *ethos* is to take up a position in relation to others. This involves comparison, relation to what is different and to what passes before us. Taking up a position, presenting oneself, therefore requires a nonthematic awareness of temporality and location. And, the intrinsic reference point for temporality, spatial orientation and, therefore, difference, is one's body. Embodiment and ethics are inseparable insofar as we understand human existence in terms of dwelling or spatiotemporal being-in-the-world.

To base ethics on bodily dwelling would seem to be at odds with a more modern understanding of ethics. We more usually understand ethics in terms of a universal set of principles that ought to govern behavior, principles that are formulated and grasped by the rational mind. Because these principles claim universality, they evoke an ethics that assumes that behavior originates in a potentially unified mind housed in a broad, homogeneous habitat. Despite this emphasis, there are some contemporary accounts of an ethics based on embodied dwelling.[3] These variously locate the body as the site of one's habitat and subjectivity, where the body is constituted by a dynamic relation with other bodies in a social context of power, desire, and knowledge. Ethics then becomes the problematic of what constitutes one's habitat, the problematic of corporeal self-formation in relation to other social beings and within the laws and discourses that regulate those relations.[4] At issue in such an ethics is the extent of injustice effected by normalization and intolerance of, and discrimination against, different modes of dwelling.

The discrepancy between an approach to ethics based on universal rational principles and ethics based on embodied dwelling is not simply a question of etymology. Related to this are different, and usually unacknowledged, understandings of the structure and dynamics of our spatiotemporal being-in-the-world. The difference pertains to whether we think human "being" is composed primarily of mind or matter; to what we understand by the relation between mind and matter; and to whether we think that the world we inhabit is homogeneous or fragmented. Underlying all these questions is some assumption about the meaning of "in" in the phrase "being in the world."[5] An ethics based on universal rational principles assumes that human being is a discrete existence separate from the world (material) so that it is "in" the world after the advent of both. An ethics of bodily dwelling, on the other hand, claims that our being and the world (always material *and* social) are constituted through the relation "in." Science, that field of knowledge which governs the formulation of the nature of our being and of the world that we are "in," assumes the first meaning of "in"—that our being and the world are primordially distinct. And, since scientific descriptions of the body and the (natural) world that the body inhabits are thought to hover above both the body and its world without effect, then ethics is thought to have no place in knowledge.

Despite this distancing between ethics and epistemology and despite a preference for an ethics based on universal rational principles, the increasing public scrutiny of the activities of biomedical science suggests a link between science, bodily being, and ethics. The link is suggestive only. Much of the recent discussion within biomedical ethics does move away from abstract, formal principles, stressing instead individual rights, particular contexts, and specific needs.[6] However, in these discussions the nature of human being is usually described in terms of individuality and sentience; rarely is there any analysis of how or why medicine and science, as modes of *knowing*, are necessarily ethical.

What is even more surprising, given the material of biomedicine, is that rarely is there any explicit reference to the significance of embodiment to biomedical ethics.

David Schenck's paper, "The Texture of Embodiment: Foundation for Medical Ethics," is one notable exception (1986). Schenck, following Merleau-Ponty, acknowledges that the body is "our centre of activity in the world" (Schenck 1986: 44). As we comport ourselves toward the world *through* our bodies then, he argues, our body is not just an instrument by which we express ourselves. Rather, the body "*is literally our selves expressed*" (1986: 46, emphasis in original). Biomedical science and medical practice are by nature ethical because they deal with our most "intimate and alienating possession"—the body as our mode of social expression: "It is the texture of bodily being that gives to medicine as social practice and medical ethics as social discourse their particular and distinctive features" (Schenck 1986: 50). The general point to be made is that it is as bodies that we make sense, that meaning and value are generated. The body therefore is the expression of one's uniqueness as finite existence; as full of meaning and value in itself and as expressing a particular style of existence. However, a point that Schenck does not stress, paradoxically, is that this uniqueness is only signified within sociality.[7] This signification of the body, its expressiveness, is inseparable from the body's openness to the meaningful world of others and to the social and scientific discourses that make up the world in which we dwell and that attempt to represent and evaluate that uniqueness.

While recognizing the social expressiveness of the body as the ethical basis of biomedicine, Schenck limits the ethics of biomedicine to its role of intervening after the texture of the body, its social "expressiveness," has been rendered incoherent:

> Medicine deals with the *brokenness* of the body. . . . The collapse of the body at once invites and necessitates care by others. It *invites* care by virtue of the social expressiveness of the body, the call the injured body makes to unimpaired others. . . . [W]hat is given over to others in these moments is that which is most intimate to one's self, most important to one's presence in the world. (Schenck 1986: 51)

Schenck recognizes that the uniqueness of one's being-in-the-world is signified by the body, and he locates medical ethics in the responsibility involved in repairing that being-in-the-world. His analysis, therefore, suggests an ethics of difference—one that recognizes the material significance of embodiment to social existence. However, the connection he makes between being and world remains unclear and "in" takes on the status of the copula between two entities that precede their conjunction. It would seem, in Schenck's account, that our being, while bodily and habitual, only encounters the world it inhabits after it is constituted. Since biomedical practices only make the body their object after it is "broken," then they are included in the world that our being encounters. By separating our being from the social discourses and practices that make up the world, Schenck's analysis seems to avoid the question of how the body is the self expressed. What is it, if not something about the body's relation to its world of other social beings, that expresses its uniqueness? What constitutes the habitat and habits that hold together one's mode of being? What makes sense if not the sense of the world in which we dwell? While providing an astute analysis of the bodily foundation of medical ethics, Schenck not only leaves these questions unanswered, but seems to contradict the tradition of thought upon which his analysis depends.

Merleau-Ponty, for example, claims that the body, which is the bearer of orientation or position, is not "in" the world after the advent of both: "Our body is not primarily *in* space: it is of it" (1962: 148). Similarly, Heidegger argues that our being is not "in" the world in the way that water is in a glass (1962: 79). Rather, our being-in is constituted by the context of meaningful relations with which we are involved (Heidegger 1962: 114–22). We can only dwell in a world, encounter objects within it, and be encountered as an object (say, by science) if we are constituted by a set of relations with which we are, thereby, familiar. This familiarity, and the world's significance, is governed by a nonthematic preontological understanding of Being. For Merleau-Ponty, this prereflexive understanding resides in the body's orientation activity; for Heidegger, it resides in a history that we cannot control but that presents us as we evoke it at every moment. For both, the objectifying practices that represent our being (including biomedical science) form part of the significant world, the horizon, within which we dwell and which makes perception, action, and dwelling possible.

Scientific ideas about the body then inform the way the body expresses existence. This is neither idealism (or social constructionism), where ideas about the body would shape it into a seamless socially recognized whole, nor realism, where scientific and other discourses about the body would represent its truth in commonly accepted terms. Rather, the body expresses these ideas through its dwelling, between body and world. For Merleau-Ponty, expression (which includes perception—including scientific perception—action, sensibility in general) assumes that the body is already caught in the fabric of the perceived world and that this openness of the body to its world is such that what is seen and felt is at the same time a being seen and a being felt (1964a: 162–163).[8] For Merleau-Ponty, this ambiguity of the body arises on the basis of intercorporeality, on the basis of being touched, seen, and felt by the other. The ambiguity of the body lights the spark of perception; perception is incarnated (rather than being based on conscious representation) and is essentially signifying, and meaning of the world is expressed through the body (and vice versa). The felt is a feeling and subject and object, culture and nature (although the distinctions are only abstract) are articulated together through the perceiving body, through sensibility (Merleau-Ponty 1964b: 167). The body and its expression are realized ambiguously and unfinished between body and world, between the touching and being touched, between sensing and the sensed. Through this expression the body is both itself (it is unique and stands alone) *and* open to, and dwelling in, the world of other bodies. Also, social discourses about bodies (including biomedical discourses) inform their expression and can thereby take hold of a body through its habitual dwelling with others within this horizon of meaning. While scientific discourses can therefore capture a body, at the same time the body's expression is ambiguous, open, and unfinished and must remain so in order to begin to make sense at all.

The body's expressiveness is the basis of ethics because it is through others that this expression (the meaning and value of bodies) is realized. Levinas puts this ethical relation as follows: the other's alterity (strangeness, irreducible, unknowable difference) is the unique sense that prompts one's entry into discourse (Levinas 1987), or that prompts the body's expression (as Merleau-Ponty would put it). The body's expression given in response, including the expression of the body of the scientist who would attempt to know the body of the other, opens a relation to the other but also holds the potential for effacing the other's alterity, and so for finishing the other off. The ethics of the body's expression through others is therefore paradoxical. Another way to put this paradox, following Jean-Luc Nancy (1993), would be to say that it is through a social relation with other bodies that bodies make sense by the formation of a limit through the touch of other bodies, a limit that both separates a body from, and opens it to, the other.[9] This limit marks the expression of a body's difference from another but also marks the point at which the limit can be dissolved by the other's touch, expression, and discourse. While it is impossible to know this limit ahead of its formation, ethics is the ethics of this limit. Ethics is about trying to maintain an openness to alterity in the expression of bodies without effacing that limit of ambiguity through which bodies make unique sense.

If Schenck is to follow this tradition, then he would need to recognize that biomedical science has a role in the expression of our being-in-the-world and is not just a mode of reparation of that being. It is as a discourse as much as in its practice that biomedicine is ethical. Biomedical science does not, of course, confess to any constitutive role in the expression of the body's unique sense. It does acknowledge a role in the observation and manipulation of that identity and difference and takes on some responsibility for ensuring that its manipulative function is not socially detrimental. This distinction between the expression of the body and its manipulation is maintained by a division between theory and practice. That is, biomedical science claims to know, at least potentially, the identity of and difference among bodies. In this theoretical mode, biomedical science supposedly represents the source of the body's identity and difference, thought to lie outside that mode of knowing. On the other hand, biomedical practice can alter the texture of the body. Only as this secondary mode of intervention does biomedical science claim a constitutive role—in its ability to modify human matter.

Nowhere is biomedical science more active in its expression and manipulation of body matter, and nowhere are the distinctions between observing and doing, theory and practice, fact and value, knowledge and ethics more pronounced than in the field of genetics. An excursion into the debate about the ethical issues surrounding modern genetics best reveals what is problematic about these distinctions for an ethics aimed at enhancing our being-in-the-world.

The Ethics of Genetics

Through an increasingly vigorous and public debate about the ethics of genetics, we have been asked to share in the geneticist's competence as well as in responsibility for the always uncertain consequences of scientific research. The reason genetics is now thought to require the critical attention of all of us is best summarized in the following terms by one exemplary popularist account: "Genetics, perhaps more than any other branch of science except brain biology, probes deeply into the identity of individual human beings" (Suzuki and Knudtson 1989: 180). Any such account of modern genetics will describe how a cell's genetic content determines its metabolic processes and physical appearance. We are thus given some insight into how and why geneticists think that genes are ultimately responsible for a body's functioning and appearance and, ultimately therefore, its identity and difference.

Rather than question the theory about the source of human identity and difference, these accounts of the ethics of genetics usually focus their critical attention on the practical application of genetic theory. The first of two principal concerns about applied genetics has to do with its manipulation of "nature." The potential for designer bodies or gene therapy—the insertion, modification, and substitution of genetic material to correct defects or enhance function—is a common cause for concern.[10] However, if eugenics is a worry, the focus should not be limited to the obvious cases. Genetic theory informs a wide range of social and medical practices. It is the condition for the possibility of immunological theory, which in turn informs the approach to diseases such as AIDS.[11] Genetics also underscores screening for "defective" individuals, such as the criminal (through DNA fingerprinting, for example) or a fetus carrying a genetically transmitted disease. Reproductive technology, the development of biological weapons, and the selective breeding of flora and fauna for agricultural production all owe their vigor, splendor, and status to modern genetics.

Yet not all genetic practice is considered to be of ethical significance and even when caution is advised, say because of the potential for eugenics, not everyone agrees. The ethical import of genetics seems to depend, in the first instance, upon the degree to which modification or manipulation of bodily being is involved. Why this matters to the guardians of science is often expressed in the following terms: "Biomedical engineering circumvents the human context of speech and meaning, bypasses choice and goes directly to work to modify the human material itself" (Kass 1973: 62). By invoking a distinction between social meaning and matter (which allows the distinction between knowledge, or observation, and intervention), such arguments claim that biomedical manipulation can institute an irreversible change to one's being-in-the-world, to one's habitat. This implies that other vehicles of social change (the alteration of meaning for example) are more flexible. The distinction between social meaning and matter also implies that there is an original and pure mode of being that resides outside of social meaning in nature.

Not all genetic practice involves the obvious manipulation of matter; sometimes it is just a matter of surveillance. However, surveillance, or genetic screening, and genetic engineering share a second feature considered to be of ethical import: a particular attitude about difference. Nobody wants to create a chimera (at least no one would admit to this); the fantastic is considered to be too perverse, too offensive to our sensibilities. Rather, as Leon Kass has suggested, both the supporters and opponents of genetic engineering have, from the time the dream began, "ground their hopes and their fears in the same prospect: *that man can for the first time re-create himself*", emphasis in original (Kass 1973: 62) This desire to double the self by reproducing the self and making the other the same, and the attendant eradication of differences, is the second major cause of concern about genetic screening and manipulation.

The preservation of diversity is the primary motivation behind David Suzuki's and Peter Knudtson's critical account of modern genetics in *Genethics* (1989). They cite numerous examples of applied genetics that intentionally or inadvertently seek to eliminate the expression of differences. The Human Genome Project (HGP) is a case in point, although perhaps not obviously so. The HGP does not expressly aim at eradicating differences, but rather aims at locating all genes responsible for disease, normal metabolic processes, and subtle hereditary differences among individuals. Still, Suzuki and Knudtson point to a link between the mapping of genetic differences and the potential use of this map for surveillance, and they caution against the possibility of establishing "wholescale genetic screening programs . . . for identifying individuals who harbor genes considered 'defective' or 'inferior'" (Suzuki and Knudtson 1989: 336). The HGP and related screening programs, they claim, place too much confidence in a direct causal link between genes and individual behavioral differences and could result in misguided attempts to normalize and/or isolate individuals considered to be inferior. If anything, this concern about the HGP has deepened as it has progressed in the years since *Genethics* was published. Most recently Timothy Murphy has summarized similar ongoing concerns about screening based on the HGP in a context "where genetic data are often understood as genetic destiny" (Murphy 2001: 204).

There is little doubt that modern genetics lends authority and sophistication to the practices that map and attempt to efface differences. Yet, as the champions of genetics will point out, we have at our disposal more efficient means to regulate human behavior and minimize the expression of difference.[12] Any sinister use of genetics, they argue, reflects the contamination of science by the ideology governing these other means of regulation. This may be the case. However, the defense of genetics here again relies on a distinction between social meaning, or a biased interpretation of differences, and differences per se. Even Suzuki's and Knudtson's caution implies this distinction in the way they separate genetic theory from practice and then question the ability to interpret in practice the meaning and value of observed differences without reference to biased and discriminatory social norms. What supposedly separates "pure" genetics from other methods of social regulation, and from the "bad politics" that may allow its misuse, is that its authority is derived from the claim to know the origin of the expression of identity and difference outside its social meaning. Presumably then, the ethically correct categorization and manipulation of bodily being in the practical application of genetics would involve, not the social evaluation of difference in terms of a social norm, but reference to the origin of identity and difference per se.

Implied in these warnings about the social evaluation of identity and difference in the practical applications of genetics is a claim that this evaluation is relational (to a social norm), rather than a direct or self-present representation, and on that basis should be avoided. However, as the tradition of philosophy beginning with Hegel reminds us, identity is always *produced* through differential relations.[13] To evaluate differences as defective or inferior relies on the (incorrect) assumption that the standard to which the evaluation refers, the "proper," stands alone. This assumption also pervades the claim that science can represent difference per se, as if the identity from which the difference differs stands apart from that relation and has an identity in itself. In both cases, the social and the scientific, the practical and the theoretical, the description and evaluation of identity and difference, and the expression of identity and difference proceed by the institution of an interval or limit between the one and the other. Insofar as this expression of identity and difference is taken as the final word and the interval between one and the other is taken as immutable empty space, expression consists in an ontological closure to the other, to difference, and the reduction of difference to the same. If this is what is considered unethical about applied genetics, then its unethical preconditions lie in the theory.

The expression of bodies through the constitution of this interval matters. What constitutes this interval between entities so that they make sense is also what constitutes the "in" between one's being and the world. It is what prevents each identity from dissolving into its other (including the subject and object of knowledge). Genetics, by referring to the origin of difference, claims to know the nature of this interval—what lies between entities so that their difference is real and absolute. However, it is the complicity of genetics in the *production*, rather than the indifferent description, of this interval or limit between different identities that requires more attention. What I will argue is that genetic theory is itself a genetic operation; it is involved in the production of identity and difference. As such it runs the risk, always there in the expression of bodies through the other, of effecting an ontological closure to otherness. Insofar as this production secures the interval between the one and the other, it reduces differences to its own terms, reproducing the normalizing and discriminatory practices of which applied genetics is accused.

On the other hand, because identity comes into being through the otherness of the other, both the subject and object of knowledge are always other than themselves, as are the identities and differences that genetics purports to describe. Hence, the genetic determination of bodily identity and differences is necessarily deferred. Insofar as genetics demonstrates this ambiguity of the expression of bodies, it remains open to the openness to difference through which bodies make sense.

Genetics That Makes Sense

Genetic theory takes place within the scientific mode of existence that assumes a distinction between the object and subject of knowledge, between the identity of our bodily being and the discourses that describe that being and that make up the world that we inhabit. So genetics, at the level of theory, is considered to have a representative rather than a constitutive function in its delineation of the origin and somatic expression of difference. It would seem that genetics, as theory, has no ethics; it does not make or modify the sensed, it makes sense of the sensed. At least its aim is to make sense.

But could genetics make sense in another sense? As a branch of science, genetics promises more complete and adequate truth of the origin of somatic identity and differences. Lurking within this promise is the same attitude about difference that is of concern in applied genetics. As Emmanuel Levinas claims: "Without doubt, the finite being that we are cannot in the final account complete the task of knowledge; but in the limit where this task is accomplished, it consists in making the other become the Same" (Levinas 1985: 91).[14] For Levinas, it is alterity (irreducible, unknowable difference) that provokes the desire to know—a claim that seems obvious in the case of genetics. Yet, the subject of knowledge, in response to this otherness, does not simply discover the nature of the interval between entities that makes them different or between itself and its object. Rather, the subject of knowledge forms and transforms this interval by expressing the other in its own terms. We may be sympathetic with the call to responsibility being made by the custodians of science toward the geneticist who puts the theory into practice. However, if, the formative activity of applied genetics is informed by a similar reduction and normalization of difference at the level of theory, then perhaps this finger pointing is slightly misplaced.

If "pure" genetics is a simple re-presentation of the origin and expression of difference, then it must uphold the basis of its authority: the assumption that it can be uncontaminated by social meaning and devoid of productive effects. Neverthless, every aspect of genetic theory is informed by the same notion of difference apparent in its practice. This is difference as complementarity that assumes a preferred identity, and where the one and its other appear to stand apart before comparison of the other in terms of the one. It is the notion of difference that has been the target of so much feminist criticism. Insofar as it operates with this economy of difference, genetic theory displays a tendency toward the doubling of self (making the other the same), which is of concern in applied genetics. As we accompany the geneticist to the origin of difference, we encounter numerous examples of this understanding of difference.[15] Beginning with sexual difference, we find that the man and the woman each contribute half the complement of chromosomes to be found in the cells of their offspring. These match up into twenty-two pairs plus two sex chromosomes (identical in females, different in males). Each chromosome consists of a DNA double helix containing two complementary strands that "are related in much the same way as a photographic print and the negative from which it is made. Each harbors the shadowy image of the other" (Suzuki and Knudtson 1989: 52). Moreover, each DNA strand is joined to the other through a series of nucleotide bases that will only link with their opposites.

Described in this way, from the macro level of sexual difference down to its microscopic expression, one would assume that the microscopic distribution of differences mimics sexual difference, or the way in which we map sexual difference at the level of the social: as opposition and complementarity where the negative is the other side of a favored image. However, according to the geneticist, the production and expression of difference is the other way around: difference as complementarity at the macro level is an expression of, and originates with, the genetic code. In other words, the genetic code grounds this mirroring effect and is what prevents each identity from dissolving into the other through its determination of difference in and for itself. At least, this is the case in theory.

However, in the pathway between the genetic code and its expression there lies another slippery operation of difference and an unsuccessful attempt to contain difference as the other side of sameness. Even the origin of difference, the gene, defies identification in itself.

While the gene is proposed as the origin of meaning, its expression is determined, not by a discrete code as one would assume, but by the *order* of nucleotide base pairs along the DNA double strand. Nor do contiguous relations alone determine the expression of difference. This sequence must first be replicated or transcribed into the form of a mirror image itself. This discordant doubling is then reversed; the message carried by the messenger is translated back by specifying the production of its own mirror image. With the appearance of the other of the other, we do not return to the genetic code from which we began. The bases that make up the transfer RNA carry with them the base units of proteins that dutifully assemble according to the order of their nucleotide base hosts—an order prescribed, via a detour through the other, by the original code. With this synthesis of proteins, the genetic message is expressed at the microscopic level. However, the message must pass through a further symphony of differential relations before difference is orchestrated at the surface of the body. In a mysterious and unknown way, the relation among proteins determines the function and shape of cells, the distribution of which determines the function and shape of different parts of the body and, hence, the morphology of the whole.

Even if the geneticist's map were complete, which it is not, the most it could explain is sameness from repetition, not difference. While this description of the origin and expression of difference indicates that the manifestation of the message is always other than itself, there is an attempt to contain the production of meaning within the paradigm of exact translation. This requires insisting, despite all indications to the contrary, upon an integrity between the code and its expression. Such integrity can only be claimed if the code is original, discrete, and can in its necessary passage through the other, completely subsume the other to itself without remainder. The cost of insisting on total incorporation of the other so that translation is exact is that diversity, which is the rule rather than the exception, tends to be understood in terms of disruption, breakdown, or mutation in the process of transmission rather than an expression of an absence of integrity in reproduction and the expression of difference. It is therefore not surprising that difference in applied genetics is understood in the same terms.

At the same time, the geneticist concedes, even within his or her own paradigm, that the expression of the code is never exact; nor the code original. There is a play of difference that is the condition for the possibility of both the original code and of the complementary difference apparently operating in its expression. For a start, the gene does not simply appear but is a product of a prior distribution of differences—sexual difference (meiosis) and prior DNA replication—and is prone to the uncertainties of both. This uncertainty is acknowledged in genetics, but is usually attributed to the limits of knowledge rather than its effect—the effect of a process of signification that divides and disperses entities as it grounds and presents them.

The effect of attempting to contain identity and difference within a notion of complementarity is also manifests in the inability of genetics to adequately explain the process of DNA transcription and translation without the production of, and reference to, other "outsides." For instance, what prior "message" draws a boundary around base sequences to indicate the beginning and end of a code? Other base sequences ("terminators" and "promoters") "which are not expressed," we are told. Who or what recognizes these boundaries so that the process of transcription begins and ends appropriately? Enzymes determine this spacing, but who or what directs the work of enzymes? There are further differential relations to which this no-longer-original code is referred, all of which account for a necessary ambiguity in the expression of meaning: the "same" code is found in multiple locations; the activity of genes can be affected by the "geographic location" of other genes; some genes are "programmed" to be "nomadic"; most genes are polymorphic and "hereditary" differences are usually polygenic (involving the interplay of many genes). The spatiotemporal relations that determine the interplay of these different terms are said to be a product of yet another set of "regulatory mechanisms," but, of these, "little is known" (Suzuki and Knudtson 1989: 48–69).

While the mapping and manipulation of identities and differences that occur in applied genetics are meant to be authorized by knowledge of the genetic origin of the expression of identity and differences, we find that the origin is always other than itself. The geneticist's dream of mapping the play of genes into a seamless whole will remain just that, a dream. This is because genetics does not re-present real differences thought to lie outside that expression; it signifies with material effects. As a mode of knowing that divides entities and claims their difference to be original and part of the same, genetics is itself a process of production of origins. This is a mode of production that Jacques Derrida would describe as a spacing that constitutes the interval, necessary for signification, between the two "things" that interval produces. It is a process that expresses identities and differences only to ensure that the discrete identity of those differences is deferred. The genetic production and expression of differences, therefore, guarantees the interruption of every self-identity.[16]

The search for the origin of identity and difference, therefore, cannot stop with the gene—an entity that the search itself produces. We are referred beyond genes to mysterious regulatory mechanisms that oversee their production and spatiotemporal distribution. Nor will the origin be found there. As each origin dissolves into its other, we get closer to where we began: to the manifestation of differences at the surface of the body and among bodies, to their sociopolitical expression, and to the author of that distribution. However, we cannot find an ultimate author or subject of this system of differences either.[17] The geneticist, like the gene, is a body expressed via its other and as an effect of the same spacing, is therefore constituted and expressed only in being divided from itself. The body may be the self expressed, as Schenck would put it, but only with a lack of certainty—only by being inscribed in a system of differences that genetics helps to produce and maintain. In other words, we find that both the subject and the object of genetics, the world and one's being, are constituted in relation to each other and are therefore always other than themselves.

The uniqueness of bodies can almost be found in the thick of this genetics and are not indifferent to its terms. The production and manifestation of differences that genetic theory attempts to describe is not outside of that description. Genetics is not simply a correct or incorrect re-presentation of real differences; it actualizes differences through their corporeal expression. On the other hand, bodily differences cannot be reduced to the genetic code. Genetics does not give us the truth of the origin of identity and difference; the genetic expression of a body is ambiguous and always other to itself. Rather, genetics is one particularly dominant mode of an infinite number of discursive practices that make differences real by the use of categories that produce and organize them through relations on the basis of sameness. The body is the homespun fabric of this process of organization and as such it is an almost coherent, but somewhat fragile, effect of power and knowledge.

Genetics is included in what Michel Foucault refers to as biopower: the technologies of power deployed with the emergence of the modern biomedical and social sciences in the nineteenth century. Without reference to law, and without displaying themselves as power, these sciences divide and assemble the body; evaluate, sort, and compare it. They thereby transform life by effecting distributions around a norm of health and well-being (Foucault 1978). The assumption of, and desire for, sameness pervades these sciences of the body. As I have argued, this urge to re-create the self informs genetic theory as well as its practice.

To the extent that the formative function of genetics is disavowed—its function of distributing differences in and among bodies—the body stands alone in the splendor of its presence. This spacing has material effects, so that the body appears to stand apart from the world or the discursive practices that constitute it and measure its difference as an apparent afterthought. At the same time, a body's specificity cannot be reduced to this objectification, and the gap between our being and the world, which knowledge opens up, cannot be maintained. The origins and causes of being, which are the objects of knowledge, multiply in this gap. Just as the border of the gene disperses into a mirror image that exceeds it at the moment it is assembled, so does the border that marks off the body from the practices that objectify it. The knowledge that effects borders within and among bodies also provides the conditions for the possibility of their "brokenness."

If the uniqueness of embodiment, of one's *ethos* or habitat, is to be found anywhere, it is not in the work of some more archaic understanding of Being or in a unified identity that exists before entering a world. Rather, it lies within the modes of knowing that present us by a spacing that simultaneously marks off as it interrupts every assemblage of self;

in between a genetics that determines a body's difference in terms of a norm and the necessary deferment of that determination. One's *ethos* is marked by a *pathos*; by the conflicts and contradictions that are living testimony to the subjection of bodies to normalization; to the impossibility of separating bodies from how they are known; and to the necessary disruption of both poles of this process of identification. It is marked by a somatic expression of difference referring to an "original" code that cannot be found in and for itself; by a description of the operation of difference that refers to the same social meaning or practice of distributing difference that it is meant to authorize or correct; by a genetics that owes its prestige to locating the source of bodily differences but confesses to only locating sameness. These contradictions feed off and reinforce the conflicts that mark the differences of bodies expressed in applied genetics, both the glamour and shame of which derives from its normative function. Hence, a project such as the HGP will, in attempting to map the origin of difference, effect and underscore the effacement of difference.

Attempting to locate a body definitely, or taking up a position by evoking one's absolute uniqueness, necessarily involves reference to an outside. In thus claiming an absolute limit or empty space between one body and another, conflict or a fundamental heterogeneity is disavowed at the moment it is produced. One's position is also one's disposition. Genetics in theory or practice is complicit with this curious mode of production; it makes sense and non-sense, literally. So, medical ethics does not begin with its role in dealing with the brokenness of bodies nor does genethics begin with the misuse of theory in the practice of effacing differences. Biomedical ethics begins with the formative function of its own modes of knowing which, by mapping what remains other to oneself, are complicit in the constitution and dissolution of borders within and among bodies. Our ways of knowing are dependent upon and multiply differences that we then attempt to contain. It is in this production and effacement of different habitats that we can locate the conditions for the possibility of what is considered unethical practice. It would seem that biomedical science is an art in all its modes and, as Aldous Huxley claimed in his early warning about genetics, "art also has its morality" (1955: 7).

Notes

1. An early version of this paper appeared in Diprose and Ferrell (1991). While much has happened in genetics and its ethics since then, the message about the impact of postmodernism on the ethics of genetics has yet to filter through to the debates and textbooks in the field. The message therefore bears repeating with some extra commentary on the French and German philosophy that carries it and with some account of the literature on the ethics of genetics that has emerged more recently.

2. For example, in *Nichomachean Ethics,* book 2, ch. 1, Aristotle defines *ethics* as character established through habitual action. See also Charles Scott's detailed etymology of *ethos* in Scott (1988).

3. See, for example, Diprose (1994), Foucault (1985), Gatens (1996), and Irigaray (1993).

4. For a more detailed account of ethics so understood, particularly in relation to Foucault's distinction between ethics and morality, see chapter 2 in Diprose (1994).

5. The meaning of "being-in" is Martin Heidegger's question in *Being and Time* (1962: s. 12, 78–86).

6. This kind of ethics of specificity is evoked, for example, by H. Tristram Engelhardt, Jr. (1986) and by various papers in a special issue of *Hypatia* on feminist ethics and medicine (vol. 4, no. 2, 1989). However, this is without reference to the problem of embodiment (with the exception of Susan Wendall's account of disability in the latter). This move away from universal moral priciples is even more apparent in recent bioethics textbooks although still without any direct link made between the human body and the need to account for differences.

7. See Jean-Luc Nancy's discussion of the body's uniqueness (singularity) and how this uniqueness is only realized through the otherness of others in "Corpus" (Nancy 1993).

8. For a more detailed account of Merleau-Ponty's model of expression from his early work and how this relates to ethics, see chapter 6 in Diprose (1994); for an account of his model of expression from his later work, see chapter 5 and 9 in Diprose (2002).

9. This is one way Nancy describes the ambiguity of the body, or the idea that the body makes sense as "singular" but only through the touch of other bodies; "to touch is to be at this limit" (Nancy 1993: 206).

10. For accounts of the ethics of gene therapy with respect to its manipulation of human identity and difference, see Elliot (1993) and Chadwick (2001).

11. For an account of genetics, difference, and HIV-AIDS, see Diprose and Vasseleu (1990).

12. Bernard Davis, for example, defends the progress that genetics can bring by claiming that the misuse of genetics is no worse than, and merely feeds into,

other politically contaminated methods for regulating individuals (Davis 1973). Charles Birch uses the same distinction between "bad politics" and scientific exploration of reality slightly differently. He claims that the use of genetics to eliminate real differences is a virtue that rectifies inequalities resulting from the biased evaluation of genetic differences in "wrong political and social systems" (Birch 1975: 8).

13. This idea pervades Hegel's work, but a brief account can be found in his *Science of Logic*, pp. 171–174 in s.119 (1975). This relational understanding of the production of identity and difference also underlies Saussure's understanding of the production of meaning (there are no positive terms, only differences) as well as Merleau-Ponty's model of the expression of the body (outlined earlier) and Derrida's idea of *différance*. The critical difference between Hegel's formulation and his poststructural critics is that for them there can be no unity of identity and difference, no final fully present expression of meaning.

14. For a more detailed discussiom of Levinas' idea of the ethical relation to alterity, see Chapter 9 in Diprose (2002).

15. My illustration is necessarily a caricature of genetic theory, drawn from texts, such as Suzuki and Knudtson's *Genethics* (1989), that applaud genetic theory while condemning unethical aspects of its practical application. I do not thereby wish to deny either the richness and complexities of the theory or the ambiguities and uncertainties that remain over the question of how genes express identities and differences. My point is rather to show how overlooking those complexities and ambiguities, which is what gives genetics its status as a science, serves to reduce difference to sameness. The complexities and ambiguities, when admitted, reveal the way science can practice a light touch in the expression of bodies by revealing the uncertainty and dynamic aspect of the limits that differentiate bodies from each other.

16. For his most concise account of this operation, see Derrida (1982). See also Vasseleu (1991) for further discussion of the effects of this operation within the discourses of the biological sciences.

17. As Derrida claims, "Subjectivity—like objectivity—is an effect of *différance*" (1981: 28). Hence, there can be no subject of the difference that conditions this distinction.

References

Birch, Charles (1975) "Genetics and Moral Responsibility," in Charles Birch and Paul Abrecht (eds.), *Genetics and the Quality of Life*. Sydney: Pergamon Press, pp. 6–19.

Chadwick, Ruth (2001) "Gene Therapy," in H. Kuhse and P. Singer (eds.), *A Companion to Bioethics*. Oxford: Blackwell, pp. 189–197.

Davis, Bernard (1973) "Prospects for Genetic Intervention in Man," in Richard W. Wertz (ed.), *Readings on Ethical and Social Issues in Biomedicine*. Englewood Cliffs, N.J.: Prentice-Hall, pp. 57–61.

Derrida, Jacques (1981) *Positions*, trans. Alan Bass. Chicago: University of Chicago Press.

Derrida, Jacques (1982) "Différance," in *Margins of Philosophy*, trans. Alan Bass. Chicago: University of Chicago Press, pp. 1–28.

Diprose, Rosalyn (1994) *The Bodies of Women: Ethics, Embodiment and Sexual Difference*. London: Routledge.

Diprose, Rosalyn (2002) *Corporeal Generosity: On Giving with Nietzsche, Merleau-Ponty, and Levinas*. Albany: State University of New York Press.

Diprose, Rosalyn, and Ferrell, Robin (eds.) (1991) *Cartographies: Post-structuralism and the Mapping of Bodies and Spaces*. Sydney: Allen & Unwin.

Diprose, Rosalyn, and Vasseleu Cathryn (1990). "Animation-AIDS and Science/Fiction," in A. Cholodenko (ed.), *The Illusion of Life*. Sydney: The Power Institute, pp. 145–160.

Engelhardt, H. Tristam, Jr. (1986) *The Foundation of Bioethics*. New York and Oxford: Oxford University Press.

Elliot, Robert (1993) "Identity and the Ethics of Gene Therapy," *Bioethics* 7: 27–40.

Foucault, Michel (1978) *The History of Sexuality, vol.* I, trans. Robert Hurley. New York: Random House.

Foucault, Michel (1985) *The Use of Pleasure*, trans. Robert Hurley. New York: Vintage.

Gatens, Moira (1996) *Imaginary Bodies: Ethics, Power and Corporeality*. London and New York: Routledge.

Hegel, G. W. F. (1975) *The Science of Logic* (trans William Wallace) Oxford: Oxford University Press.

Heidegger, Martin (1962) *Being and Time* (trans. John Macquarrie and Edward Robinson) New York: Harper & Row.

Huxley, Aldous (1955) *Brave New World*. Harmondsworth, UK: Penguin.

Irigaray, Luce (1993) *An Ethics of Sexual Difference* (trans. C. Burke and G. C. Gill) London: Athlone Press.

Kass, Leon R. (1973) "The New Biology: What Price Relieving Man's Estate," in Richard W. Wertz (ed.), *Readings on Ethical and Social Issues in Biomedicine*. Englewood Cliffs, N. J.: Prentice-Hall, pp. 62–71.

Levinas, Emmanuel (1985) *Ethics and Infinity: Conversations with Philippe Nemo* (trans. Richard A. Cohen) Pittsburgh, Pa.: Duquesne University Press.

Levinas, Emmanuel (1987) "Meaning and Sense," in *Emmanuel Levinas: Collected Philosophical Papers* (trans. Alphonso Lingis). Dordrecht, the Netherlands: Martinus Nijhoff, pp. 75–108.

Merleau-Ponty, Maurice (1962) *Phenomenology of Perception* (trans. Colin Smith) London: Routledge & Kegan Paul.

Merleau-Ponty, Maurice (1964a) "Eye and Mind," (trans. Carleton Dallery) in James M. Edie (ed.), *The Primacy of Perception*. Evanston, Ill.: Northwestern University Press, pp. 159–190.

Merleau-Ponty, Maurice (1964b) "The Philosopher and His Shadow," in *Signs* (trans. Richard McCleary) Evanston, Ill.: Northwestern University Press, pp. 159–181.

Murphy, Timothy F (2001) "Mapping the Human Genome," in H. Kuhse and P. Singer (eds.), *A Companion to Bioethics*. Oxford: Blackwell, pp. 198–205.

Nancy, Jean-Luc (1993) "Corpus," in *The Birth to Presence,* trans. Brian Holmes et al. Stanford, Calif: Stanford University Press, pp. 189–207.

Schenck, David (1986) "The Texture of Embodiment: Foundation for Medical Ethics," *Human Studies* 9: 43–54.

Scott, Charles (1988) "Heidegger and the Question of Ethics," *Research in Phenomenology* 18, pp. 23–40.

Suzuki, David, and Knudtson, Peter (1989) *Genethics: The Ethics of Engineering Life*. Sydney: Allen & Unwin.

Vasseleu, Cathryn (1991) "Life Itself," in R. Diprose and R. Ferrell (eds.), *Cartographies: Poststructuralism and the Mapping of Bodies and Spaces*. Sydney: Allen & Unwin, pp. 55–64.

Weldon, Fay (1989) *The Cloning of Joanna May*. London: Collins.

13

Queer Kids: Toward Ethical Clinical Interactions with Intersex People

Katrina Roen

Medicine should be at the service of intersexed people rather than a power that operates on our bodies to normalize us whether we want to be normalized or not.
—(Hegarty and Chase 2000: 128)

Poststructuralist feminist approaches to bioethics offer opportunities for analyzing how we are constituted as "women" through medical discourses. Such approaches may disturb the foundations of ethically questionable practices and knowledges. This disturbance must be the starting point for feminist analysis of intersex treatment.

For the sake of not laboring analytical themes that reappear throughout this volume, I will state briefly what I consider to be pivotal aspects of a poststructuralist feminist approach to biomedical ethics and sexed embodiment. According to such an approach, human subjects are not understood in terms of mechanistic models of body and mind, where components may be isolated and manipulated (treated). Rather, medical practices and processes are situated in a discursive and politicized context by which "bioethics . . . [becomes] fully implicated in the inscription of the very body it seeks to describe, and ostensibly to protect" (Shildrick 1997: 214). If the discursive and sociopolitical context is part of clinical practice, then medical technologies must be developed concurrently with rigorous analysis of their broader implications, including their ethical implications.

Within such a framework, notions of normalcy and of health may be critically reviewed so that the latter is not defined in terms of the former. Dominant understandings about "sex" and "gender" may be problematized, and clinical approaches to people who live outside of normative sex and gender constructs would reflect a sensitivity to their experiences and their medical needs, over and above any medical imperative to set everything straight. Clinicians, and people who seek clinical services, would be regarded as complexly gendered, embodied subjects. Decisions that clinicians and families make about the care of atypically sexed children would take place in a context where all genders are in question, every body is queer in some way.

The understanding of "intersex" used throughout this chapter is very broad and inclusive, referring to any body whose sex may be perceived as sufficiently atypical to raise the possibility of cosmetic treatment. The concept of "queer" is useful here insofar as it signifies the liberatory possibility of claiming non-normative ways of being, the radical opportunity to redefine sexes and genders, and the potential of poststructuralist thought to rework notions of sexed embodiment and identity.

Intersex Debate

[A] queer body . . . throws into question even the possibility of surgical and hormonal "correction." (Turner 1999: 474)

During the latter half of the twentieth century, the anatomies and identities of children born with sexually atypical features have come under specific kinds of discursive and surgical regulation. In North America, Australasia, and the United Kingdom it has become standard medical practice to surgically and hormonally "correct" intersexed anatomies from infancy. These regulatory practices have come under criticism from ethicists (Dreger, 1998), medical practitioners (Diamond and Sigmundson 1997), and intersexed people themselves (Mitchell 2000; Chase 1998; Holmes 1994). The way that ethical questions about intersex medical treatments have been framed by clinicians and by intersex activists suggests an impasse. Clinicians have an ethical responsibility to respond to parents' requests—and they do this by surgically "correcting" infants' ambiguous genitalia. Activists, nonetheless, argue forcibly for a moratorium on cosmetic genital surgery on infants.

The standards of practice that have been emerging since the 1950s grew directly from the work of John Money, who proposed that sexual reassignment would be possible if carried out before a critical age, and if the child was raised unambiguously within the gender role consistent with its new sex (Money et al., 1955). The late 1990s, however, saw a rapid increase in interest and new concerns about the medical treatment of intersex infants and children. One forum for discussion on this topic was the *Journal of Clinical Ethics'* special issue on intersexuality in 1998. Authors in this issue urged "above all else, that surgeons no longer operate on infants born with ambiguous genitals to create 'more normal looking' genitals" and "if surgery should be done at all, it should be done much later, when children . . . can consent" (Howe, 1998: 337). In his overview of the debate between intersex adults and clinicians who support infant genital surgery, Howe describes clinicians as seeking (1) to enable genitally ambiguous children to "acquire an intact sexual identity" (1998: 337), and (2) to enable parents to overcome ambivalent feelings and love their child.

Kipnis and Diamond, who have researched the clinical management of intersex infants from a medical ethics perspective since the early 1980s, proposed three significant changes with regard to medical approaches to intersexuality:

> 1. That there be a general moratorium on [the surgical assignment of intersex people] when it is done without the consent of the patient. (1998: 405)
> 2. That this moratorium not be lifted unless and until the medical profession completes comprehensive look-back studies and finds that the outcomes of past interventions have been positive. (1998: 406)
> 3. That efforts be made to undo the effects of past deception by physicians. (1998: 406)

Their third point refers to the effects of deception, which echoes numerous texts (e.g., Moreno 1997; Wilson and Reiner 1998; Kitzinger 2000) critiquing the aspect of intersex treatment that demands a level of secrecy. Kitzinger cites stories reflecting the secrecy, confusion, and humiliation against which many intersex people battle.

> Doctors have lied to parents (and, later, to the daughters), with stories of "twisted" or "cancerous" ovaries, or a "diseased uterus," leaving women to grapple with, as one woman expressed it, "the sense of being an outsider without knowing just what kind of outsider I was." (Kitzinger 2000: 388)

At the heart of the clinical imperative to keep the surgical assignment of gender secret is an understanding about the "naturalness" of gender. This understanding was articulated in the work of Garfinkel (1967) and Kessler and McKenna (1978). "In order for gender to be perceived as "natural" . . . it must not be seen as passing . . . [as it is understood that] real men and women do not pass" (Kessler and McKenna 2000: 18). The assumption of clinicians is that conscious passing is not enough (for them or for the child). The optimal solution is to get the child to "be" a girl or a boy, and that requires secrecy about the measures taken to enable their bodies to pass. Ironically, in the attempt to provide intersex people with a normative sense of gender, medical practices and prescriptions leave some intersex people with a great deal of emotional pain and confusion.

Kipnis and Diamond's second point concerns the failing of outcome studies, about which Kessler's work is particularly informative. She claims that "in spite of the thousands of genital operations performed every year, there are no meta-analyses from within the medical community on levels of success" (Kessler 1998: 53). From her own analysis of clinical follow-up studies, Kessler describes how surgeons tend to evaluate their own procedures, "rarely comparing across procedures and never comparing results with a control sample—the intersexed who did not receive surgery" (1998: 53).

From her review of twelve clitoroplasty and vaginoplasty follow-up studies published between 1974 and 1995, Kessler (1998) concluded that evaluations of surgical success, in the case of intersexed children and infants, rest not on the experiences, preferences, or later adjustments of the intersexed person concerned, but on the cosmetic appearance of the surgically constructed genitalia, and on parents' and clinicians' satisfaction with that appearance.

What of the first of Kipnis and Diamond's recommendations, calling for a moratorium on intersex surgery? For those critical of intersex treatment, many of whom are intersex adults, the call to stop surgery is made passionately and repeatedly, and articulated as an ethical imperative. Yet for clinicians who carry out the treatment, and who navigate emotional interactions with the parents of intersex children, the need to do *something* to enable the child to be accepted by its parents, and ultimately by its peers, is sometimes expressed as an ethical imperative to use surgery.

In response to the call for a moratorium, clinicians working in the field argue, first, that recent technological developments will ensure that the next generation of intersex adults is likely to be more satisfied with their treatment than those who came before,[1] and second that any surgical complications point to technological failure, not to an error in deciding to embark on the surgery per se. Further in defense of intersex surgery, clinicians suggest that technological failures are not the norm. The reason we hear horror stories about surgery going wrong, and about intersex adults who claim they should not have been surgically altered in childhood, is because stories of successes are defined precisely by their silence. Based on assessment criteria that favor rates of (cosmetic) success over severity of emotional trauma, clinicians who defend intersex surgery conclude that current treatment approaches are not sufficiently unsatisfactory to be stopped. And so the impasse persists between those who practice or enable, and those who speak out against cosmetic genital surgery for intersex patients.

While recent intersex writings have considerable points of overlap with poststructuralist feminism,[2] feminism in general does not necessarily sit easily with intersex issues. Some strands of feminism have too willingly worked within binary notions of gender to be obviously useful for an analysis of intersex treatment. Feminist approaches, which rely on a fixed and clearly demarcated identity for women (e.g., Jeffreys 1997; Raymond 1979), are explicitly hostile to those whose politics rest on a deconstruction of the man or woman binary, such as transgender and intersex people. Nevertheless, recent expositions of intersex concerns present a strong case for the importance of these concerns to feminists.

A key proponent of U.S. intersex politics, Chase, considers the ethics and practices of intersex surgery to be important areas for feminist analysis and critique because such practices are "incredibly sexist. They're based on the idea that men have sex; women are penetrated by men and have babies" (Hegarty and Chase 2000: 124). Chase articulates her own feminist analysis, suggesting that, in a clinical setting, "women's" pain is regarded as less important than "men's" pain. According to her, this differential perception of women's and men's experiences underpins the logic of intersex treatment.

> [W]hen doctors are presented with a boy whose penis is very small and pees from the underside rather than from the tip, they ask themselves: "what can we do

> about this boy's pain? That's going to be an emotionally painful thing to live with." And I agree that's going to be painful to live with. They say: "we'll chop off his dick, and cut out his balls and tell everybody he's a girl and give him estrogen and then stitch a piece of colon into his crotch and have him live as a woman. That will be less painful." What you produce is somebody who has a body that is vaguely female, is infertile, doesn't menstruate, probably doesn't have any sexual function, might have genital pain, and has been lied to and shamed. That is supposed to be less painful than having a small dick? I think it is taken to be less painful because female pain is discounted. Once it has been transformed into female pain it doesn't bother us so much. (Hegarty and Chase 2000: 124)

Chase speaks as one of many intersex people—and, indeed, as one of many patients—who are now politicizing their involvement in medical processes. In the U.S. context, where the intersex debate has been gaining significant momentum in recent years, Chase serves as a key point of contact for intersex people and a key voice.

What I am calling the intersex debate is part of a wide-ranging movement in which sophisticated medical technologies are sought by some and critiqued by others. Through this debate the voices of marginalized, medicalized Others are being heard. This typically postmodern movement plunges biomedicine (and clinicians themselves) into an unprecedented and ethically fraught dilemma. With regard to this dilemma, feminist poststructuralist analysis may contribute usefully by offering a critical analysis of sexed embodiment and ethics.

Increasingly, advanced technologies are sought for a variety of reasons, by a number of parties. Sometimes these technologies are sought for reasons of scientific progress or health care. Sometimes they are sought by those for whom they bring wealth and prestige, and sometimes by those who seek a medical solution to the troubling problems of sexual and gender diversity. Some critics of this technologizing of sexed embodiment suggest that clinicians—eager to try out their new practices on ideal candidates[3]—pressure their clients to consent to treatment. Other critics point to instances where prospective clients put pressure on clinicians to deliver on the fantastic promises of medical science.[4]

The tug-of-war dynamics between what is demanded of medical science and what medical science can offer is well established (Meyerowitz 1998). The considerable forces that are in tension with standard medical practice make it increasingly complex to find ethically sound courses of action. What is a clinician to do when faced with an atypically sexed infant who may experience life-long stigma because of her or his difference? What is a clinician to do when presented with a boy who insists he is a girl and who faces bullying to the point that his schooling is jeopardized? Or, to give the question a different spin, what is a clinician to do when approached by an adult female who wishes to have surgically constructed male genitalia so that "he" can have sex with other men? Is it the business of clinicians to be eliminating—or creating—queer sexes?

Each of these clinical scenarios has something important to tell us about how sexed beings are understood, regulated, and normalized in medical contexts. Each of these scenarios helps to expose how power relations operate in the clinical setting to (1) maintain normative understandings of what is ethical practice and (2) create and maintain (hetero)normative forms of maleness and femaleness. In what follows I present two scenarios in which clinicians respond to opportunities to regulate, normalize, or embrace the queerness in their clients. The first scenario concerns transgender people who seek sex reassignment with the understanding that they will be post-transitionally bisexual, lesbian, or gay. The second scenario focuses on children brought to clinicians because their parents are concerned about their gender-atypical behavior.

Embodied Desire

> It is a rather amazing fact that, of the very many dimensions along which the genital activity of one person can be differentiated from that of another (dimensions that include preference for certain acts, certain zones or sensations, certain physical types, a certain frequency, certain symbolic investments . . . etc.), precisely one, the gender of object choice, emerged from the turn of the century, and has remained, as the dimension denoted by the now ubiquitous category of "sexual orientation." (Sedgwick 1990: 8).

In previous work I have noted that psychomedical constructions of transsexuality depict transsexuals as postoperatively heterosexual (Roen, 1998). During their development, the classification of, and diagnostic criteria for, transsexuality were validated through a framework that clearly differentiated "true transsexuals" from transvestites and homosexuals. Indeed, the inclusion of transsexuality in the American Psychiatric Association's *Diagnostic and Statistical Manual for Mental Disorders*

(*DSM*) happened simultaneously with the withdrawal of homosexuality from the *DSM*.[5] At that time (1974), after decades of trying to "cure" homosexuality, and after fierce protest from gay, lesbian, and bisexual political groups, clinicians forced to acknowledge that homosexuality per se was not grounds for a psychiatric diagnosis. In order to justify the entry of transsexuality into the *DSM* however, it was important that transsexuality and homosexuality be clearly distinguished from one another. By defining transsexuality and homosexuality as mutually exclusive, psychomedical professionals who work with transsexuals attempted to divorce gender identity from sexuality (e.g., Stoller 1971 and Pauly 1974). According to this logic, sex reassignment supposedly reinstates normative heterosexual relations.

The assumption of postoperative heterosexuality is perhaps most crudely and blatantly played out through surgeons' postoperative assessments where the ability to engage in penis–vagina intercourse is considered to be the mark of successful surgery. An instance of this heterocentric approach to sex reassignment surgery (SRS) is outlined by Hale (1998), who reports critically that "[p]rior to performing penile inversion vaginoplasty (in which penile skin forms the inner lining of the neo-vagina), Eugene Schrang (Neenah, Wisconsin) measures the penises of his mtf patients to ensure that they are long enough to provide 'adequate vaginal depth.'[6] If they are not, he grafts skin from other parts of the bodies to achieve 'adequate vaginal depth'" (1998: 107). Through such constructions of transsexuals' erotic desires, psychomedical treatment of transsexuality (like the surgical assignment of intersexuals) enables gender disordered people to maintain healthy (read "normative") social and sexual relationships.

Just as clinicians are eager to ascede to, and to create, parental demand for normal looking and, ultimately, heteronormative children, so too are clinicians often unwilling to alter bodies in ways that seem to create queer sexual possibilities. From the points of view of transpeople, and particularly those who identify as post-transitionally bisexual, gay, or lesbian, the tardiness of psychomedical professionals in recognizing the overlaps between homosexualities and transsexualities "has caused a great deal of suffering and psychiatric mismanagement" (Rosario 1996: 43)

Listening to the experiences of transpeople who have sought sex reassignment reveals that some of them have purposely kept quiet about aspects of their sexuality that went against the grain of dominant theories of the time. "[I]n follow-up conversations, some model patients admitted having shaped biographical accounts to exclude discrediting information, including homosexual and erotic, heterosexual pasts" (Billings and Urban 1982: 274; Hausman 1995; Turner 1999). Some transpeople do, however, choose to be open with clinicians and discover that this can work to their detriment.

> I told [the clinicians] I am bisexual but I prefer women. . . . I don't think that that was particularly the best thing to say. I thought, "Why in hell should I lie and present all the classic case history that I'm supposed to present?" I tried to be as honest as I could. Which probably wasn't the best policy. So it took a long time [to access reassignment surgery]. I felt that I lost five years of my life. (Nataf, quoting "Caroline" 1996: 20)

While normalizing SRS is performed on intersex children without their knowledge, transgender adults who seek SRS may have difficulty obtaining this surgery unless they play a role that depicts the surgery as normalizing (e.g., by claiming "I am a heterosexual woman trapped in a man's body"). The common theme here is that clinical practice seeks to create bodies that approximate normative ways of being sexed and of expressing sexual desire. That treatments for maintaining gender and sexual normativity continue despite the existence of individualized protocols seeking consent raises ethical concerns in relation to questions of identity. What role can medical practices ethically take in shaping the identities of people who are subject to those practices?

The Straight and Narrow Path of Gender

The imperative to ensure that boys be real boys and girls be real girls concerns not only surgical alterations but also psychotherapeutic practices. This kind of psychotherapeutic work with children is justified by the *DSM* classification of childhood gender identity disorder (CGID), which is, in diagnostic terms, the childhood parallel of transsexuality. The focus on gender identity disorders of childhood has been driven by clinicians and researchers who perceive that where transsexuality is concerned, psychotherapeutic prevention during childhood is far more effective than surgical treatment during adulthood.

As with the treatment of intersex children, the treatment of children diagnosed as having CGID occurs in the context of negotiations between parents and clinicians. As with the intersex case, parents may look to clinicians for information, support, advice, and reassurance. Essentially, parents want to know "Is my (queer-looking or queer-acting) kid OK?" As with intersex treatment, the accepted clinical response is not primarily to offer (queer-positive) information, support, advice, and reassurance to parents (or even to the children concerned), but to institute a normalizing program of treatment. Through this treatment, the child is not unlikely to develop the impression that something is wrong with him or her and subsequently to experience shame and distrust.

The classification and treatment of CGID has drawn concern from transsexual, transgendered, and gay people (Wilson, 1997). Psychomedical professionals, aware of this concern, are quick to assure that:

> Gender Identity Disorder . . . is not meant to describe a child's nonconformity to stereotypic sex-role behaviour as, for example, in "tomboyishness" in girls or "sissyish" behaviour in boys. Rather, it represents a profound disturbance of the individual's sense of identity with regard to maleness or femaleness. Behaviour in children that merely does not fit the cultural stereotype of masculinity or femininity should not be given the diagnosis unless the full syndrome is present, including marked distress or impairment. (*DSM* 1994: 536)

Despite this reassurance, it is left unclear how, exactly, the boundary between deviating from a stereotype and being profoundly disturbed is determined. What kind of impairment might result from childhood gender-crossing? How can this be validated as a mental disorder when the marked distress or impairment could result, not from the disorder itself, but from the horror and disapproval of homophobic or transphobic parents, teachers, and peers?

Not only has the gender-normatizing imperative of CGID raised concern, but some critics see it as a way of sneaking homosexuality back into the *DSM*. In relation to this, the fourth edition of the *DSM* states:

> By late adolescence or adulthood, about three-quarters of boys who had a childhood history of Gender Identity Disorder report a homosexual or bisexual orientation, but without concurrent Gender Identity Disorder. Most of the remainder report a heterosexual orientation, also without concurrent Gender Identity Disorder. (*DSM* 1994: 536)

Or, put more bluntly, "studies have shown that effeminate boys more often grow up as homosexuals than as transsexuals" (Gelder et al. 1996: 507). This raises questions about precisely which adulthood disorder is being targeted through the treatment of CGID: homosexuality or transsexuality. And as with intersex surgery, the emphasis of CGID treatment appears to be on defending the boundaries of masculinity. The high proportion of boys, relative to girls, who undergo treatment for CGID suggests that the treatment is aimed at ensuring that boys conform to masculine stereotypes.[7]

Reading between the lines of psychomedical texts on CGID tells a familiar story of two genders, of children who mistakenly take off on the "wrong" gender path, and of treatment programs designed to steer them back to the "right" path. This is the story that underpins dominant ethical justifications for the treatments of concern in this chapter—treatments intended to relieve people of the stigma of abnormality in a social context where there is assumed to be a normal (read "right") way to be gendered and an abnormal (read "wrong") way to be gendered.

In the absence of critical (and queer-positive) analysis, dominant clinical practices rest firmly upon ethical justifications that look alarmingly reminiscent of moral principles. The tendency to think in terms of right and wrong is thinly veiled in the language of (ab)normality. The emotionally evocative image of queer embodiment, along with the assumption that to suffer such embodiment would be a terrible fate, serves to convince clinicians and parents that normalizing treatments are for the best. If one were to scratch the surface of the ethical justifications for treatment, one might find space for another ethics: an ethics that acknowledges the importance of normative gender constructs for the developing child, as well as the inevitability that no one truly embodies such norms; an ethics that respects the parents' fear of having queer kids, as well as envisaging the possibility that those kids will become vibrant, creative, resilient adults with the ability to contribute enormously to current understandings of sexual diversity.

Normalizing treatments for variously queered individuals persist despite continuing efforts to challenge and change such clinical approaches. Modernist psychological theorizing of identity as stable and unitary provides a rationale for clinical processes intended to eradicate the specter of queerly sexed beings. Such theorizing proposes that gender identity will (or should) develop in a way that is consistent with socialization (as a girl or boy) and anatomy (as female or male). When that consistency or correlation is threatened, clinicians step in with processes intended to straighten things out. Ironically, in carrying out these processes, clinicians (surgeons, endocrinologists, psychiatrists, and others) inevitably create newly queered beings. Surgical and psychotherapeutic processes carried out in childhood are not forgotten. Even when carried out on newborns, the body remembers. No matter how much the technological procedures are perfected, the experience of treatment is not erased. Furthermore, for adults who are able to articulate their own understandings of identity, the surgical reconstruction of queer bodies does not ultimately determine what, or how, those bodies become (Holmes 2000; Stryker 1994). Such *becoming* relates to the subjectivity of the person who has undergone surgical reconstruction, not to the technological sophistication of the surgery or the medical discourses through which the reconstruction may have been deemed ethically justifiable.

Medical science attempts to bend bodies and minds to fit into a simplistic grid of male or female, man or woman, where these concepts are necessarily defined in heterosexist terms. Ironically, in trying to perform such a feat, clinicians only demonstrate the impossibility of either regulating or categorizing people in these ways. As Turner observes: "Genitals and genders that evade categorization invite sexual desires and behaviors that also resist description and, thus, regulation" (1999: 476). Given that the imperative to regulate and categorize persists, and given that medical practice has become a primary vehicle for this task, it is necessary that bioethics be able to theorize diverse and atypical forms of embodiment, as well as embrace the concept of undecidability. The following discussion of identity elaborates the importance of that undecidability and its relation to diverse forms of embodiment.

Foreclosing Identity

I didn't want to be different. I longed to be everything grownups wanted, so they would love me. . . . But there was something about me that made them knit their eyebrows and frown. No one ever offered a name for what was wrong with me.

That's what made me afraid it was really bad. I only came to recognize its melody through the constant refrain: "Is that a boy or a girl?" (Feinberg 1993: 13).

[I]t is up to those of us who are intersexed . . . to seize the name "intersexual" as our own and take away its pathologizing power. (Holmes 2000: 106)

Intersex and transgender activists' desire to "seize the name" represents a postmodern twist of the writing of medical discourses on queer bodies. While some clinicians and parents seek to foreclose the question of identity, intersex and transgender activists continually reopen that question, while psychoanalytic theorists argue that it cannot be foreclosed.

The quest for certainty, the assumption that one may be known to be a "boy" or a "girl," the assumption that gender can be articulated so simply and conclusively, is pervasive. This assumption underpins clinical responses to intersex and transgender people. Despite the tremendous influence of the imperative of gender certainty, outside the clinical setting transgender and intersex people make it explicit that no such certainty exists:

I've been raised with the notion that gender is a very clear thing, but my experience doesn't tell me that. My experience says it's a very vague, very nebulous [thing] . . . at some times I'm actually aware of a multiplicity of aspects of myself. And some of those can be both the maleness and the femaleness and the genderlessness. (Mimi, transsexual research participant)[8]

In trying to find a language for expressing the unknowability of gender, Mimi broaches a topic of critical importance. As she observed, the difficulty in defining what it is to be a wo/man extends well beyond transsexuals. She said, "My experience of observing other people is that most other people are rather fuzzy about their gender. Even though they say: 'Yes I'm female,' when you try and pin them down, it's sort of fuzzy. It's like trying to grab a ghost."

Undermining the assumption that gender can be certain and knowable brings into question the truth of gender categories. If gender is no longer certain, then how can there be a call for a one-to-one relationship between gender and sexual anatomy? It is this very imperative—to be certain about one's gender and to ensure its consistency with one's sex—that underlies the ethical concerns of interest here.

This imperative to choose—to *be*—one sex or gender or the other underlies clinicians' justification for normalizing treatments. In the absence of a critical stance in relation to this imperative, conventional ethics becomes yet another building block in the monument to normativity. Here, ethics can be used to justify treatments that reduce, or render invisible, difference. A critical stance, however, enables a different kind of ethics to be formulated. Here, ethics can be articulated in relation to diversely sexed and gendered subjects who struggle together to make sense of—to live within and live outside of—normative, binary categories. This kind of critical ethics would enable clinicians, clients, and their advocates to have respectful discussions in which the available options are expanded and not defined primarily in terms of normative appearances and the likelihood of cosmetic success.

Aspects of psychoanalytic theory highlight the risks and implications of psychomedical assumptions about gender certainty.[9] Two authors who contribute specifically in this area are Shepherdson (1994) and Millot (1990). Of central importance in Shepherdson's thesis is the distinction between the body and the organism. The body is that which is born through the process of signification, while the organism is the biological or organic aspect. Millot argues that sex reassignment focuses primarily on changing the organism (anatomical change) rather than changing the body.

While Shepherdson and Millot's critiques of sex reassignment and of medicalized gender certainty focus on the surgical treatment of transsexuality, their key concerns are equally pertinent with regard to the sex reassignment of intersex children. Failing to acknowledge the distinction between the body and the organism allows medical professionals to intervene on transsexual and intersex anatomies without considering the significatory aspects of sexed embodiment. The psychoanalytic approach to transsexuality described by Millot and Shepherdson hinges on a resistance to providing certainty. That is, psychoanalysis refuses to give answers, whereas psychomedical approaches come with ready-made answers, which the applicant has only to repeat convincingly.

Millot contrasts the uncertainty, the refusal to foreclose questions of identity within psychoanalysis, with medical science's persistent desire to provide an answer, a remedy, truth. According to her, the attempt to resolve transsexuality (or, I suggest, intersexuality) by operating on the organism fails to address issues of signification. What kind of subject does the postoperative transsexual or intersex person become? Medical science expresses little interest in this. Follow-up studies are necessarily limited by difficulties in maintaining contact with postoperative patients over a long period of time, and by medical professionals' assumptions about what constitutes a successful outcome of SRS.[10] Despite repeated references to the theory that the purpose of early intersex sex reassignment is to facilitate healthy gender development, in terms of clinical practice, questions of signification—of becoming—hardly figure at all in the psychomedical picture.

In contrast to psychoanalytic approaches that resist the foreclosure of identity, medical models assume that once surgically resolved, the identity question will be closed. Chase points to this during an interview with Hegarty:

> Hegarty: It seems that doctors are very unprepared to deal with intersexed adults.
>
> Chase: Doctors refer to adults as "formerly intersexed." Once they have done the surgery, intersexuality is over. (Hegarty and Chase 2000: 120)

Yet how medical practitioners address the psychoanalytic refusal to foreclose identity profoundly affects the ethics of medical treatment. "To forgo the myth of identity, to undo the binary of order/disorder must result in a very different ethic . . . in which normalisation would be meaningless" (Shildrick, 1997: 214). Operating from normative understandings of identity leaves little room, as Shildrick observes, for problematizing embodied subjectivity. Conventional bioethics' "privileging [of] . . . patient autonomy as the appropriate goal of ethical practice amounts to little more than a narrow and overdetermined focus on consent" (Shildrick, 1997: 215); and the focus on controlling bodies leaves little room for thinking of medical experiences as creating new forms of embodied subjectivity.

Medical Management of Monstrosity

Historically, the dominance of dualistic frameworks enabled medical science to conceptualize the body as mechanistic—machinery made up of parts, any one of which may become dysfunctional and need repair.[11] This created a context in which the body could be treated in various ways without moral issues arising. More recently, psychology (specifically socialization theory) conceived of the child's mind as plastic, and as something that can be purposely shaped by adults. Through behaviorism, aspects of the mind's workings were reduced to basic mechanistic elements, just as the body had been. With theories of gender socialization, gender identity could be isolated as one aspect of the mind that was understood to be plastic, and therefore manipulable, prior to a critical age. According to this framework of understanding, gender is open to being shaped without raising ethical concerns, as long as normative one-to-one gender-sex mapping is maintained.

Through the collaboration of these aspects of medical science and psychological theorizing was born contemporary intersex medical treatment. Mechanistic approaches to both mind and body, in conjunction with a firm belief that non-normative sexes were abhorrent, enabled intersex treatment to be ethically justified despite the lack of follow-up studies demonstrating long-term success, the physical and psychological pain it inflicted, the loss or diminishing of sexual sensation and functioning it caused, and the complete absence of medical advantages of treatment.

The marriage of psychological and medical advances promised clinicians ultimate control over the bodies and minds of their patients. The dream of such control and scientific advancement was brought even closer by the desperate willingness of parents terrified of having queer kids. In their desperation, they have handed their babies over to the care of contemporary science. Clinicians would have been barely able to find a more ideal situation: highly suggestible, consenting parents; highly malleable infants whose physical ambiguity made them easy targets for experimental treatment; and grand theories that pictured the growing child being successfully moulded by the powers of scalpel, psychotherapy, and socialization into something new yet something remarkably resembling a "real" woman or girl.

That such practices still occur highlights the urgency of addressing questions about the ethics of the clinical processes through which queer bodies are reconstructed. What are the conditions and understandings that make intersex surgery appear ethically defensible? What are the understandings that make it ethically indefensible to cut into a normal infant's penis? The purpose of bringing a poststructuralist feminist analysis to this issue is neither to condemn the work of those who perpetuate this treatment approach nor to propose a miracle solution. Rather, the purpose of this analysis is to offer a conceptual platform from which the issue may be rethought, and on the basis of which better courses of action and clearer ethical frameworks may be navigated. As one intersex theorist writes, the irony of intersex surgery is that rather than eliminating abnormality, such "surgery *creates* . . . abnormality" (Holmes, 2000: 104, emphasis in original).

Acknowledgment

I would like to thank Michael Lloyd for his discussion and feedback on this chapter.

Notes

1. Chase counters this claim by writing: "the argument that 'surgery is better now' ignores the lack of informed consent . . . inherent in the old model. [This] argument . . . gives surgeons a perpetual license to ignore patients . . . voices" (1998: 391).

2. Poststructuralist feminist and intersex writings overlap in challenging dominant notions of binary forms of sexed embodiment, and considering the relationship between identity and embodiment from a politicized, discursive perspective.

3. Twins and ambiguously sexed infants have provided fertile grounds for the testing of numerous theories of sex and gender.

4. Meyerowitz (1998) thoughtfully traces the development of surgical sex change procedures and demonstrates how fantastic medical claims create a demand for what is medically unattainable.

5. In January 1974, the board of trustees of the American Psychological Association voted to delete homosexuality as a mental disorder from the *DSM* (Friedman et al. 1976).

6. mtf stands for male-to-female transsexual.

7. For a transgender critique of the so-called sissy-boy research and clinical programs, see MacKenzie (1994). See Wilson (1997) for a critique of the discrepancy between boys' and girls' treatment for GID.

8. Aspects of this discussion draw from my doctoral research on transsexuality. During that research, I carried out interviews with eleven transpeople living in New Zealand. One of these interviewees, referred to as Mimi, is quoted here.

9. I am grateful for Patricia Elliot's contribution to my understanding of this psychoanalytic approach to transsexuality. Aspects of this chapter have been informed by our work together (Elliot and Roen, 1998).

10. See Abramowitz (1986) for detailed descriptions of sex reassignment surgery follow-up studies and their limitations.

11. In referring to monstrosity in this way, I am invoking both Annas (1987) and Stryker (1994). Annas described the "the monster approach" in writing about clinical practices that take place when the patient's atypical features lead to their being seen as "so grotesque that they are not really human" (1987: 28). Stryker reclaims the idea of the monster in the context of arguing that what the postoperative transsexual becomes has to do with subjectivity and signification, and is not dictated by the medical discourses and processes that enable SRS. Here, the monster is a figure of empowerment and subversion.

References

Abramowitz, Stephen (1986) "Psychosocial Outcomes of Sex Reassignment Surgery," *Journal of Consulting and Clinical Psychology* 54(2), 183–189.

Annas, G. J. (1987a) "Siamese Twins: Killing One to Save the Other," *Hastings Center Report* 17, 27–29.

Billings, Dwight, and Urban, Thomas (1982a) "The Socio-Medical Construction of Transsexualism: An Interpretation and Critique," *Social Problems* 29(3), 266–282.

Chase, Cheryl (1998) "Surgical Progress Is Not the Answer to Intersexuality," *Journal of Clinical Ethics* 9(4), 385–392.

Diamond, Milton, and Sigmundson, Keith (1997) "Management of Intersexuality: Guidelines for Dealing with Persons with Ambiguous Genitalia," *Archives of Pediatric and Adolescent Medicine* 151, 1046–1050.

Dreger, Alice Domurat (1998) *Hermaphrodites and the Medical Invention of Sex*. Cambridge, Mass.: Harvard University Press.

DSM (1994) *Diagnostic and Statistical Manual for Mental Disorders* (4th ed.). Washington, D.C.: American Psychiatric Association.

Elliot, Patricia, and Roen, Katrina (1998) "Transgenderism and the Question of Embodiment: Promising Queer Politics?" *GLQ: A Journal of Lesbian and Gay Studies* 4(2), 231–261.

Feinberg, Leslie (1993) *Stone Butch Blues*. Ithaca, N.Y.: Firebrand Books.

Friedman, Richard C., Green, Richard, and Spitzer, Robert L. (1976) "Reassessment of Homosexuality and Transsexualism," *Annual Review of Medicine* 27, 57–62.

Garfinkel, Harold (1967) *Studies in Ethnomethodology*. Englewood Cliffs, N.J.: Prentice-Hall.

Gelder, Michael, Gath, Dennis, Mayon, Richard, and Cowen, Phillip (eds.) (1996) *Oxford Textbook of Psychiatry* (3rd ed). Oxford: Oxford University Press.

Hale, C. Jacob (1998) "Tracing a Ghostly Memory in My Throat: Reflections on Ftm Feminist Voice and Agency," in Tom Digby (ed.), *Men Doing Feminism*. London and New York: Routledge, pp. 99–129.

Hausman, Bernice (1995) *Changing Sex: Transsexualism, Technology, and the Idea of Gender*. Durham and London: Duke University Press.

Hegarty, Peter, and Chase, Cheryl (2000) "Intersex Activism, Feminism and Psychology: Opening a Dialogue on Theory, Research and Clinical Practice," *Feminism and Psychology* 10(1), 117–132.

Holmes, Morgan (1994) "I'm Still Intersexual," *Hermaphrodites with Attitude* 1(1), 5–6.

Holmes, Morgan (2000) "Queer Cut Bodies," in Joseph A. Boone, Martin Dupuis, Martin Meeker, Karin Quimby, Cindy Sarver, Debra Silverman, and Rosemary Weatherston (eds.), *Queer Frontiers: Millennial Geographies, Genders, and Generations*. Madison: University of Wisconsin Press, pp. 84–110.

Howe, Edmund (1998) "Intersexuality: What Should Careproviders Do Now?" *Journal of Clinical Ethics* 9(4), 337–344.

Jeffreys, Sheila (1997) "Transgender Activism: A Lesbian Feminist Perspective," *Journal of Lesbian Studies* 1(3/4), 55–74.

Kessler, Suzanne J. (1998) *Lessons from the Intersexed*. New Brunswick, N.Y.: Rutgers University Press.

Kessler, Suzanne and McKenna, Wendy (1978) *Gender: An Ethnomethodological Approach*. New York: Wiley.

Kessler, Suzanne J., and McKenna, Wendy (2000) "Gender Construction in Everyday Life: Transsexualism," *Feminism and Psychology* 10(1) 11–29.

Kipnis, Kenneth, and Diamond, Milton (1998) "Pediatric Ethics and the Surgical Assignment of Sex," *Journal of Clinical Ethics* 9(4), 398–410.

Kitzinger, Celia (2000) "Women with Androgen Insensitivity Syndrome (AIS)," in Jane Ussher (ed.), *Women's Health: Contemporary International Perspectives*. Leicester, UK: British Psychological Society, pp. 387–394.

MacKenzie, Gordene Olga (1994) *Transgender Nation*. Bowling Green, Ohio: Popular Press.

Meyerowitz, Joanne (1998) "Sex Change and the Popular Press: Historical Notes on Transsexuality in the United States, 1930–1955," *GLQ: A Journal of Lesbian and Gay Studies* 4(2), 159–188.

Millot, Catherine (1990) *Horsexe*, trans. Kenneth Hylton. New York: Autonomedia.

Mitchell, Mani B. (2000) "Fifty Years: The Untold Intersex Story," unpublished conference paper, New Zealand Venereological Society Conference.

Money, John, Hampson, Joan G., and Hampson, John L. (1955) "Hermaphroditism: Recommendations Concerning Assignment of Sex, Change of Sex and Psychological Management," *Bulletin of the Johns Hopkins Hospital*, 97, 284–300.

Moreno, Angela (1997) "In Amerika They Call Us Hermaphrodites," *Chrysalis: The Journal of Transgressive Gender Identities* 2, 11–12.

Nataf, Zachary I. (1996) *Lesbians Talk Transgender*. London: Scarlet Press.

Pauly, Ira B. (1974) "Female Transsexualism: Part I," *Archives of Sexual Behavior* 3(6), 487–507.

Raymond, Janice (1979) *The Transsexual Empire*. Boston: Beacon Press.

Roen, Katrina (1998) "Constructing Transsexuality: Discursive Manoeuvres through Psycho-Medical, Transgender, and Queer Texts," unpublished doctoral dissertation, University of Canterbury, New Zealand.

Rosario, Vernon A., II (1996) "Trans (Homo) Sexuality? Double Inversion, Psychiatric Confusion, and Hetero-Hegemony," in Brett Beemyn and Mickey Eliason (eds.), *Queer Studies: A Lesbian, Gay, Bisexual and Transgender Anthology*. New York and London: New York University Press, pp. 35–51.

Sedgwick, Eve Kosofsky (1990) *Epistemology of the Closet*. Berkeley: University of California Press.

Shepherdson, Charles (1994) "The Role of Gender and the Imperative of Sex," in Joan Copjec (ed.), *Supposing the Subject*. London: Verso, pp. 158–184.

Shildrick, Margrit (1997) *Leaky Bodies and Boundaries: Feminism, Postmodernism and (Bio)Ethics*. London: Routledge.

Stoller, Robert (1971) "The Term 'Transvestism,'" *Archives of General Psychiatry* 24, 230–237.

Stryker, Susan (1994) "My Words to Victor Frankenstein Above the Village of Chamounix: Performing Transgender Rage," *GLQ: A Journal of Lesbian and Gay Studies* 1, 237–254.

Turner, Stephanie (1999) "Intersex Identities: Locating New Intersections of Sex and Gender," *Gender and Society* 13(4), 457–479.

Wilson, Bruce E., and Reiner, William G. (1998) "Management of Intersex: A Shifting Paradigm" *Journal of Clinical Ethics* 9(4), 360–369.

Wilson, Katherine K. (1997) "The Disparate Classification of Gender and Sexual Orientation in American Psychiatry," unpublished paper, Gender Identity Center of Colorado, Inc., Denver.

Contributors

Carol Bacchi
Associate professor in politics
University of Adelaide

Chris Beasley
Senior lecturer in politics
University of Adelaide

Lisa Diedrich
Assistant professor in women's studies
State University of New York at Stony Brook

Rosalyn Diprose
Senior lecturer in philosophy
University of New South Wales

Isabel Karpin
Senior lecturer in law
University of Sydney

Helen Keane
Research fellow
National Centre for HIV Research, University of New South Wales

Roxanne Mykitiuk
Associate professor of law
Osgoode Hall Law School, York University, Toronto

Sylvia Nagl
Senior lecturer in oncology
University College London

Karen O'Connell
Doctoral candidate in law
Columbia Law School, New York and acting Director of Human Rights Unit
Human Rights and Equal Opportunities Commission
Australia

Nancy Potter
Associate professor of philosophy
University of Louisville, Kentucky and Executive Council member of the Association of Philosophy and Psychiatry

Katrina Roen
Lecturer in Research Methods
Clinical Psychology Programme
Institute for Health Research
Lancaster University
Lancaster

Marsha Rosengarten
Lecturer in Sociology
Goldsmiths College
University of London

Philipa Rothfield
Senior lecturer
School of Philosophy
La Trobe University, Melbourne and co-editor of the journal *Hysteric: Body, Medicine, Text*

Jackie Leach Scully
Lecturer in bioethics
Institute for History and Ethics
of Medicine
University of Basle
Switzerland

Margrit Shildrick
Senior Researcher
Women's Education, Research
and Resources Centre
University College Dublin and
Adjunct Professor of critical disability
studies
York University, Toronto

Index